Daily Dose of Positivity™

Daily Dose of Positivity™

Mental Supplements for Better Health

Craig S. Travis, Ph.D.

iUniverse, Inc.
New York Lincoln Shanghai

Daily Dose of Positivity™
Mental Supplements for Better Health

Copyright © 2006 by Craig S. Travis, Ph.D.

All rights reserved. No part of this book may be used or reproduced by any means, graphic, electronic, or mechanical, including photocopying, recording, taping or by any information storage retrieval system without the written permission of the publisher except in the case of brief quotations embodied in critical articles and reviews.

iUniverse books may be ordered through booksellers or by contacting:

iUniverse
2021 Pine Lake Road, Suite 100
Lincoln, NE 68512
www.iuniverse.com
1-800-Authors (1-800-288-4677)

The author and publisher do not guarantee that this material will change you overnight, solve all problems, cure medical diseases, reconcile marriages, and the like. What we do believe is that you will continue down the same path in life unless you actively do something different. This book can be the beginning to that journey into Positivity.

Keep on doing what you've always done, and you'll keep on getting what you've always gotten.

ISBN-13: 978-0-595-39987-1 (pbk)
ISBN-13: 978-0-595-84375-6 (ebk)
ISBN-10: 0-595-39987-8 (pbk)
ISBN-10: 0-595-84375-1 (ebk)

Printed in the United States of America

To my son, Nathan, who has shown me the importance of attitude and how I perceive things in life. May you live in a world that prospers in Positivity.

PERSONAL ACKNOWLEDGMENTS

There are so many people to thank for making this book possible; more people to thank than is possible in such a short space. However, I would like to honor several people and express my thanks in their contributions to this book.

First and foremost, I would like to thank my brother, Todd Travis, who had it not been for him, I never would have had the idea nor courage to write this book. I would also like to thank my parents, Alan and Fiona, for all the support they have continued to give me throughout my life, and especially for teaching me what is important and showing me how to see things healthily.

Special thanks goes to Deidre (Dee) Smith, who has shown me the effect that this book truly can have on people. And who has also contributed a number of ideas as well as being a sounding board for many of the positivities I have written.

To Regina Gray, thanks for the feedback and direction in writing this set of DDP's. I value your judgment and perception.

Thanks to Ken and Jacqui Hamilton for listening to my endless promotion of this book. I appreciate your feedback and support. You are great neighbors and better friends. Also, thank you to Amy Osborne, who graciously gave her opinion on the subject matter. To Julie Baumer, I appreciate your feedback in letting me know how helpful the DDP's have been to you personally and the encouragement to keep pursuing publication.

Thanks to iUniverse, for everything they have done to help me spread the word of Positivity.

Finally, thanks to my lovely wife, Heather, whose patience and support throughout this project have meant much more than words could ever express. Thank you for believing in my ideas and me. I love you.

PROFESSIONAL ACKNOWLEDGEMENTS

I would like to take the opportunity also to acknowledge the thinkers, researchers, and authors whom have greatly influenced my thinking and professional development. Robert Sapolsky, professor of biological and neurosciences at Stanford; his writings on stress and the mind body interconnection; Joseph Ledoux, his research on emotions; Candace Pert, her work in neuroscience; Donald Meichenbaum and Albert Ellis, their contribution to cognitive behavioral theory; Martin Seligman, Ed Diener, David Myers, and Barbara Frederickson for legitimizing the science of positive psychology, positive emotion, and happiness. Of course, there are many more, too numerous to mention in such a short space. But, to all: thank you for sharing your wisdom.

CONGRATULATIONS!

If you are reading this book, that means you have taken the first step in changing your life; a step in the direction of better health emotionally, physically, and behaviorally. You have begun the journey into the world of Positivity. Keep moving forward and you will meet your dreams! Again, congratulations on embarking on your new journey!

CONTENTS

Preface xxv
How Did We Get Here? xxvii

1: NEW DIRECTIONS FOR A NEW AGE 1
2: NEW "MEDICINE" FOR THE NEW AGE 2

PART I: THE PAST—Psychology's Heritage: Building the Foundation of
Evidence for the Effectiveness of Positivity 3

3: IMPORTANCE OF ATTITUDE 5
4: HISTORY OF MIND/BODY THEORY 6
5: STRESS THEORY 8
6: THE FUNCTIONALITY OF ANXIETY AND DEPRESSION ...12
    CURRENT THINKING 16
    SEND IN THE MARINES: THE DAMAGE CONTROL MODEL—
    UNDERSTANDING PSYCHOLOGICAL THREATS &
    EGO WOUND REACTIONS 23
    'SAVING FACE'—PRESERVING YOUR EGO:
    REAL WORLD EXAMPLES IN ACTION 41
7: WHAT WAS ONCE OLD IS NEW AGAIN 43
8: POSITIVITY IN UNCOMFORTABLE "NEGATIVE" FEELINGS 47
9: THE CARDS WE'RE DEALT 50
10: THE SCIENCE BEHIND THE THOUGHT 53
    RATIONAL EMOTIVE BEHAVIOR THEORY (REBT) 56

Daily Dose of Positivity™

RECENT CHANGES TO REBT 65
WHAT'S IN A NAME? THE NAME CHANGE DEBATE 67
BELIEFS AND PHYSICAL ILLNESS 69

PART II: THE PRESENT—THE POSITIVE PSYCHOLOGY MOVEMENT 71

11: POSITIVE PSYCHOLOGY: WHAT IS IT AND WHY WEREN'T WE DOING IT BEFORE? 73
POSITIVE PSYCHOLOGY 75
THE PSYCHOLOGY OF YESTERYEAR AND REESTABLISHING THE SCIENCE OF OLD 77
POSITIVE PSYCHOLOGY: FROM TREATMENT AND PREVENTION TO WELLNESS AND FULL POTENTIAL 80
SO, WHAT ARE WE SUPPOSED TO FEEL? 83

12: IN PURSUIT OF HAPPINESS 90
THE EVOLUTION OF HAPPINESS 91
THE SCIENCE OF HAPPINESS: SUBJECTIVE WELL-BEING 95
HAPPY HUNTING 98
SO, WHO IS HAPPY? 100

13: EFFECTIVENESS OF COGNITIVE THERAPY: WHAT DOES RESEARCH TELL US? 101

14: COMBINING PAST AND PRESENT: THE PSYCHOPHYSIOLOGY OF NEGATIVITY VS. POSITIVITY 104

PART III: THE FUTURE—Daily Dose of Positivity™ 113

DDP1: EACH DAILY JOURNEY BEGINS WITH ATTITUDE 115

Craig S. Travis, Ph.D.

DDP2: CHANGING YOUR BEHAVIOR STARTS WITH CHANGING YOUR THOUGHTS 116

DDP3: AWARENESS IS THE KEY TO ALL CHANGE 117

DDP4: REACH FOR YOUR DREAMS 118

DDP5: ATTITUDE IS WHAT MAKES YOU SUCCESSFUL 119

DDP6: YOU ARE WHAT YOU THINK 120

DDP7: DON'T GIVE UP, DON'T EVER GIVE UP 121

DDP8: SUCCESS IS YOUR RESPONSIBILITY 122

DDP9: ACTION IS FUNDAMENTAL FOR SUCCESSFUL ACCOMPLISHMENT 123

DDP10: HAPPINESS IS JUST A THOUGHT AWAY 124

DDP11: LIFE IS ONE BIG CHOICE 125

DDP12: MOTIVATION IS THAT DEEP DESIRE WITHIN 126

DDP13: START LITTLE, BUT THINK BIG 127

DDP14: POSITIVE BEHAVIOR BEGINS WITH POSITIVE THOUGHTS 128

DDP15: ATTITUDE IS THE ONLY THING 129

DDP16: ADVERSITY MAKES US STRONGER 130

DDP17: LIFE IS A JOURNEY 131

DDP18: MAKE YOUR GOALS CLEAR 132

DDP19: WHAT YOU SEE IS WHAT YOU GET 133

DDP20: YOU SET YOUR OWN DESTINY 134

DDP21: YOUR FUTURE LIES IN WHAT YOU ENVISION TODAY 135

DDP22: IDENTIFY YOUR DREAMS AND GOALS 136

DDP23: HAPPINESS IS A CHOICE 137

DDP24: CHALLENGE YOURSELF EVERYDAY 138

Daily Dose of Positivity™

DDP25: PERSONAL GROWTH MEANS LEARNING FROM YOUR MISTAKES 139
DDP26: PERSISTANCE IS WHAT MAKES PEOPLE SUCCESSFUL 140
DDP27: WORDS ARE TOOLS OF POWER 141
DDP28: ENTHUSIASM IS A CHARACTERISTIC OF SUCCESS 142
DDP29: LIFE IS WHAT YOU MAKE IT 143
DDP30: ACTION AND THINKING ARE CONNECTED 144
DDP31: YOU DETERMINE YOUR OWN DESTINY 145
DDP32: HAVE FAITH IN YOURSELF 146
DDP33: DON'T JUST DREAM IT, BE IT 147
DDP34: IMAGINATION IS THE SEED OF SUCCESS 148
DDP35: DON'T LET FEAR BE THE MASTER OF YOUR LIFE 149
DDP36: DON'T WAIT UNTIL TOMORROW, START TODAY 150
DDP37: CHANGE IS ALL AROUND YOU 151
DDP38: YOU MUST SEE IT, TO BE IT 152
DDP39: IF YOU PUT YOUR MIND TO IT, YOU CAN ACCOMPLISH ANYTHING 153
DDP40: BE FULL OF HOPES ABOUT YOUR FUTURE 154
DDP41: REPETETIVE ACTION PAVES THE ROAD TO SUCCESS 155
DDP42: SUCCESS IS A MATTER OF EXPECTATION 156
DDP43: THERE IS NO FINISH LINE WHEN IT COMES TO PERSONAL GROWTH 157
DDP44: YOU HAVE WHAT IT TAKES TO BE SUCCESSFUL 158
DDP45: FEEL THE POWER OF YOUR MIND 159
DDP46: TRAIN YOUR BRAIN FOR SUCCESS 160
DDP47: MOVEMENT MAKES YOU HEALTHY 161
DDP48: IT'S THE THOUGHT THAT COUNTS 162

DDP49: HAPPINESS IS NOT AS ELUSIVE AS YOU THINK 163

DDP50: PUSH IT TO THE LIMIT 164

DDP51: UNLEASH YOUR POTENTIAL BY UNLEASHING
YOUR PASSION 165

DDP52: KEEP MOVING FORWARD AND YOU WILL MEET YOUR
DREAMS 166

DDP53: STICK TO IT 167

DDP54: SET YOUR MIND TO IT AND YOU'LL DO IT 168

DDP55: KEEP MOVING FORWARD NO MATTER WHAT 169

DDP56: DARE TO PAVE A NEW PATH 170

DDP57: HAVE FAITH IN YOUR ABILITIES 171

DDP58: DO A LITTLE EACH AND EVERY DAY 172

DDP59: YOUR EMOTIONS ARE TO BE MANAGED, NOT FEARED 173

DDP60: GOOD HABITS COME FROM REPETITIVE BEHAVIOR 174

DDP61: YOU SHAPE YOUR DESTINY BY
THE CHOICES YOU MAKE 175

DDP62: YOU DETERMINE WHAT WILL BE 176

DDP63: YOU HAVE THE KEYS TO OPEN THE DOOR
TO YOUR FUTURE 177

DDP64: HAPPINESS IS YOURS FOR THE TAKING 178

DDP65: INVENT YOUR OWN FUTURE 179

DDP66: SEEING IS BELIEVING 180

DDP67: THE MOST VALUABLE ASSET YOU
CAN POSSESS IS A POSITIVE ATTITUDE 181

DDP68: BEHOLD THE POWER OF YOUR MIND 182

DDP69: CHANGING YOUR LIFE STARTS WITH
CHANGING YOUR MIND 183

DDP70: YOU CAN IF YOU THINK YOU CAN 184

DDP71: POSITIVE THOUGHTS AND ACTIONS BRING POSITIVE RESULTS	185
DDP72: HEALTHY CHOICES ARE NOT ALWAYS EASY	186
DDP73: YOUR ATTITUDE IS ALL THAT MATTERS	187
DDP74: AVOID YOUR RESPONSIBILITIES AND SUCCESS WILL AVOID YOU	188
DDP75: GIVE IT YOUR BEST SHOT	189
DDP76: SUCCESS IN LIFE INVOLVES RISK	190
DDP77: SUCCESS DEPENDS ON ACTION	191
DDP78: NO AMOUNT OF BELIEF WILL OVERRIDE INACTION	192
DDP79: BELIEVE IN YOUR ABILITIES AND YOU CAN CONQUER YOUR GOALS	193
DDP80: IT PAYS TO KNOW YOUR LIMITATIONS	194
DDP81: YOUR POSSIBILITIES ARE ENDLESS	195
DDP82: FOR FUTURE DREAMS TO BE POSSIBLE, PLAN TODAY	196
DDP83: MOVE BEYOND MENTAL BARRIERS	197
DDP84: LIFE IS FILLED WITH OPTIONS	198
DDP85: EXPECTATIONS ARE POWERFUL	199
DDP86: SUCCESS CAN BE FOUND IN MANY THINGS	200
DDP87: IT PAYS TO BE PREPARED	201
DDP88: IT PAYS TO THINK THINGS THROUGH	202
DDP89: HOW YOU THINK DETERMINES YOUR SUCCESS IN LIFE	203
DDP90: ATTITUDE MAKES THE DIFFERENCE	204
DDP91: BELIEVE IN FAITH, NOT LUCK	205
DDP92: SPEAK YOUR MIND, YOUR BODY WILL FOLLOW	206
DDP93: CHANGE HAPPENS EVERYDAY	207
DDP94: SET GOALS FOR YOURSELF, NOT OTHERS	208

Craig S. Travis, Ph.D.

DDP95: YOUR ATTITUDE IS A GIFT 209

DDP96: YOUR VALUE AS A PERSON IS IMMEASURABLE 210

DDP97: KNOW WHAT IS IMPORTANT TO YOUR HEART 211

DDP98: IT AIN'T OVER UNTIL (UNLESS) YOU GIVE UP 212

DDP99: BRAVERY INVOLVES RISK 213

DDP100: INTERPRETATION REFLECTS ATTITUDE 214

DDP101: YOUR MIND IS POWERFUL 215

DDP102: HONESTY AND INTEGRITY ARE AMONG YOUR BEST ATTRIBUTES 216

DDP103: TRUST YOUR INTUITION 217

DDP104: EXPECT THE UNEXPECTED 218

DDP105: WHATEVER YOU DO, BE SECURE IN YOURSELF 219

DDP106: ATTITUDE IS WHAT GETS YOU THROUGH LIFE 220

DDP107: SUCCESS IS BUILT ON UNITY 221

DDP108: BECOME THE PERSON YOU DREAM TO BE 222

DDP109: TRUST IN YOUR FEELINGS 223

DDP110: DON'T WAIT, START NOW 224

DDP111: CALL UPON YOUR STRENGTH 225

DDP112: POSITIVITY MEANS REACTING POSITIVELY TO A NEGATIVE SITUATION 226

DDP113: HAPPINESS STARTS WITH BELIEVING IN YOURSELF 227

DDP114: KEEP YOUR GOALS IN MIND AND YOU WILL BE SURPRISED 228

DDP115: DISCOVER A PASSION FOR WHAT'S POSSIBLE 229

DDP116: WHEN FACED WITH ADVERSITY, STILL BELIEVE 230

DDP117: INTENSITY, FORSIGHT, AND ACTION ARE ESSENTIAL FOR SUCCESS 231

DDP118: SATISFACTION COMES WITH A JOB WELL DONE 232
DDP119: SUCCESS IS A WAY OF LIFE 233
DDP120: ORGANIZED PEOPLE ARE SUCCESSFUL 234
DDP121: SUCCESS IS MARKED BY EACH
           SMALL ACCOMPLISHMENT 235
DDP122: POLITENESS NEVER GOES OUT OF STYLE 236
DDP123: WORTHWHILE THINGS ARE WORTH THE EFFORT 237
DDP124: YOU CANNOT GET AHEAD IF YOU ONLY LOOK BACK 238
DDP125: DON'T JUST THINK IT, DO IT 239
DDP126: LIFE IS AN ADVENTURE 240
DDP127: A KIND THOUGHT GOES ALONG WAY 241
DDP128: GENEROSITY IS A GESTURE OF SUCCESS 242
DDP129: PUT YOUR THOUGHTS OF POVERTY BEHIND YOU 243
DDP130: YOU CAN ACHIEVE HARMONY IN YOUR LIFE 244
DDP131: DARE TO BE DIFFERENT 245
DDP132: LIFE'S ADVENTURE AWAITS YOU 246
DDP133: LIFE IS NOT A ONE WAY STREET 247
DDP134: GET IN THE GAME 248
DDP135: THERE ARE NO SHORTCUTS TO HONOR 249
DDP136: VOW TO ACCOMPLISH ONE GOAL A DAY 250
DDP137: WHEN YOU GIVE UP, YOU MISS OPPORTUNITIES 251
DDP138: CHEERFUL DISPOSITION IS A GIFT 252
DDP139: GENUINE VISION MAKES YOU EXCEL 253
DDP140: A TASTE OF SUCCESS LEADS TO MORE SUCCESS 254
DDP141: PUT FAITH IN YOUR ABILITY TO DO ORDINARY THINGS
           EXTRAORDINARILY 255

DDP142: FAVORABLE RESULTS START WITH A GOOD PLAN 256

DDP143: THAT WHICH TAKES NO EFFORT TO ACHIEVE REWARDS AS MUCH 257

DDP144: FRIENDSHIP MAKES YOU SUCCESSFUL 258

DDP145: ACTION ENABLES ACHIEVEMENT 259

DDP146: FOOLISH ACTS COME FROM FOOLISH THOUGHTS 260

DDP147: YOUR ACTIONS DETERMINE WHO YOU ARE 261

DDP148: IF IT WORKS, KEEP DOING IT 262

DDP149: HAPPINESS IS A JOURNEY NOT A DESTINATION 263

DDP150: KEEP LIFE'S SIMPLE PLEASURES IN MIND 264

DDP151: ENJOY LIFE BY ENGAGING IN LIFE 265

DDP152: COMPASSION IS NEVER OUT OF STYLE 266

DDP153: SUCCESS IS YOURS IF YOU WANT IT 267

DDP154: MAKE NO EXCUSES 268

DDP155: FIND SUCCESS YOUR OWN WAY 269

DDP156: EMBRACE YOUR DIFFERENCES 270

DDP157: MASTERY COMES FROM PRACTICE 271

DDP158: LIFE IS TOO SHORT NOT TO HAVE FUN 272

DDP159: ENJOY WHAT YOU ALREADY HAVE 273

DDP160: ADMIT YOUR VULNERABILITIES 274

DDP161: YOUR LIFE IS FILLED WITH LESSONS 275

DDP162: THERE IS MORE TO SUCCESS THAN REACHING A GOAL 276

DDP163: PURSUE YOUR DREAMS 277

DDP164: IT'S NOT ABOUT WHAT HAPPENS, BUT RATHER YOUR RESPONSE TO IT THAT MATTERS 278

DDP165: CHANGE STARTS WITH YOUR ATTITUDE 279

DDP166: KNOWLEDGE IS POWER 280
DDP167: EXPERIENCE CAN BE A GREAT TEACHER 281
DDP168: WHAT IS, IS NOT ALWAYS WHAT MUST BE 282
DDP169: LIFES MEANING IS SET BY YOUR ATTITUDE 283
DDP170: YOUR GREATEST ACHIEVEMENT IS
 A POSITIVITE ATTITUDE 284
DDP171: BE THE CHANGE YOU WANT TO SEE IN THE WORLD 285
DDP172: DISCOVER PEACE OF MIND 286
DDP173: DELVE INTO YOUR DREAMS 287
DDP174: YOUR SUCCESS LIES IN YOUR GROWTH 288
DDP175: CHANGE YOUR ATTITUDE AND YOU
 CHANGE YOUR WORLD 289
DDP176: CHOOSE APPROPRIATE COURSE OF ACTION 290
DDP177: THERE IS STRENGTH IN
 ACKNOWLEDGING WEAKNESS 291
DDP178: SET YOUR MIND ON YOUR GOALS AND THEY CAN BE
 ACHIEVED. 292
DDP179: DARE TO CHASE YOUR DREAMS 293
DDP180: SUCCESSFUL CHANGE IS MIND OVER MATTER 294
DDP181: YOU CAN CHANGE YOUR LIFE IN AN INSTANT 295
DDP182: PICTURE YOUR SUCCESS IN YOUR MIND 296
DDP183: KNOW YOUR DREAMS; SEEK YOUR VISION 297
DDP184: CHANGE STARTS WITH CHOICE 298
DDP185: CONFIDENCE GOES A LONG WAY 299
DDP186: WHERE THERE IS A WILL, THERE IS A WAY 300
DDP187: GO AFTER YOUR DREAMS 301
DDP188: YOUR MIND CAN WORK AGAINST YOU, OR FOR YOU 302

DDP189: VALUES, NOT PLEASURE, BRING TRUE HAPPINESS 303
DDP190: TAKE THE RISK TO TRY NEW THINGS 304
DDP191: YOU CHOOSE YOUR ATTITUDE 305
DDP192: POSITIVITY STARTS WITH YOU 306
DDP193: YOUR REPUTATION IS YOUR LEGACY 307
DDP194: PUT FORTH THE EFFORT 308
DDP195: GROWTH IS RESPONDING INSTEAD OF REACTING 309
DDP196: SUCCESS IS MORE ATTITUDE THAN APTITUDE 310
DDP197: YOU NEVER KNOW WHAT YOU MIGHT ACCOMPLISH UNLESS YOU TRY 311
DDP198: FAILURE BRINGS WISDOM 312
DDP199: TAKING RISK MAKES YOU SUCCESSFUL 313
DDP200: BELIEVE IN YOURSELF, KNOW WHAT YOU WANT, AND MAKE IT HAPPEN 314
DDP201: WHAT IS HEALTHY ISN'T ALWAYS WHAT IS EASY 315
DDP202: ATTITUDE IS EVERYTHING, EVERYTHING IS ATTITUDE 316

References: Part I 317
References: Part II 323

PREFACE

A word about Positivity. I must admit that I find it truly ironic that as I write this book on being more positive, the word Positivity is not recognized as a valid descriptor by my computer; however, *negativity* is recognized by the spelling and grammar software. Perhaps that is an indication of where the state of our society is currently. Negativity is too easily recognized (technologically and otherwise). Perhaps, it is time for a change…

HOW DID WE GET HERE?
(OR, WHY DID I WRITE THIS BOOK?)

While I was working for a family medicine residency program in the mid 1990's (different than my current program), one day my brother sent me a motivational message by e-mail. He informed me that he intended to send me these inspirational messages on a daily basis. He subsequently sent more and I began to share them with patients and colleagues. At the time, a weekly intradepartmental newsletter was produced and the "editor" had asked for contributions to be able to layout a complete second page. I submitted a daily motivation that my brother had sent me and did not think twice about it. However, the response I got was overwhelmingly positive. People were saying things like, "That's what we need around here," and the editor asked if I could contribute a message each week, that "that is the kind of thing people will read". I began writing my own and I titled the column "Weekly Dose of Positivity." Being in a medical environment, I figured the physicians would appreciate the medication analogy. The Weekly Dose of Positivity soon developed into the idea for a *Daily Dose of Positivity*. Since I had this kind of impact on a few people, I thought that if I could prescribe Daily Doses of Positivity to the general population and if people followed those prescriptions, then they would be happier and more self-fulfilled and achieving greater pleasure out of life. That is why I wrote this book. I hope that you succeed in achieving a more healthful life through these Daily Doses of Positivity.

1

NEW DIRECTIONS FOR A NEW AGE

As the new Millenium is upon us, so too is each of our own destinies. The year 2001 marked a new beginning to a new life, a new age and time, a time of Positivity. What direction do you want to go: Forward into the realm of Positivity, or remain stagnated in the darkness of negativity?

The purpose of this book is not to solve the mind/body connection issue, nor to understand, in great detail, the complex specific interactive mechanisms that explain how thoughts and emotions affect behavior, physical health, and well-being. Rather, its purpose is to provide a fundamental building block to help you establish better health, emotions, and behavior. It is intended to be simple but serious in its impact. I have found that most people whom I have treated over the years, although they may have complex problems, want simple answers. Life can be hard, but sometimes you can make things more complicated than they need to be. If you are suffering, this book is designed to help. However, it is not designed to replace professional help. We strongly encourage you to seek treatment if the severity of your situation warrants professional intervention. This includes the use of medication if and when appropriate.

The ideas in this book are not intended to be a panacea, a cure-all for everything that ails you. This book is but the cornerstone for you to begin to build the foundation for a more positively motivated healthier lifestyle. Simply put, this book is designed to help you be all you can be. That means achieving peak performance, reaching your optimal potential everyday, not just avoiding illness. Growth, change and continued development lie within you. If you believe it, you can achieve it!

2

NEW "MEDICINE" FOR THE NEW AGE

Ours is a society that wants a quick fix, a pill or potion, a supplement that fixes everything immediately. Americans spend $23 Billion dollars a year on "dietary" supplements to make themselves feel better. Physicians prescribe medicines at approximately $6.39 billion each year to make our mood better (this is only a fraction of the estimated costs in that this figure includes only the top 3 selling SSRI's which are currently the most popularly prescribed psychiatric medication). View this material as a mental supplement, a dose of "mental medication"; a "Dose of Positivity" that is prescribed every day. *Daily Dose of Positivity* can ward off toxic negativity, anxiety, and depression just as a flu shot can help prevent catching the flu. As with any "medication", if you do not take it as prescribed, it will not work to its maximum benefit. Just as with antibiotics, blood pressure, and/or heart medication, the "prescription" of a *Daily Dose of Positivity* achieves maximum benefit only if taken as directed: Daily. This book gives you the ammunition/antidote to win the war over negativity. What your mind perceives, you are destined to achieve.

PART I: THE PAST

PSYCHOLOGY'S HERITAGE: BUILDING THE FOUNDATION OF EVIDENCE FOR THE EFFECTIVENESS OF POSITIVITY

3

IMPORTANCE OF ATTITUDE

"The greatest discovery of my generation is that human beings, by changing the inner attitudes of their minds, can change the outer aspects of their lives"

William James (1842-1910)
"Father" of American Psychology

William James wrote of the significance of people's thought processes impacting their lives more than 100 years ago. In fact, this is the very nature of the field of psychology: the science dealing with the mind and mental and emotional processes. The interaction between thoughts, feelings, behaviors, and the impact these all have on your health, although makes common sense today, has proven over the years to be difficult to establish scientifically. What to study and how to study it has been the topic of debate ever since psychology first emerged as a profession in the late 1800's. One thing is for certain: Attitude is extremely important to happiness, health, and well-being.

The following sections are not intended to be all inclusive of mind/body theory, health psychology, positive psychology, nor the comprehensive history of psychology. Rather, the following are a synopsis of the theoretical and historical assumptions in psychology and medicine that built the foundation for providing evidence for the efficacy of thinking Positivity.

4

HISTORY OF MIND/BODY THEORY

> Anybody knows that when you are stressed and having negative thoughts, self-doubt and anxiety, the body does not feel good in response. People may have palpitations or muscle tension. So we know our state of mind affects us physically. In the 70's, scientists began to discover that the brain produces chemicals in response to thinking processes. These chemicals affect our immune system, endocrine system, cardiovascular system and other functions. Every cell in our bodies has receptors for these molecules in these chemicals.
>
> Deepak Chopra

If you were to poll the general public, most of you would probably agree with the idea that what you think affects how you feel and consequently how you behave, and some may even agree that it all impacts your physical health. In fact, this seems to be common sense. What we know to be "true" today has its antecedents in the past.

Mind/body concepts date back to ancient beliefs that external forces can affect the body. The roots to scientific intellectual approaches to mind body medicine theories can be traced to the ancient Greeks; Hippocrates, Aristotle, Socrates, and Plato all addressed mind body relations in their teachings.

Mind body concepts in modern medicine can be traced most notably to Sigmund Freud whose psychoanalytic theories seemed to confirm the role of psychological factors causing and determining the manifestations of such conversion reactions as paralysis and blindness. In fact, this notion has become so acceptable in popular psychology that in the early 1970's the popular rock band The Who wrote the hugely successful rock opera Tommy. The plot in this artistic piece centers on the idea that psychological conflict can manifest itself in physical ways. In Tommy, the main character is rendered "deaf, dumb and blind" as a child as a result of witnessing the traumatic event of seeing his father kill his mother's lover. The thought of this event is so distressing to Tommy that he becomes imprisoned by these physical ailments well into adulthood. His only solace: pinball.

Freud and subsequent psychoanalysts popularized the notion that the mind can have profound affects on the physiology of the body and subsequent behaviors. What were once known as "hysteria" symptoms are now reflected in psychosomatic medicine and functional disorders; physical symptoms with no *known* medical cause or etiology. In the mid 20th century, Franz Alexander took this notion a step further in explaining specific physiological disorders. He differentiated between "hysterical" conversion reactions and what were so-called organ neuroses. For Alexander, emotional distress was thought to contribute to a variety of physical ailments such as essential hypertension, rheumatoid arthritis, thyrotoxicosis, peptic ulcer, ulcerative colitis, bronchial asthma and neurodermatitis. Alexander's theoretical assumption was that specific types of unconscious conflicts were purported to cause these specific types of disease as a result of stress that causes autonomic arousal that leads to chronic emotional and physiological distress. Medicine and psychology of the past had difficulty showing this theoretical connection between mind and body scientifically. In fact, Alexander's specificity theory has since been debunked; however, he always maintained a multifactorial approach to disease vulnerability emphasizing the importance of contributing and interacting factors such as genetics, environment, and various psychosocial factors.

Around the same time as Alexander, Adolph Meyer developed a parallel theory that continues to have a powerful influence on mainstream mind body theory. Meyer's psychobiological approach attempted to integrate mind and body into one psychobiological unit. His approach encouraged evaluating each aspect of the person's life – physiological, developmental, psychological, social and environmental. Meyer's psychobiological theory formulated the basis for the biopsychosocial approach to medicine proposed by George Engel in 1977. The biopsychosocial approach is the cornerstone to the Family Medicine specialty. It essentially proposes that all aspects, biological/physiological/genetic, psychological, and social, are interacting and affect one another. This approach suggests that illness is rarely separated from psychosocial processes and that the body is a container for emotional mental suffering.

5

STRESS THEORY

"It's not stress that kills us; it is our reaction to it."

Hans Selye

The notion of stress has been instrumental in the formulation of mind body theory. Walter B. Cannon is often credited as being the first researcher to recognize the role of emotional reactions in the development of illness. Cannon, a Harvard physiologist, first coined the term "fight-or-flight response" in 1927 describing the body's internal adaptive response to threat. Cannon believed that under certain circumstances, physical or emotional stimuli could strain animals and human beings beyond their ability to adapt successfully. In this fight-or-flight response, the body secretes catecholamines or stress hormones that immediately arouse certain key organ systems, preparing the person under threat to fight or flee. Early in our history, this "emergency reaction" was essential to survival and self-preservation. This response was appropriate at a time when human beings faced many physical threats, such as wild animals, that caused acute stress and could be handled effectively by fighting off the threat or running away to safety. Anxiety and fear based on this kind of threat, impending real physical danger, makes sense and most people do not have a 'problem' experiencing this sensation. The logic is: I am threatened physically and my adrenaline starts flowing. However, the threats you face today are often less recognizable as they are much more likely to be psychological in nature. Anxiety and fear based on psychological threats are much harder to recognize, thus making the emergency reaction of the body confusing. The logical thought with psychological stress is: why should my adrenaline be pumping, I am not in any (physical) danger. You have more of a problem with this kind of feeling because if you haven't made the conscious connection to the psychological threat, then the feelings and bodily sensations of the alarm reaction do not make sense. In addition, psychological threats are often more subtle and less intense than immediate physical dangers, thus are harder to recognize.

Social isolation, public humiliation, being ridiculed, emotional invalidation, and negative perception of oneself can be categorized as psychological threats or threats to your ego. Each chip taken out of your ego, your sense of self, is threatening, and like taking an ax to a tree, weakens it. Continue to keep chopping and the tree falls. Similarly, you get chopped down with each psychological swing of the ax. This reflects what I call the annihilation of self syndrome. The thought (albeit unconscious) may go something like this: "if my sense of self keeps getting smaller and smaller as a result of ego threats (that is, my self-esteem is dwindled down to nothing), then at some point I won't exist psychologically." This is very frightening. The pending thought that you might "lose your mind" and become "nothing" psychologically is very threatening. So you often behave, react, or respond in ways to protect yourself from these psychological threats. The fight or flight, emergency reaction, kicks into gear automatically. This process can however be counteracted by awareness and interpretation. Awareness of what is happening and an interpretation that is more positive.

Hans Selye was the first to demonstrate that the body responds to today's psychological stress as though it were still facing a real physical threat. Selye defined stress as "the nonspecific result of any demand upon the body". Stress was used to define the body's response to stimuli and the term stressor referred to the stimulus that elicited a response. Selye also formulated the concept of the General Adaptation Syndrome (GAS), which explains the body's nonspecific attempt to defend itself against noxious agents. The GAS involved three phases: The alarm stage, the resistance stage, and the exhaustion stage. The alarm phase occurs when a stressful stimuli is first encountered and is characterized by the triggering of the release of epinephrine (adrenaline) by the sympathetic nervous system which prepares the body to take action ("fight-or-flight"). The resistance phase is the period in which the body adjusts to deal with the stressor, and exhaustion refers to the phase when the body's defenses are no longer capable of dealing with the stressor. Selye believed this last stage could result in death. In reality, the first two phases are more common than the third stage. Selye also proposed the notion of eustress as opposed to distress. He believed that some stresses were positive (e.g. physical exercise) and called this type eustress. He reserved the term distress to refer to harmful demands on the body (e.g. extreme temperatures). Selye focused most of his work on the physiological response, failing to acknowledge other important factors such as coping skills, thought patterns and appraisal's as well as other individual characteristics. Richard Lazarus introduced a more complex theory that included coping mechanisms and appraisals of stress. He believed that a person's perception of stress was far more important than the actual event in determining the impact of the stressor. This theory involves the importance of thought processes in the management of stress, particularly psychological stress.

Unfortunately, the fight-or-flight response that was once very effective and adaptively appropriate (and in some cases still is—e.g. a barking, snarling dog) is no longer the best mechanism for coping with the psychological stress of today. It is not considered socially appropriate to beat up (fight) or run away (flight) from our boss during a negative performance review (no matter how much we may want to do so). So what do you do? You often engage in a psychological behavioral translation of the fight or flight emergency reaction. You respond by being passive-aggressive (fight) and/or with internalization and avoidance (flight). Internalizing the anxious feelings and thoughts that result from the psychological threat tends to lead you into depression.

So what is the nature of psychological stress? Taking a cognitive view, one may say our interpretation, our perception, our attitude is what perpetuates chronic psychological stress. There are two ways of "thinking" about the stress response and threat: there is the automatic emergency reaction or alarm system that is a preconscious sense perception that is immediate and self protective. That is, you are not consciously aware that it is triggered until you have the "symptoms" that accompany it (increased breathing, rapid heartbeat, muscular tension, etc.), at which time you make an automatic appraisal of the situation as threatening. This is triggered in milli-seconds before you consciously know it and has allowed human beings to survive for millions of years. This automatic perception is also largely tainted by your overall attitude and general perception of the world. If you tend to view the world negatively, then your automatic response tends to lean toward the negative. If your view of the world is more optimistic, then your response is more positive and growth-oriented.

There is also the mechanism by which conscious thought, your internal dialogue, triggers, or at least maintains, the same stress reaction although this may be more subtle. This is a manifestation of psychological stress. An example might be when you are excited about expressing your opinion at a work presentation and they say, "we're going with the other proposal." You might think to yourself, "they hate it, I am such a loser." Or giving the same proposal you get no immediate verbal response. What goes through your head when you express your opinion about something and nobody says anything? This can be perceived as invalidating, being "hung out in the wind," so-to-speak. This is an ax chop to your ego; the perceived lack of approval can be threatening to your ego. This type of threat still triggers your body's protective defense system of fight-or-flight.

You can also maintain the fight-or-flight reaction to real physical danger long after it would normally be shut off by what you think. "Road Rage" was a popular media term in the late 1990's to describe what might be seen as the fight end of the emergency reaction. The protective emergency reaction is triggered because of the physical threat of injury due to a potential car crash. What happens afterward, may be driven by what you think or what you are telling yourself about the situation. Once you recognize the threat no longer exists (the accident was avoided) the alarm reaction shuts off. Or does it? When someone cuts you off in traffic narrowly missing totaling your car, how do you respond? Slam on the breaks and breathe a sigh of relief that you were not fatally injured? Or do you curse the other driver and tailgate them to show how angry you are that you were violated by them. The latter response may be due to the thoughts, appraisal, or interpretation of the situation. What meaning do you assign it? Do you personalize it in a negative way? Most people would agree that the automatic thought or perception might be "Holy shit, I'm going to get killed!" Once you recognize that you are all right, that you are safe, the self preservation of fight-or flight shuts down. Unless you interpret the situation as, "that son-of-a-bitch did that on purpose. He intentionally cut me off." This personalized negative attitude would lead to a more passive-aggressive behavioral response such as tailgating, and perhaps an even more aggressive response, such as has been reported by the media in several incidences of car shootings. The negative thoughts are what maintain the stress response. This is an overly simplified version of the mind body connection related to psychological stress, but illustrative that you have the power to choose to respond with attitudes programmed toward negativity or Positivity. It is your choice.

6

THE FUNCTIONALITY OF ANXIETY AND DEPRESSION

"The mind is its own place, and in itself
Can make a Heav'n of Hell, a Hell of Heaven"

Satan, in Milton's Paradise Lost

Often you hear how problematic anxiety and depression are. You might have even seen commercials on TV targeting these problems by various pharmaceutical companies. Furthermore, public service and educational programs from the NIH and NIMH have helped legitimize the seriousness of these medical conditions. You can also find information regarding the crippling effects of such disorders on the Internet. In fact, this very book addresses the significance of these topics. Anxiety and depression are no doubt problematic, whether they are merely symptoms or full-blown disorders, but the better you understand them the better you are able to attend to them, thus making them less problematic. Let me be clear; this is not meant to trivialize how disruptive and paralyzing anxiety and depression can be. But, I am a believer that information is knowledge and knowledge applied is power, power for *your* life. The material in this section (the entire book, really) is designed to help you gain control. As a colleague of mine likes to say, "Forewarned is forearmed." So, let's get you ready for battle!

The medical model has been the predominate view in tackling the problems of mental and emotional conditions. The medical model posits that such disorders as anxiety and depression are medical illnesses due to chemical imbalances in the brain. Originally, researchers thought that the chemical imbalances in anxiety and depression were the result of structural abnormalities in the brain. With the advent of brain imaging technology, we are now concluding that although there may be structural differences in people who suffer from mental and emotional conditions, we are still faced with the proverbial chicken or egg dilemma. We do not know which comes first, the condition or the structural and chemical difference. For example, major, long-term depression has been connected to shrinkage in the area of the brain called the hippocampus, in some cases as much as 20%. And this region doesn't seem to bounce back after the depression remits. Scientists are not entirely sure why this occurs: Neurons may die or shrink, or creation or replenishment to the region may not be happening. Whatever may be the case, it seems linked to the stress hormone called cortisol. Furthermore, research indicates that the likelihood of further depressive episodes increases the more episodes you have. For instance, after the first episode of major depression, you have a 50-60% chance of having a second episode; after the second your risk of a third episode increases to 70% and after a third your chances of a fourth increase to 90%. It seems plausible that cortisol shrinks the hippocampus and that without intervention to replenish this region, you are at risk for subsequent stress induced depressive episodes. The good news is that studies have shown cognitive therapy, some principles upon which DDP was developed, can prevent recurrent depression. The German antidepressant tianetpine, counters this hippocampal shrinkage, also increasing the likelihood of preventing future depression. I suspect that this is also true of other medications. And, while structural differences and chemical changes in the brain may in fact exist, research now indicates this may be due primarily to how the brain functions (i.e. how you think), and this is either adaptive or maladaptive. Specifically, anxiety and depressive symptoms may be due more to brain function rather than structure. For example, negative thinking patterns have been shown to contribute to both anxiety and depressive disorders. Furthermore, different thinking patterns have varying effects on your brain's chemistry. I will elaborate on this further in the Negativity Vs. Positivity model explaining the psychophysiology of the mind body interaction. This research evidence may explain the chronic nature of anxiety and depressive disorders and lends support to the stress–induced ego wound Damage Control Model that I propose in later sections.

In the attempt to better understand such stress related emotional disorders as anxiety and depression, research has also focused on genetic influence and researchers are currently examining the plausibility of gene etiology in these conditions. But, as Robert Sapolsky, professor of biological sciences and neurology at Stanford University, states, "the environment you grow up in is as important as your DNA in determining the person you ultimately become." Experts agree that your development, personality, way of thinking, function and behavior, are a complex mix of biological, genetic, psychological, social and environmental factors. But, because you can control your own psychology, you can greatly influence the other factors to weigh in your favor, rather than against you.

Finally, chronic stress has been shown to have an influence on brain function, as well. The hypothalamic-pituitary-adrenal axis (HPA axis) is the area of the brain that modulates the human stress response and has been implicated in anxiety and depressive symptoms. For example, The Journal of the American Medical Association reports that childhood abuse may create a hormonal predisposition of anxiety and depression. Women who suffered severe stress early in life, which was reported as a history of childhood abuse, had nervous system hyper–reactivity as adults. They showed an increase in pituitary adrenal (HPA axis) and autonomic responses to stress. Think about this for a moment. This makes evolutionary sense. It benefits you to have imprinted in your brain information based on experience (especially experiences that threaten your survival) so that when you encounter a similar situation you can recall that stored blueprint of information, retrieve it automatically, and act accordingly. The problem is that you tend to over generalize the applicability of this stored blueprint of information. That is, anything that even remotely is sensed as a threat, including the more subtle and abstract ego threats, triggers the mental-emotional-behavioral survival schema blueprinted in your brain as a result of those earlier experiences, especially if they were particularly intense to begin with. This may explain why cognitive therapy, identifying and restructuring underlying schemas, is an effective strategy for coping with stress and helps to prevent recurring depression. This kind of current research, and the work of noted scientists such as Dr. Sapolsky, Antonio Damasio, Joseph LeDoux, Candace Pert, (and the list goes on) provide recent scientific evidence supporting the current thinking regarding anxiety and depression as functional, but mismatched maladaptive responses to stress. So, let's get a better understanding of the way this works.

Fear is essential for survival. It is a vital emotion preserved through evolution because it can be life-saving. In other words, cautious people live on to pass down their 'fear genes'. Fear allows for evasive action in a dangerous situation that may otherwise prove fatal. While the ability to regulate levels of fear may be adaptive and thus evolutionary prerequisites, scientists who study the functionality of emotions, such as Joseph LeDoux and Antonio Demassio, are now discovering that fear is the root problem in anxiety and panic *disorders*. While fear is a realistic response to a genuine threat, in contrast, anxiety is usually considered an unrealistic 'over-reaction' to a non-life-threatening situation (e.g., breaking out in a panic attack because you have to give a speech). Fear and anxiety, as defined, may have some physiologic similarities, such as the activation of the adrenal gland in the so-called "fight-or-flight" response; however, there may also be differences in terms of brain regions that are activated in fear vs. anxiety. If, because of our evolutionary heritage, an overactive fear response is the cause of anxiety disorders and panic attacks, does this mean these disorders are inherited? To some degree, the answer is yes. Studies involving twins suggest a genetic predisposition, a risk factor, for developing anxiety disorders. These studies show that an anxiety disorder in one twin probably predicts development of an anxiety disorder in the other. While the propensity for an anxiety disorder may be inherited, the form it takes would depend mainly on the environmental circumstances and learned coping mechanisms for stress. Having healthy coping mechanisms firmly in place may be able to help prevent the development of these crippling but ever-increasing problems. Given the right tools and strategies, these conditions are quite manageable.

You don't have to have a familial predisposition to be susceptible to anxiety and depression – your biologically driven stress response and survival mechanism may contribute as well. Let us now turn to the current thinking behind this explanation.

Daily Dose of Positivity™

CURRENT THINKING

"Human life is the only thing that takes care of itself."

—Napoleon Bonaparte

Current thinking now suggests an alternative yet intriguing explanation for how and why anxiety and depression are problematic. The current theory is that anxiety and depression are failures to regulate normal adaptive responses. Failures of the more advanced and complex structures of the frontal cortex, your 'primate-human' brain, to regulate or modulate the more primitive structures, your 'mammalian' and 'reptilian' brains. These normal adaptive responses are evolved survival mechanisms for dealing with the stress of threat to your physical well-being and safety; they become problematic when mismatched to the situation or environmental circumstances. In previous sections, I addressed this evolutionary adaptive function of the fight-or-flight survival mechanism or emergency reaction, your body's innate system to defend itself from physical danger, threat and potential bodily damage. When faced with physical danger, this system automatically at a preconscious level kicks into gear and protects you. You do not question your adrenaline pumping, your heart racing, your breathing quickening, or you muscles tensing in preparation for defending yourself in a physically threatening situation, such as when being attacked by a vicious barking, growling, snarling, dog, with bloodstained teeth! This system is part of the more primitive survival structures buried deep in the layers of your brain. What is more difficult to recognize is that this same system and physical experiences and behavioral desires or actions are triggered when your ego is threatened. But it is. The same physiology and behaviors and actions are triggered when our ego is threatened (e.g., you are picked last for the team, breakup with a boyfriend/girlfriend, teased for your appearance, hair, clothes, weight, etc., overlooked for a raise or promotion, 'dissed', and the list goes on…). Your neocortex, with the proper training, is designed and has evolved to modulate your more primitive impulses; it is just having a hard time keeping up with the advances of the evolution of society. The interaction and regulation (or lack there of) of your various systems is of course more complicated than this, but this is the general idea behind the current thinking.

Craig S. Travis, Ph.D.

The fight-or-flight survival response seems to explain the evolutionary functionality of anxiety, but what about depression? Depression and anxiety symptoms and disorders are very closely related. Research abounds regarding the high co-occurrence of anxiety and depression. Literature on comorbidity rates in the medical field suggest that anxiety and depressive symptoms overlap so much that patients with just one disorder may be the exception rather than the rule.

The following two diagrams are conceptual representations of this co-occurrence dynamic between anxiety and depression.

Daily Dose of Positivity™

Comorbid disorders in a 12 month period (50% of patients with major depression also had an anxiety disorder)

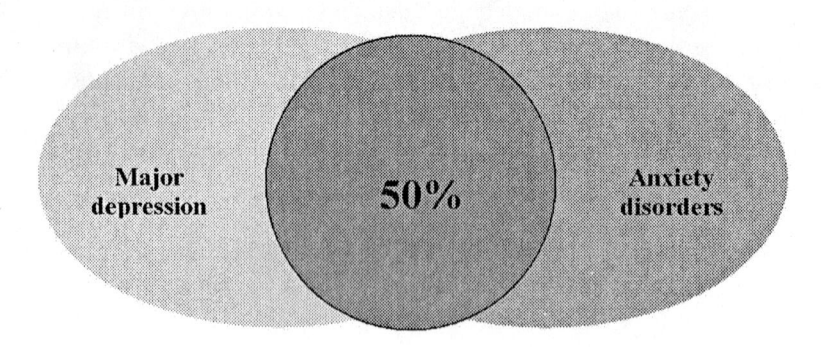

```
          Major         50%        Anxiety
         depression                disorders
```

When looking at symptoms and not full-blown disorders, the co-occurrence increases from 50% to 90% further supporting the current thinking and the ego wound analogy and Damage Control Model elaborated in the next section.

Conceptual representation of overlapping anxiety and depressive symptoms

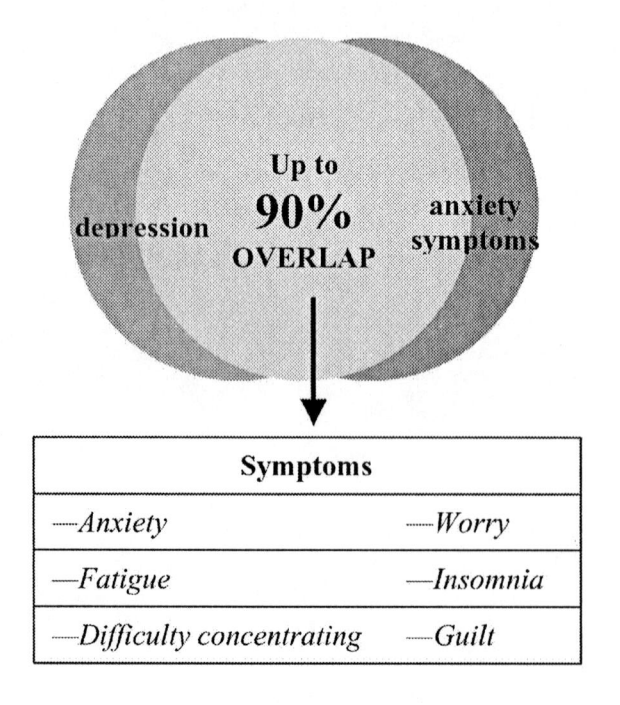

```
                    Up to
   depression       90%         anxiety
                   OVERLAP      symptoms
```

Symptoms	
—*Anxiety*	—*Worry*
—*Fatigue*	—*Insomnia*
—*Difficulty concentrating*	—*Guilt*

So, how is depression functional? What purpose does it serve? Is it just a part of anxiety? Andrew Solomon, author of *The Noonday Demon: An Atlas of Depression*, concludes that depression is an essential component of human life, and that it serves a biological role. He theorizes that just as pain is an essential sign of physical injury, so depression may be a personal indicator of psychological injury, or as I have phrased it, an ego wound. If this is accurate, it may very well explain the evolutionary preservation of the 'depressive gene' rather than its suppression. This is very similar to the following statement by Aaron Beck, one of the pioneers in developing cognitive behavioral theory, regarding anxiety: "Anxiety is not *the* pathological process in so-called anxiety disorders any more than pain or fever constitute the pathological process in an infection or injury". These theories provide compelling evidence to support the ego wound theory and damage control model I propose in the next section; that is anxiety and depression are not THE pathological problem; they are merely symptoms and warning signs of the problem, that which is a threat and subsequent damage to your ego! And your body is just taking care of it as best it knows how. It is trying to heal an abstract wound, one with very real physical aspects, thus the problem lies in a primitive system trying to defend itself against an advanced threat. Let me clearly state that I am not implying that you should treat the 'pain' or 'fever' of anxiety and depression *without* medication. Just as you might treat fever and pain from an infection or injury with medication, so too it is true that you might treat your psychic pain (anxiety and depression) with medications. But, as it is with pain and fever in an infection or injury, you want to get at the root cause. That is you would not only treat the pain from a broken ankle; if you want it to heal right (i.e., not cause problems in the future), then you need to treat the source, the broken bone. So too it is true for the injury and infection of an ego wound; indeed, you may need to alleviate the symptoms of anxiety and depression through medication, but if you don't treat the source, the 'broken heart', if you will, then the injury doesn't heal. If you want it to heal right, you must treat it, not ignore it or deny its significance as we so often do with our feelings. To prevent infection after you cut yourself, you clean and then bandage the wound. Depending on the severity you might put over-the-counter antibiotic ointment on it, or as is often the case with surgery, your physician may prescribe a preventative oral antibiotic. Just as we need to treat the physical wound to ensure proper healing and to prevent infection and future problems, we need to treat the ego wound similarly, to prevent infection and subsequent problems (i.e., recurring anxiety and depression) in the future.

Clean and bandage your ego wounds and beware of infection! The risk of infection after ego wounds results from negativity, particularly in the form of self-doubt and negative self-criticism. It is true that you are your own worst enemy in that you have the capacity to use your mind against you. Infectious negative thinking will trickle down from your mind and into your body and can infiltrate virtually every system and cell. So, when you do get your feelings hurt, treat them. When your ego is 'cut', put on an 'ego bandage'. If you see it happen to children, do it for them. While writing this book, some relatives were visiting from the east coast. My aunt and uncle, cousin-in-law and her 18-month-old daughter came out to visit so the 'younger' generation of second cousins would have some memories of each other. My son, who was 3 ½ years old at the time, intentionally fell off his bike to pull the attention away from his younger cousin. In doing so, he fell on his bottom. He cried, because he was injured, not physically, but emotionally. He didn't feel he was important because his uncle Todd was paying attention to his cousin. Having experienced and thus learning the nurturing treatment of parental attention when he has been physically hurt or sick with an ear infection, being an only child at the time, he behaved in a way he unconsciously (and maybe even consciously) knew would get him what he wanted and needed, nurturance to his ego wound. His pride from losing his uncle's attention was hurt more than his bottom from intentionally falling off his bike! But, he indeed got what he needed and wanted! Instead of uncle Todd dismissing his feelings ("quit acting hurt, you fell on purpose, you're not hurt"), he hugged him and continued to hug him until he stopped crying and then they talked about what had happened; they recognized the ego wound (feelings hurt through less attention), the subsequent attempt at damage control (get attention by falling off bike—act wounded and you'll get what you need!), and necessary treatment (the hug, the nonverbal message encoded at the primitive brain level). Talking about it processed it at the advanced level helping lead to clean, healthy, and bandaging thoughts (I am important to uncle Todd) rather than infection of negative thoughts and poor self-image (uncle Todd hates me and I am unlovable and worthless). They then talked about better behavioral ways to get attention, like saying, "Uncle Todd, look at me!" If you are not fortunate enough to have had this kind of healing environment and relationship while growing up, learn to either do it for yourself (e.g., use the DDP strategies in this book), and/or create an environment by surrounding yourself with others who can, now!

For some reason, we don't like to admit when our feelings get hurt. This may be instinctual; to thwart any would be predator if we were to expose our vulnerabilities. What happens to a wounded antelope on the African plains; or the hurt deer in the American forests? They fall prey to the lions, cougars, tigers, and other would be predators, in essence they become dinner. From a survival perspective, it benefits the wounded animal to not show its vulnerability, to limp away and hide, to lick and heal its wounds. This is adaptive for your physical survival. But why don't you admit when your feelings get hurt? Why not expose your emotional vulnerabilities and admit when your ego is wounded? Your primitive brain, the part responsible for your ancestor's physical survival and thus evolutionarily passed on to you, kicks in and often overrides the newer parts of your brain. So, again you can see that you take a normally physically adaptive response—don't show your wounds to predators—and misapply it to the psychological world. Yes, some people will and do prey on your emotional vulnerabilities, but most do not. And even so, more advanced and adaptive psychobehavioral responses are available and more suitable than the misapplied primitive physiobehavioral ones connected with your emergency reaction. Another reason we may hide expressing our 'negative' feelings of emotional pain and vulnerabilities is because it is risky; risky because we often do not get the response that we want, acceptance and validation. We risk the ego wound of rejection of our true selves, our feeling selves. So we are simply trying to protect ourselves from a wounded ego, it is our attempt at damage control. The problem is that by doing so, we miss the opportunities to get what we need to ensure a strong identity and sense of self: emotional validation. While this protective mechanism of hiding your wounds may be instinctual and at one time adaptive with physical injuries, the opposite is true for hiding your emotional pain and anxiety. Chronically suppressing your emotions contributes to a number of physical ailments such as chest pain, headaches, indigestion, diarrhea, etc. Habitually hiding your negative feelings also leads to disease susceptibility and is related to decreased immune function and increased risk of cardiovascular disorders, colitis, Rheumatoid Arthritis, and cancer. For example, Karen Weihs, from George Washington University, recently presented her research at the 2002 American Psychiatric Association detailing the benefits of expressing negative feelings and anxiety as a protective factor in the progression of breast cancer. Weihs' research reveals a link between a woman's emotional state and disease outcome; suboptimal ways of coping with stress lead to a greater risk of disease progression. In addition, women who have experienced stressful events in the year before breast cancer diagnosis tend to have a poorer outcome. This appears to be related to high levels of the stress hormone cortisol. However, women with breast cancer can increase the length of survival by learning how to regulate their emotions and better cope with stress by expressing their anxiety and distress and admitting that they need support. Weihs also addresses the problem of denial. When doctors ask how they are coping, and inquire whether they are feeling anxious or depressed, many women will say no, because they 'don't want to distract their doctor from the cancer'. However, this is not to say that all women who appear to be coping are in denial. It seems to be the 'superfunctioning' women that are often at risk. Being diagnosed with breast cancer is stressful and emotional, thus it is perfectly normal for these women to feel anxious. Weihs recommends women with breast cancer to sit down with their family, as early as possible after diagnosis, to discuss and rearrange family roles. This provides the opportunity for areas of stress to be identified and removed from the patient. While this example specifically addresses women, other data suggests similar relationships and dynamics for both men and women who have some form of cancer. The example of cancer and negative emotions provides evidence for the value of sharing your emotional pain to properly treat ego wounds. You need to let them out even though the instinctual thing is to keep them in to protect yourself; but keeping them in is not really protective, it leads to more health problems. So we instinctually have an ill-fated logic, don't show your ego pain so that you may survive predators only to become sick with other disease from suppressing the hurt. Remember what I said about the positivity of negative feelings; Positivity is not about eliminating these feelings but rather not allowing them to dominate your life. All emotions are developmentally important because they evolved to alert you to specific kinds of problems. Emotions become negative when they consume and control your life.

Perhaps we hide our emotions due to sociocultural influences, keeping the British 'stiff upper lip' in times of adversity. Regardless, it happens. The problem is that what at one time might have been adaptive and natural has not caught up with the evolution of society. We are a more sophisticated culture and humane society that need not worry so much about the primitive threats and dangers that our ancestors used to face. But as you may well know personally, old habits and patterns die hard.

Therefore, I propose that anxiety and depression are merely physiobehavioral reactions of your body's natural defense system against physical threat, but they are maladaptively attached to a more sophisticated and often unrecognizable (or at least consciously un-acknowledgeable) ego threat. Your body/minds attempt to repair the damage. In other words, you try to use a primitive system designed for specific, concrete, physical threats (e.g., bacterial and viral infection, cuts, bruises, etc) to defend against more sophisticated, abstract, diffuse psychological threats (e.g., social rejection, teasing, invalidation, etc.). Simply put, your hurt emotions (injured ego) 'ask' your body to protect it, to repair the damage, when it would be more adaptive to 'ask' the brain/mind through higher processing (rational, logical, thoughts/cognitions) to do it.

Craig S. Travis, Ph.D.

SEND IN THE MARINES: THE DAMAGE CONTROL MODEL— UNDERSTANDING PSYCHOLOGICAL THREATS & EGO WOUND REACTIONS

"I have not yet begun to fight."

Captain John Paul Jones

"The Marines have landed, and the situation is well in hand."

Richard Harding Davis,
war correspondent (1885)

    I would like to now further develop the current thinking behind anxiety and depression as your body's natural defense system gone awry (i.e., failure to modulate normal adaptive responses), and expand it into what I like to call The Damage Control Model, or defending the ego wound. As you have seen, the human body is quite remarkable in its ability to take care of itself naturally, without a lot of conscious thought on your part. That is, you don't spend a lot of time thinking about digesting your food, breathing, resisting bacteria and viruses, etc. No, your body's natural defense systems operate in an unconscious natural state, and for the most part, do extremely well. As you have read, under moderate conditions of stimulation, you thrive. But, excess stress, and your body's system is taxed, and without corrective action begins to breakdown, showing signs of wear and tear (you just don't always pay attention to those signals). It is through stress and your response to stress, mentally, emotionally, and physiobehaviorally, that you can witness the damage control model and the functionality of anxiety and depression.
    Imagine this: your best friend, your spouse, your partner, boyfriend or girlfriend, brother or sister, maybe even your mom and dad, perhaps your boss, comes up to you and says, "What in the world are you wearing? That outfit makes you look fat and old." Or the more blatant comment, "I hate you," or "You suck." These comments are not physical assaults (certainly the later two could easily be seen as real warnings of potential physical harm), but ouch!

What a verbal/emotional punch in the gut! Certainly could be construed as a metaphorical chop to the ego tree. You may literally have a knee-jerk reaction and subconsciously sensing the threat, lash out in fear and anger or want to slink away in despair. Depending on the perceived severity of the stressor, you go through the 3 natural motions of the stress response: higher processing (cognition/thought), physio-emotional action (fight/flight-anxiety), and withdrawal or shutdown (depression). This dynamic is easy to see when dealing with a real threat to your physical safety. Unfortunately, you often do not consciously recognize the threat, as it is subtler due to the psychological nature (the ego wound).

The following diagram displays a conceptual framework of the biologically instinctive human stress response.

Damage Control Model—Inverted Triangle Stress Response

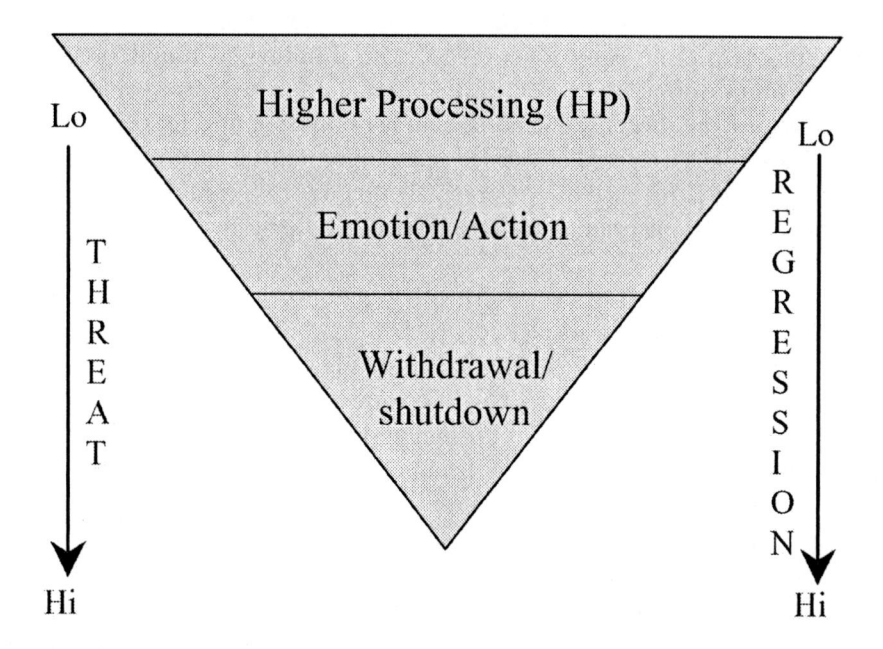

```
Lo                                              Lo
 |    Higher Processing (HP)                     |
 |                                               | R
 |                                               | E
 | T        Emotion/Action                       | G
 | H                                             | R
 | R                                             | E
 | E        Withdrawal/                          | S
 | A         shutdown                            | S
 | T                                             | I
 |                                               | O
 ▼                                               | N
Hi                                               ▼
                                                Hi
```

Although you may think you only have one, in fact, you have three brains. Your brain carries the story of human evolution and consists of an intricate web of three distinct clusters of various parts that stack on top of one another. The evolution of your brain is hierarchical and has formed a 3-tiered system that is complexly interwoven. The 3 components roughly correspond with the 3 levels of the inverted triangle stress response diagram above; the bottom tier is smallest and most primitive in function followed by a hierarchical development in form and function. The foundation of your brain starts with the reptilian brain, which includes the brain stem and cerebellum; this is the oldest and most primitive part of your brain. The reptilian brain is mechanical and unconscious; it drives the basic survival instincts (eat it or be eaten!). Surrounding the reptilian brain, the next level is the mammalian brain, which involves the limbic system and is responsible for emotion. Your emotions are generated in the mammalian brain but not experienced here, as it is not conscious. Because it is connected to the reptilian brain, this level also generates survival behavior but branches out and adds more complex emotions and sophisticated behaviors (love, anger, sadness, fear, happiness, nurturance, etc.), not just simply reflex. The mammalian brain is more advanced than the reptilian brain, but not quite as sophisticated as the next level, the primate/human brain. The primate/human brain is much larger and complex than the other two lower levels and consists of the cortex and neocortex. Your primate/human brain is most concerned with thinking, planning, organizing and communicating. It is responsible for the higher processing coping responses to stress. Because each of the three brains is connected, their specific functions still get triggered as needed (e.g., physiological survival) and oftentimes these mechanisms that are largely designed for physical survival (reptilian and mammalian brains) are triggered psychologically when your ego is threatened.

When coping with stress, you start with higher processing. That is you enlist the help of your more advanced neocortex, the complex outer primate/human brain. Higher processing (e.g., conscious thinking, connected awareness, problem solving, attitude, etc.) is gradual; it is slower, adaptive and more creative in its ability than the primitive mammalian and reptilian brains. As you can see by the diagram, higher processing is larger and has more possibilities in its repertoire. It monitors and mediates the lower brains until stimulation becomes 'stress'. Higher processing is asking 'what would be a good idea/choice given my situation?' It is appropriate for most of today's stress, which is largely psychological in nature. As pressure increases (stimulation transforms to stress), you regress back to more primitive biological coping mechanisms. You have a built in safety valve; your body does what it 'thinks' is necessary for survival. So, under increased pressure, your mammalian and reptilian brains are enlisted and become activated. You move downward in the triangle and as the diagram indicates, coping responses become more limited, narrow and focused. Your primitive brains are more deliberate and purposeful; their function is survival at all cost (especially the reptilian brain). There is no thought of future consequences. The primitive brain is extremely here-and-now; it only knows the past and present. It is not designed to think in the future. It does not think of the possible ramifications in the future based on you're current coping choices; what it 'thinks' is: If I don't preserve myself right now, there is no tomorrow! Your primitive brains are responsible for triggering the fight-or-flight emergency reaction. There is increased fear (anxiety), energy, agitation, and motion; your adrenalin starts flowing, your heart races to pump necessary blood to your muscles in preparation to flee or defend against your predator. In addition, the body prepares itself for potential physical damage; the immune system kicks into gear producing more natural killer cells, your blood gets thicker and coagulates preparing itself to clot in case you get an open wound or laceration of some sort. Adaptive physiologically if you suffer an open wound during the ensuing battle. But with chronic psychological stress, perpetuated by negative thinking, there is no obvious real predator, no literal wound nor bacterial or viral infection for the immune systems natural killer cells and the other various survival systems to attack, so they end up attacking your own body. You simmer, stew, and boil in your body's own chemicals. This is what leads to and is meant by stress related physical health conditions. And often is the case that the predator, the threat of injury or infectious agent is you in the form of negative hypercritical self-judgment. You can be your own worst enemy. And as you can see, we often attack our enemies in order to survive them. The irony being that with psychological threats, often we are attacking and defeating ourselves, hence the phrase self-defeating circle or cycle.

Sometimes you need the emotion. When you are in a life-threatening situation, you want that reptilian fight-or-flight. You want action. Emotion is what triggers your arousal; you can't move that fast in higher processing. Higher processing was designed and evolved for a different purpose, psychological stress. Again the problem seems to be a mismatch of coping response to the situation or stressor. Same goes for higher processing, it is not most adaptive when you need to act quickly, like moving out of the way of that speeding bus that is about to hit you as you cross the street. In such a situation, you better be in fight-or-flight (preferably flight, I wouldn't want to fight a bus), not thinking about what manufacturer made the bus, or how many stops the bus is making, or wondering if the bus driver sees you, or how many people are on it. No, you want to get the hell out of the way.

As you move downward in the triangle, and the stress of pressure increases, you continue to regress biological and physiobehaviorally, finally reaching withdrawal or shutdown. This is when your body shuts down to conserve energy for the vital organs to make sure they keep working. Think of what happens when two animals get into a fight. They start by attempting to deter their enemy or attacker before the fight begins using gestures, grunts, growls, and assorted animated behavior. The idea, perhaps if I warn them loudly enough I can scare them away and avoid the physical confrontation. (Perhaps you even know some people who act this way) After all, they are usually just protecting their territory. If the attempted warning doesn't work, the fight ensues, sometimes leading to the death of one or the other. Often, the fight stops when one is severely wounded at which point that animal limps, hobbles, or slinks away. And then what do you see? The wounded animal withdraws, finds a quiet safe place to lie down and hide, conserve energy, and lick to heal its wounds. Or, the wounded animal waits to die. So you can see that from a biological perspective, you are simply attempting to control the amount of damage to your body, hence the Damage Control Model.

Looking at this dynamic from a *psychological* perspective in trying to understand anxiety and depression, we see the following diagram:

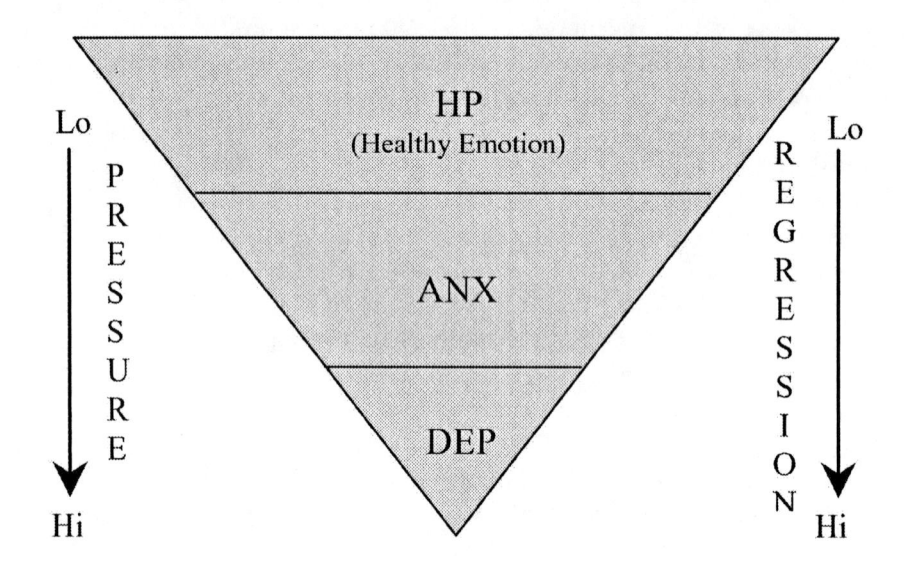

Lo
P
R
E
S
S
U
R
E
Hi

HP
(Healthy Emotion)

ANX

DEP

Lo
R
E
G
R
E
S
S
I
O
N
Hi

Higher Processing (HP) explanation

The mind is a glorious and wonderful, yet tricky entity; it can work for you or work against you. As a human being, you have the capacity to think both healthily and unhealthily, to conjure up negativity and positivity. The beautiful thing about your mind is that you get to put into it exactly what you want to get out of it! You have the power to think whatever you want. Make your mind work for you or make it work against you. It's your choice!

Higher Processing (HP) means using your capacity for more rational consciously deliberate and healthy thought processes and this leads to ensuing healthy emotions and behaviors. HP is what keeps you from 'flying off at the handle' and acting impulsively, which usually gets you in trouble. You engage the more advanced and sophisticated outer brain, the cortex. You use this part of your brain to regulate the more primitive parts responsible for anxiety and depression. With moderate stimulation, you function well and are able to manage and handle pretty much whatever life throws at you. Higher processing is a greater conscious awareness about how you function and how your mind and body are connected. It is more than specific beliefs and automatic thoughts in particular situations. It is an attitude; it is how you carry yourself through the day. It means using the power of your mind to overcome your obstacles, whether they're physical, or psychological. It is built on knowledge, common sense and reasoning skills (deductive and inductive) and like any other behavior is a learned skill that can be honed. *Daily Dose of Positivity* is one way to hone that skill to develop that positive 'sphere of attitude' that will infiltrate all aspects of your life, personal, physical, and social. It can be subtle, but it is transformational. Higher processing leads to healthy emotions, physiology, and behavior, which has a reciprocating and self-promoting cycle.

ANXIETY explanation

If you do not intervene and stop the stress cycle by developing healthy coping strategies, you will move into and eventually stay stuck in the anxiety (emotion/action—fight-or-flight) and depression (withdrawal/shutdown) mode of the Damage Control Model. This is because the mind/body perpetually perceives and interprets everything as threatening, whether it is physical or psychological. You essentially become hypersensitive to anything deemed a threat including your own thoughts, feelings, and behaviors. You live in anxiety because you think everything is threatening. Negative internal dialogue, self-talk that is hypercritical, unfairly judgmental, invalidating, and devaluing, is very threatening to your ego. Continue to view yourself and the world in such character assassinating terms, and you live in a constant state of arousal; the fight-or-flight emergency reaction survival mechanism never shuts off, it continues to operate at a subtle level. You may have grown up in an emotionally invalidating environment. Or, perhaps you are experiencing invalidation in a current relationship or work environment, and subsequently, your feelings are hurt. As a result, you may be stuck in the mindset 'I must be alert and on guard—I can't trust (sharing how I feel with) anyone!' Due to this negativity, understandably a natural impulse, you don't allow yourself to recuperate, to escape the danger, the danger of continued ego wounds. So you invariably slip into depression, the primal mind and body's way of trying to escape the threat, danger and subsequent wound.

DEPRESSION explanation
When it's chronic psychological stress, usually kept alive by the infection of negativity, your body decides it can't take any more and needs to recuperate; it needs to remove itself from the 'fight' and shut down to heal. The body is just trying to take care of itself from a phsyiobehavioral perspective. Without the overt threat and ensuing battle and consequent physical injury, it looks like depression. But if you are the enemy, the infection through your own negative thinking, how do you remove yourself from the battle? Use DDP or other methods to stop beating yourself up!

I have used the following surgery anecdote with patients, medical students, and physician residents to help explain how anxiety and depression could possibly be functional. While writing this book, my father was diagnosed with an abdominal aortic aneurysm (AAA). If you don't know what this is, suffice to say it is a very serious medical condition that without treatment can lead to rupture, which almost certainly leads to death. A ruptured AAA killed Lucille Ball of *I Love Lucy* fame. My father's surgeon educated him on what would happen from a physiological perspective. He described the procedure; essentially they would make an incision about 11-12 inches long in his abdomen, remove or slide his organs over, repair the damaged aorta, and then return his organs and close the incision. My dad likes to refer to it as, "they gut you like a fish." It took 48 external metal staples to hold the exterior wound closed; we are not sure how many interior sutures were used. The incision ran from his pubic bone up to his breastbone. In essence, he would be responding and healing from a major intrusive wound as if a sword had sliced him. To paraphrase his surgeon, it's the cave man reflex; something that was part of your evolutionary journey. The body says, 'You have just been gored/clawed by a wooly mammoth or saber-toothed tiger!' Stop all leaking of blood. Save all bodily fluids. The kidneys tend to or actually shut down to preserve fluid. No fluids out, and no fluids in due to the body saying, 'we got major damage here, shut down 'til we figure this thing out.' So, the body signals organs and other systems to shut down, don't pump any fluid, keep it, you need it to survive. In the surgery, when your abdominal aorta is clamped off, it puts a significant strain on the heart. However, the retention of fluids is more of a problem. If they are unable to reduce the fluid buildup, after about two days of the heart straining to move all the excess fluid (blood) around, there is a significant possibility of a myocardial infarction or heart attack. Ironically, my father was at a greater risk of dying, not from the actual wound itself, but after the surgery as his body tried to recuperate. This surgical wound would have a significant effect on his energy and activity level. He would be fatigued and could expect to tire easily, probably sleep a lot, lose his appetite (he lost 10 pounds from hardly eating), act lethargic, move slowly, he would be weak physically, and was restricted in what he was allowed to lift. My father having been through other hospital procedures before respectfully diminished the significance of the impact of such a physical wound. He said the day he got home from the hospital he went right to bed. He slept until 11 a.m. the next morning, he then got up, showered, ate breakfast and was back in bed by 12 p.m. and slept the rest of the day! He said he was wiped out.

It was after his surgery and he was recuperating at home that I had my epiphany about the functionality of anxiety and more so depression. You see, such a physical wound/injury slows you down; you get tired easily. Your body conserves its energy and puts it where it needs it, toward the wound healing. So, everything slows or shuts down due to the physical stress your body goes through. When you look at this dynamic (the inverted triangle stress response) from a physical, biological, and survival perspective, that is a real physical threat and subsequent wound (bruise, laceration, broken bone), it makes sense. In my father's case the threat of surgery and subsequent surgical wound followed by withdrawal for healing. But without the real danger, without the overt physical wound, it doesn't make sense. Taking a closer look perhaps it does. Using the ego wound Damage Control Model, anxiety looks like fight-or-flight, you just don't see or consciously recognize the danger. The threat is most likely psychological in nature and is often internally generated, or at least kept alive, through negative thinking and interpretation, although you are probably not aware of it. Constant threat and bombardment on your ego resulting from negativity, whether from an actual invalidating negative environment or internally driven through hypercritical self-judgment, devaluing, hopeless, helpless thoughts, and you move into depression, or shutdown mode. Instinctually, you want to retreat, to remove yourself from the battle and bombing of your ego. Given this and depression looks a lot like limping away, curling up to lick and heal your wounds. If my father hadn't been through a major surgery with an 11-12 inch scar as a reminder, and his response to it would have looked a lot like depression (sleeping all the time, weight loss, fatigue, lack of energy, decreased motivation, thoughts of death, loss of appetite, etc.). Depression, from this mind/body, physiological-immunological sense, may be considered an attempt at wound healing. Just as in a severe physical wound where your system shuts down to recuperate and rejuvenate itself, and you withdraw to conserve energy, depression, resulting from psychological battle and wounds, is an attempt to conserve energy, a shutting down of your system, to go to the wound so it can heal. The problem is, where is the wound? It is too diffuse and abstract for your body to figure out, yet it tries to from a primitive physiological sense. Comparing the physical wound to the psychological ego wound and it triggers some of the same physiological machinery, but you don't validate the significance of the psychological wound because you can't see it, it is too abstract. I mean, where is the ego? Go ahead, point to it. Not easy is it? So just as we can engage in physical battle and suffer subsequent damage, we can do psychological battle and also are inflicted with psychological damage. Often, the other person does not intentionally do this, that is to say they are just trying to take care of their ego damage, but it has the impact of intentional physical damage. And you can engage in your own personal battle, caused by negativity, equally impacting your self with your own damage. And so, after the battle, you either curl up to lick and heal your wounds, or wait to die. Perhaps that is the instinctual motivation behind suicide, but the last bastion of attempt at regaining control: you killed me with your assault, but I will decide when I die from it! But what if, through your own negativity, you are the insult/assault? Withdrawing from the toxic environment is an illusion; you cannot escape yourself. Depression does not get you away from the assault if you have fallen victim to negativity, although you think it does. And I understand how easy it is to get caught in this vicious self-defeating, negative cycle.

Since my epiphany about my dad's surgery, I have run across other authors who share a similar view about the functionality of negative emotions and anxiety and depression. In particular, University of Colorado, Boulder professor Steven Maier's work in psychonueroimmunology is interesting. He suggests the fight-or-flight stress response is a relatively recent development from an evolutionary perspective. He believes the body's emergency reaction borrowed from physiological machinery already in place used to fight infection. Your immune system acts as a diffuse sense organ that when activated by stress most likely plays a role comparable to hormones (e.g., cortisol, etc.) in altering mood and cognition. The association with the immune system highlights depression's apparent adaptive value from a biological evolutionary perspective. Just as a fever might, depression engineers an organismic change that reduces energy output and conserves resources. Depression might be viewed as the body's psychological attempt at repairing damage. Preserve everything within itself—nothing out, nothing in—until the danger is gone. But rather than bacterial or viral infection of a physical wound, what is infectious to the ego is negativity and emotional invalidation! 20 years of stress research by Dr. George Chrousos, Chief of the Pediatric and Reproductive Endocrinology Branch at the National Institute of Child Health and Human Development, and Philip Gold of the Clinical Neuroendocrinology Branch at the National Institute of Mental Health, also lend support to the functionality of but misapplied physiobehavioral stress response of anxiety and depression. Drs. Chrousos and Gold theorize a complex interplay between the nervous system and stress hormonal system known as the hypothalamic-pituatary-adrenal axis (HPA). Think of the HPA axis as a feedback loop similar to a thermostat to warm and cool your house, but instead, it regulates your body's stress 'temperature'. The HPA feedback loop via signals from the brain trigger the release of hormones needed to respond to stress (cortisol, CRH, ACTH, adrenaline, etc.) thus priming your body to be alert and ready to escape danger. Remember, this is an evolutionary adaptive primal response to physical threats; it is the body's natural defense system and gives you the strength and speed to ward off (fight) or escape (flight) the impending threat. The HPA axis communicates with various regions of the brain, including the limbic system, which controls motivation and mood, with the amygdala, which is responsible for the fear response to danger, and with the hippocampus, which plays a role in memory as well as motivation and mood. Normally, with short tem physical stress (threats to safety), cortisol exerts a feedback effect to shut down the stress response after the threat has passed. But when stress persists, via more subtle psychological threats and the infection of negativity, the HPA axis does not shut down as it is supposed to, thus doing more harm than good. Chrousos and colleagues, through their research, suggest that an overactive HPA axis may be responsible for melancholic or chronic depression, of which a cornerstone feature is chronic anxiety. He has shown that people with depression have a blunted ability to "counterregulate," or adapt to the negative feedback of increases in cortisol. In essence, your body turns on the 'fight-or-flight' emergency response but is prevented from shutting it off again. This in turn produces constant anxiety and overreaction to stimulation, and is followed by the paradoxical response of 'learned helplessness' in which you lose all motivation, a phenomenon attributed to research by psychologist Martin Seligman.

Daily Dose of Positivity™

Remember that anxiety and depression occur together so frequently that experiencing one without the other may be the exception rather than the rule. Why is this? Well, following the inverted triangle stress response and you see that each level or stage can have overlapping symptoms as you move through them. The more pressure, the more damage to your ego through infectious negative devaluing, hypercritical thoughts about yourself and your competence and ability to cope (I can't handle this, I am such a loser, what a @#$&-up, I'll never be able to do anything right, what a piece of shit I am!). Those who are depressed only and show no signs of anxiety have reached the bottom; depression or shutdown mode. This is the body's unconscious innate survival instinct. Conserve as much energy as possible to heal the wound. Perhaps the following military analogy will help show the apparent function of this dynamic.

Inverted Triangle Stress Response Showing Overlap of Anx/Dep Sx's

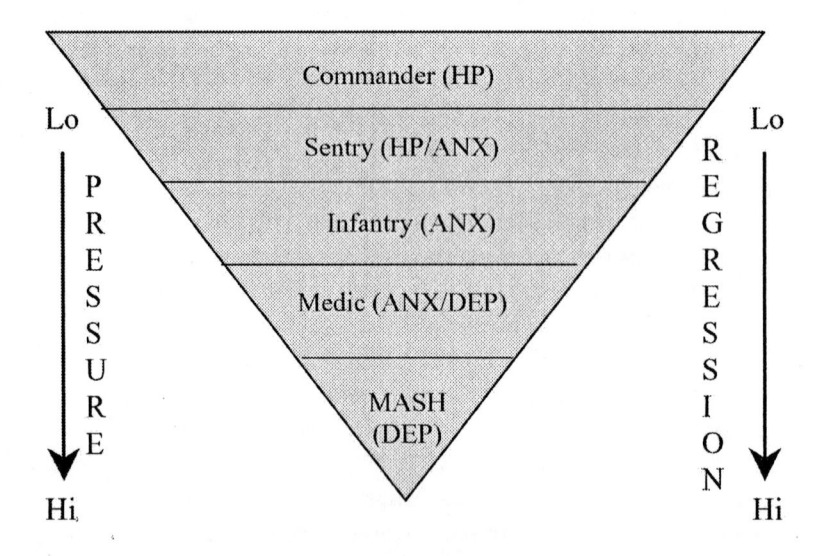

```
                  Commander (HP)
Lo                                              Lo
 |              Sentry (HP/ANX)                  |
 P                                               R
 R              Infantry (ANX)                   E
 E                                               G
 S                                               R
 S             Medic (ANX/DEP)                   E
 U                                               S
 R                                               S
 E                 MASH                          I
 |                 (DEP)                         O
 v                                               N
Hi                                              Hi
```

HP represents The Commander in Chief: confident and resourceful, fully functional and adaptive. Think of it as being stationed stateside and at base camp or the barracks. You feel safe. When operating from this base, your commander uses healthy coping strategies, finds positive meaning, and is grounded in more objective positive thinking. Your Commander in Chief experiences a full range of healthy emotions, identifies them, acknowledges them as significant and valid, accepts them, and expresses or releases the feeling in personal ways deemed reasonably appropriate (shares them with others, vents, journals, exercises, draws, etc.). Your commander is not afraid to neither feel nor show emotion, but does not allow emotion to run roughshod over your life. You are able to ride the waves of the seven seas: calm, cool, collected, control, confident, competent and, connected. Your commander is able to recognize the difference between physical threat and ego threats and can healthy cope with both types of damage quite well. Your commander waits to hear from the sentry that there may be a possible threat and then determines the appropriate course of action. If the threat is minimal, the stress is not perceived as overwhelming, healthy coping ensues and you are able to break the anxiety/depression downward spiral, or triangle as the case may be.

HP/ANX is the sentry. You shift to this level with slight increase in percieved stress. This is the part of your brain that is on watch but there is no overt sign of threat. Your sentry has increased awareness but has not necessarily sounded the alarm. There is a greater alertness to your surroundings and potential threat (e.g., that suspicious looking character lurking in the shadows may potentially attack and hurt me, but there is no immediate danger). Your sentry is quicker to act and sound the alarm than your commander.

ANX is similar to the infantry. Threat detected and alarm is sounded. Once your sentry sounds the alarm, the infantry without question prepares for and enters battle (e.g., He has lunged at me from the shadows! I'm in danger! Fight him off or run away). The fight or flight emergency reaction kicks in and your body prepares for damage. The battle is often chaotic and you do not care about tomorrow or three days from now (let alone preparing for the long-term future by setting up your mutual fund account); your immediate concern is fight now, flee now, live now! Of course, if you are in battle long enough, you are bound to get wounded.

ANX/DEP represents the medic. This suggests that you are still on the battlefield fighting, but there is an attempt at retreat (withdrawal) and triage repair. You do your best at treating the wound given the limited resources and hostile surroundings. You feel like you can't quite fight back or flee the situation without outside help. And the ironic part is that you are being patched up and assessed to see if you can return to battle! If the damage is not severe enough, you are put right back into harms way. The difficulty is determining the severity of the ego wound and when you are able to continue about your business after a quick triage and bandage, and understanding when you may need surgical repair. Sometimes triage is enough attendance to the wound, but if the wound is great enough, you need more attention, conservation and concentration of energy to attend to the wound. So you move down to depression because that is what the body knows; that given a serious enough wound you have to withdraw and shutdown to recuperate.

DEP is analogous to MASH (mobile army surgical hospital). If your medic is not able to repair the damage, or you get hit with another 'artillery shell' to the same spot (ego wound) after returning to battle, and the damage is severe enough, you are withdrawn from battle and potential further assault and injury. You are taken to a place where the sole purpose is specified for healing and recuperation. Energy is conserved and focused on healing the specific damage so you can get on your feet again. But as indicated, physical injuries and illness tend to be easier to 'see' then psychological ones.

What makes overcoming past stressors, damage, and ego wounds so difficult? Neuroscientist and emotion researcher, Joseph Ledoux, has shown that the neural pathways in the brain that lead from the bottom-up are more numerous and stronger than top-down connections. What this means is that the connections from the deeper more primal parts of the brain, the reptilian mammalian brains, that go up to the more sophisticated advanced part of the brain, the neocortex primate brain, are stronger and larger in number than the top down connections. This means in times of increased stress and perceived potential threat-danger, your emotions are more powerful in influencing your behavior than your rational thoughts. This allows for inherent survival of the organism (you) from a biological perspective. Your primal instinctive survival mechanisms kick into gear; survival at all cost right now or there will be no tomorrow. The good news, research shows that you can 'retrain your brain' using principles like those addressed in this book. Essentially, you rewire your brains connections so the top-down connectors overpower the bottom-up. Using your more sophisticated brain and higher processing you can regulate and 'cool-off' the deeper primitive parts. In the world of psychological therapy, we call this 'corrective experiences'. Recent research reported in the *Archives of General Psychiatry* suggests that cognitive behavioral therapy (CBT), similar to DDP training, has a positive effect on the brain regions subserving bodily defense reactions to threat. Improvement in social phobia was accompanied by a decrease in regional cerebral blood flow (rCBF) in the amygdala and hippocampus. These are the areas of the brain implicated in the biologically driven threat-danger fear response. The authors conclude that thorough reduction of neural activity in this area of the brain resulting from CBT is associated with favorable long-term outcome and may need to occur for clinical improvement. This supports the notion that you can use the more advanced higher processing to retrain your brain or rewire your brain's neural connections.

As I have indicated, medications are very effective in treating anxiety and depression, and in many cases may be needed for you to gain control.

Craig S. Travis, Ph.D.

However, I propose that this method alone is simply treating the symptoms, like aspirin treats the pain, and not targeting the whole problem, thus explaining the high recurrence rates and chronicity of these problems. I have long stated that medications mostly target the somatic (physiological) or body symptoms of anxiety and depression. Recent research seems to support this notion. Helen Mayberg and colleagues at the University of Texas Health Science Center used functional brain imaging to show the effect of antidepressant medication (fluoxetine) and placebo on brain activity levels in different areas of the brain. Both fluoxetine and placebo showed an increase in activity in the cortex, 'top' area of the brain, and decreased activity in limbic regions, lower areas of the brain. While both treatments were effective, medication showed unique changes in even lower, more primitive areas of the brain. I propose that this supports medications targeting the more physiological somatic symptoms of depression. Interestingly, placebo responders showed the increased activity much quicker, at week 1, than the antidepressant responders, at week 6. As the authors indicate, this supports the idea that treatment with placebo is not the absence of treatment, just absence of active medication. They state that possible benefits of change in environment and supportive, therapeutic relationships may contribute to the efficacy of placebo. Other studies comparing antidepressants to placebo confirm that there appears to be a different mechanism of action between placebo and 'active' medications. And the really fascinating thing is that changing how you think has a similar effect as medication, it just might take a different path. With continued research, I predict that what we find is that placebo and non-drug cognitive approaches (e.g., changing thinking patterns) enlist similar parts of the 'sophisticated' brain and harness the power of your mind thus enhancing brain function; in essence you harness the power of positivity. Mayberg and colleagues note that medications that take a 'bottom-up' approach or non-drug, cognitive 'top-down' interventions should work equally well. Other research supports this statement that cognitive therapy and medication are equally effective in relieving depression symptoms. And in some cases, cognitive therapy may even be better. Meta-analyses, a statistical procedure that allows researchers to combine and compare numerous studies at once, has shown cognitive therapy to be slightly superior to antidepressants in treating unipolar depression and more importantly, one year after treatment discontinuation, depressed patients treated with cognitive therapy had half the relapse rates of those treated with antidepressant medication. Recent reports from the APA 2002 convention on the long-term management of mood disorders, confirms prior data suggesting differences in relapse and recurrence rates between medication and cognitive therapy. Susan Kornstein, from Medical College of Virginia,

Virginia Commonwealth University found that while antidepressants were effective for most patients in preventing relapse and recurrence, discontinuation can lead to relapse and recurrence within six months in 40% to 60% of patients. Furthermore, Dr. Robin Jarrett, from the university of Texas Southwestern Medical Center, reported that cognitive therapy, behavioral therapy, and interpersonal psychotherapy can not only reduce depressive symptoms, but also prevent relapse and recurrence and continuation/maintenance cognitive therapy can reduce relapse/recurrence after acute medication. This supports the proposal I made that antidepressant medications to treat anxiety and depression, like aspirin to treat pain or fever, targets the somatic symptoms and signs, but may not treat the actual wound (the psychological injury) thus the higher relapse/recurrence, but that psychotherapy (specifically, cognitive therapy) treats the ego wound and better protects against relapse and recurrence of its symptoms, the infection of negativity, anxiety and depression. If you are on medication, THIS IS NOT PERMISSION TO STOP TAKING MEDICATION! Nor does it mean you may not benefit from medication. I think it means that there is a difference between 'feeling better' (alleviating symptoms) and 'getting better' (healing the wound). If you are concerned about the intensity of your anxiety and depression, please consult your doctor or a therapist.

If anxiety and depression are inherently human dynamics, that given the preceding argument are natural adaptive albeit misapplied stress responses, then why doesn't everyone get anxious and depressed and develop full-blown mental/medical disorders? In short, my answer is: genetics, individual differences, learned adaptive coping, and environment. I propose the hypothesis that those who do not develop crippling, problematic anxiety and depressive disorders, intervene some how. This may be that you may be lucky enough to have the 'right' genetic influence and biological make-up that precludes a full-blown disorder. Or, innate, individual differences make you more stress hardy. I mean, why do siblings from the same family turn out so very different? Perhaps, it's learned coping. This may have been formally taught in the family or learned informally on your own; that given your life experiences, you learned to adaptively cope with the demands, challenges, and obstacles the world puts in front of you. Maybe you learned to create positive meaning from unfortunate circumstances and even tragedy; construe beneficial interpretations of your circumstances; put things into perspective; get validation and emotional support; essentially you use your mind to help rather than hurt you. And of course, from a mathematical explanation, it always could be chalked up to pure chance! Whatever the means, suffice to say that you have discovered mechanisms to treat the (ego) wound, before it gets infected seeping ooze and puss!

I had a close friend of mine years ago ask me one time why I thought people got depressed, that probably once a month he would get a little down, but didn't understand why people couldn't keep from having it get worse. My response, a simplified one that did not figure in all the complex factors of depression but sums it up really well, was "probably because you have family and friends that you can talk to about what troubles you." He had people around him that gave him the message through their interaction and validation of who he was that fed and nurtured his ego; he knew people cared about him. Who knew I was laying the ground work for my ego wound damage control model? As my son and I now say to each other when we feel vulnerable and want hugs "Let's feed the need." "What's that need?" you ask. The need to be loved and know you are lovable, no matter what. That nurtures the ego; and more importantly replenishes it, heals and bandages it when it takes a hit, when it gets injured. You see the physical contact of a hug is processed and understood by the brain at the preverbal, somatic (body), primitive level, thus countering or silencing the alarm of your body's natural fight-or-flight defense system. Your mind, because it has a need to make sense of the world, then creates meaningful, healthy positive, thoughts or mental schemata about yourself, These 'ego bandages' then infiltrate to others and the world and you view things in a more positive light.

When you do get emotionally 'cut', how do you keep it from getting infected? The infection of such a wound is negative thoughts; they creep into your mind and body in the form of self-doubt and criticism and wreak havoc on your entire system. In medicine, there is a rule of thumb when it comes to skin conditions; If it's dry wet it, if it's wet dry it. In other words, treatment is to do the opposite of what appears to be the problem. So if negative thinking, pessimism, and an all around negative attitude are the infection from an ego wound, then treat it by doing the opposite. *Daily Dose of Positivity* treats the negativity infection of ego wounds; it prevents infection of and builds immunity against the negative thoughts of self-doubt, anxiety, and depression.

It is true—you live in a stressful society. Your world, through technology and other means, has rapidly transformed your environment and the world you live in. From an evolutionary and biological perspective, you are still catching up in terms of adjusting to this rapid change. Stress is less physical and more psychological. That does not mean psychological stress does not have a real impact on your physical health. An estimated 75% of primary care doctor's visits are for stress related health problems. Infectious disease has been replaced by chronic illnesses as the majority of today's health problems, problems that are largely psychological or behavioral in nature (e.g., high blood pressure, heart disease, diabetes, etc). Are we seeing a stress epidemic in our society? Perhaps, but stress is not the problem per se; adequate recovery and healing from stress is the issue. That is to say, the wound is not the problem; psychological wounds in-and-of-themselves are not fatal. What can become fatal is the consequent maladaptive thinking and behavior, the negativity, which indirectly leads to unhealthy coping choices, and as brain-imaging research has shown, directly leads to subsequent negative physiology.

Craig S. Travis, Ph.D.

'SAVING FACE'—PRESERVING YOUR EGO: REAL WORLD EXAMPLES IN ACTION

"Anyone can get angry—
that is easy…but to do this to the right person, to the right extent, at the right time, with the right motive, and in the right way, that is not for everyone, nor is it easy"

Aristotle

You don't like it when your feelings get hurt; nobody does. But believe me, it happens to all of us! Even the big macho tough guys get their feelings hurt (they just won't admit it; sorry guys, but it's true). And, we all have ways we cope with such threats to our ego, some natural some learned. On some level, you probably get angry; you just may not always show it (or even know it). You deal with your hurt and anger in your own way, but there are some fundamental coping strategies that all of us share. Sigmund Freud developed the concept of ego defense mechanisms as ways that you and I handle such emotional wounds. There is a hierarchical order to them where the more advanced ones are conscious coping strategies and thus healthier than the more primitive and unconscious ones. I am not going to list them here; if you are interested, any intro to psychology book will have them. Then there is also the body's innate physical survival mechanism that I have mentioned earlier. This is highly adaptive for preserving your physical safety, but unfortunately also gets triggered by emotional/psychological or ego threats, at which point it loses its adaptability. The short of it, when faced with a danger, you run away from the danger (flight), hide from it (freeze—"if I'm still enough, no one will notice me"), or pummel it into oblivion (fight). This is a natural reaction as any one with a toddler can attest. Every parent either goes through their child having a 'hitting' phase, a 'withdrawing' phase or both, as their children learn to manage their emotions and behaviors; some more successfully than others. You may have learned not to physically retaliate when your ego is wounded, but still might verbally assault the person you think is responsible, or at least jab at them sarcastically. Or perhaps you slink away in avoidance for fear of being hurt again. To demonstrate this natural human dynamic, I think of the classic example of teenage romance and break-ups (and for many of us, this still happens well into adulthood.)

Daily Dose of Positivity™

Think back to an example of breaking up in high school. What happened? The reason for the breakup is less the issue rather than the response to it; obviously, certain circumstances may create more emotional, mean, and nasty responses than others, but in general you may remember something like this: Johnny and Susie break-up, for whatever reason. The break-uppee then goes around saying bad things about the break-upper. You remember the rumors and nasty things that were spread around in high school. It is that attempt at saving face ("she's a slut", "he's an asshole") to preserve your ego and cover up your hurt, the 'fight' part of the emergency reaction when your primitive brain detects a threat, in this case, the threat of rejection. I have come to the conclusion that this is a natural human dynamic, albeit not the most healthy; that to lessen your pain you will make someone else feel bad, that way, somehow you figure you will feel better. You might think, "at least I don't feel as bad as you". As Pinker points out, a certain amount of your happiness lies in another's misery. At least, the relieving of your pain lies in the unconscious desire to inflict pain on others. I was privy to an example of this several years ago in what I like to refer to as the 'real world laboratory'. I have always been fascinated in 'observing' others' behavior (go figure, I'm a psychologist). While accompanying my wife on a visit to her hometown for her to attend a bridal shower, the groom to be hosted the spouses for a boy's night. We all gathered in the kitchen of the host. This particular home had a center island in the kitchen. The host's son, who was 4 years old at the time, was just tall enough that the corner of the kitchen counter on the center island was right at forehead level. Yep, you guessed it, he walked his forehead right into that sharp, pointy corner! Now, no one else saw this as they were busy chatting, but I did see it. What I saw next, lead me to the epiphany that humans have some innate primitive coping mechanisms for dealing with threat, pain, and damage, and that we don't always make conscious sense of it. The host's son, immediately after hitting his head on the counter, reacted by going over to his dad and punching him in the leg! His father's response, "What the hell did you do that for?!" The son, being only four and not having the advantage of the fully developed cognitive/behavioral coping skills of an emotionally mature adult, was not able to sufficiently communicate with his father to let him know he had hurt himself and was thus attempting to relieve his pain. Having witnessed this reaction leads me to this conclusion about the unconscious logic of natural human behavior: "If I hurt, somehow, I'll hurt less if you hurt more than me". Of course, you may also respond with the 'flight' part of the emergency reaction, and if the wound is damaging enough, withdrawal into depression because the pain is too great to bear. B.F. Skinner's supposition about motivation in human behavior sums this up well: "people do things for one of two reasons—to gain pleasure or avoid pain." There are just healthy and unhealthy ways to do it. Find the healthy ones!

7

WHAT WAS ONCE OLD IS NEW AGAIN

There has been a revolution in medicine concerning how we think about the diseases that now afflict us. It involves recognizing the interactions between the body and the mind, the ways in which emotions and personality can have a tremendous impact on the functioning and health of virtually every cell in the body. It is about the role of stress in making some of us more vulnerable to disease, the ways in which some of us cope with stressors, and the critical notion that you cannot really understand a disease *in vacuo*, but rather only in the context of the person suffering from that disease.

Robert M. Sapolsky

The revolution that Dr. Sapolsky refers to was built upon the works of earlier practitioners previously mentioned. It seems that pioneers in this field, such as Freud, James, Meyer, Engel, and the like, were correct in their assumptions that the mind could have profound effects on an individual's physiology, affect, and behavior. There now is medical data to support this notion.

Mind body medicine continues as a "hot" area of research today. The 1990's were dubbed the decade of the brain. Researchers were to have discovered and understood the biomechanical workings of the human brain. Although we have not unlocked all the mysteries of the structure of the brain, we certainly know more than before and now have compelling "hard" scientific evidence of how the brain functions. This is especially true of the biochemical impact of conscious and unconscious thought and ones emotional reactions.

Medical science has established that the mind does indeed affect the body. During the mid 1990's, Mark George, M.D., from the National Institute of Mental Health demonstrated this phenomenon through a remarkable study of brain function. This landmark study recorded the effects of negative thinking on brain chemistry. Dr. George studied brain activity in normal women under three separate conditions: while thinking happy thoughts, neutral thoughts, and sad thoughts. He found that during happy thoughts the women demonstrated a cooling of the deep limbic system, and during sad thoughts, he recorded a significant increase in deep limbic system activity (the limbic system is responsible for setting the emotional tone of the mind and modulates motivation). Dr. George was able to show what occurs biochemically when you think negative and positive thoughts. In essence, every time you have a "negative" thought (i.e., an angry thought, a spiteful thought, a sad thought, a cranky thought, a fearful thought, etc.) your brain releases chemicals that make your body feel bad (cortisol and other stress hormones are released making muscles tense, hearts race, hands sweat, etc.). I use the term *negative* because most people describe the emotional consequences to these types of thinking as unpleasant. Most people don't like the emotional and physical sensation of feeling mad, scared, hurt or sad. Thinking positively had the reverse effect creating a relaxing more rejuvenating feeling. This is powerful evidence that your thoughts have an impact on your emotions, your body, and body function. So, what you think, does count!

Through brain imaging, such as positron emission tomography (PET) scans, single photon emission computerized tomography (SPECT) scans, and magnetic resonance imaging (MRI), researchers have documented that your cognition's, thought processes, emotional reactions, and subsequent behaviors can influence brain chemistry. Specifically, SPECT and what is called functional magnetic resonance imaging or fMRI studies seem to have significantly contributed to unlocking the mysteries of the function of the human brain. In essence, every thought and action/behavior you engage in gets translated into a biochemical message and is carried through the body. Individually, these chemical responses may not have enough "umph" to impact you by themselves. That is, one negative thought is not going to kill you. However, collectively, if you continue to function from a negative mind and behavioral set, this takes its toll on your mind, body, and spirit. As Gestalt psychology suggests, the whole is greater than the sum of its parts.

fMRI and SPECT studies are a branch of medicine called nuclear medicine. Nuclear medicine uses radioactive compounds to "map" images of the brain. SPECT and fMRI scans can actually show the parts of the brain which are activated when you think, concentrate, laugh, cry, fantasize, get mad, are scared, sing, play a piano, imagine, and perform other functions. SPECT and fMRI studies have helped neuropsychiatric researchers recognize that many psychological disorders are not disorders of the brains anatomy, but problems in how the brain functions. Nueropsychiatrist Daniel Amen, M.D., documents this in his groundbreaking work *Change Your Brain Change Your Life*. Dr. George has also been credited with applying brain imaging to the study of psychological mood disorders.

Researchers at the University of Wisconsin-Madison have recently applied these neuroimaging techniques to study a wide variety of brain function including anxiety disorders, depression, the effects of antidepressant medication, and areas of the brain that are involved in negative thinking. Director of the HealthEmotions Research Institute (HERI), Ned Kalin, believes this new technology will greatly help to identify brain mechanisms involved in emotions that are responsible for illness as well as good health. He states, "This information should spur new advances in preventing and treating mental disorders, as well as other problems affecting cognitive abilities." Some of the researchers at HERI are also studying the power of 'positive outlooks'. One study will examine what happens after a diagnosis of a serious medical illness by comparing the symptoms and physiology in women with two debilitating conditions, fibromyalgia and rheumatoid arthritis. The goal of the study will be to determine the benefits of maintaining a positive emotional outlook. Other research at HERI focuses on understanding how the brain experiences emotion and how positive states of mind influence the body by spotlighting positive emotions and health. The imaging techniques used at HERI can be used to track the physical changes that occur in the brain resulting from sustained training and learning (i.e., retraining the brain using DDP or cognitive therapy strategies, etc.) thus, helping show how the brain is "plastic" and capable of overcoming diseases or deficiencies. This technology can provide 'pictures' to support prior research suggesting the efficacy of changing your thinking on health. For example, it has been shown that retraining your brain by using cognitive therapy methods was as equally effective as using medication in the treatment of depression. In a large study of patients who were treated for depression, The National Institutes of Health compared antidepressant medication to cognitive therapy. Researchers discovered that each of these treatments was equally effective in treating depression. In addition, interpersonal therapy (enhancing relationship skills) was as effective as the others in treating depression. Not surprising was the fact that combining all three had an even greater effect on reducing depressive symptoms. This is powerful evidence that what you think and how you relate to others can affect your overall health and behavior.

Other current examples of mind body research include the works of Elissa Epel, Julienne E. Bower, Jeff Burgdorf, and Jack B. Nitschke. Elissa Epel's research explores the possibility that Positivity (positive psychological factors such as, positive emotion, meaning based coping, optimism, spirituality, and psychological growth after facing stress) may buffer against chronic stress by increasing anabolic hormones and vagal tone, while Julienne E. Bower's research has shown that individuals who find positive meaning following a stressful life experience also show positive changes in immune status and health. Her current research investigates positive meaning of current stressful circumstance (history of diagnosis of breast cancer), subsequent (experimental) stressors and how meaning may minimize prolonged activation of biological stress response systems. Jeff Burgdorf uses brain imaging to study the neurobiology of positive emotions. His studies have shown the relationship between brain chemical's (dopamine) and self-reported positive affect. Jack Nitschke has also studied the neural circuitry of positive emotion by using fMRI to examine brain activity of new mothers while viewing images of their own infants versus unfamiliar infants. Results of this study paralleled one at the University of Wisconsin-Madison—various different areas of the brain 'lit-up' when viewing their own infants as opposed to other babies.

The area of brain imaging is really in its infancy. As technology in this area continues to develop, I predict we will have an explosion of vast amounts of information about the human brain, thoughts, emotions, behavior and health. Stay tuned!

8

POSITIVITY IN UNCOMFORTABLE "NEGATIVE" FEELINGS

In the last decade or so, science has discovered a tremendous amount about the role emotions play in our lives. Researchers have found that even more than IQ, your emotional awareness and abilities to handle feelings will determine your success and happiness in all walks of life, including family relationships.

John Gottman, Ph.D.

"Look not back in anger, nor forward in fear but around you in awareness."

Ross Hersey

"Nothing in life is to be feared. It is only to be understood."

Marie Curie (1867-1934)

"All learning has an emotional base."

Plato

Take a minute to try to define emotion. What exactly are feelings? Authors, artists, philosophers, and the like, never have quite been able to reach an agreement on the true definition of emotion. And, even the experts can't agree. Varying authors' have lists of basic universal emotions that range anywhere from four to eight. These usually include the following: surprise, happiness, anger, fear, disgust, and sadness. Resolving this debate is beyond the scope of this book. For the sake of simplicity, suffice to say that there are four primary, or what I like to call primal, human emotions: Anger, fear, sadness, and joy.

Daily Dose of Positivity™

We'll call these the Big 4. Most people classify the first three as negative. Indeed, they are unpleasant sensations. However, I do not like to call them "negative" for that implies they are bad and should be avoided at all cost. Avoiding these feelings and sensations by "stuffing" or suppressing them, although natural in impulse, may not be healthy. In fact, this natural impulse to not want to experience unpleasant sensations may not be positive. Research shows that suppressing these emotions puts you at risk for developing a variety of physical illnesses as well as developing emotional and behavioral problems. Positivity is not about eliminating these feelings but rather not allowing them to dominate your life. It is acceptable and healthy to be sad, angry or scared about something. These emotions in and of themselves are neither negative nor positive, they simply exist. The human body is quite adaptable and can handle these "negative" emotions a little at a time without great harm being done. All emotions are developmentally important because they evolved to alert us to specific kinds of problems. (In Part II, *Positive Psychology*, I will discuss the recent work on 'positive emotions' and the broaden and build hypothesis of Barbara Frederickson and how positive emotions serve an evolutionary function just as negative emotions do). Emotions become negative when they consume and control your life. It is true that, three of the four are uncomfortable and you probably don't want to feel them. Anger, fear, and grief rarely feel good, but if you allow yourself to smoothly flow between them as nature intended (much like the tides of the ocean) without judgment, then they would not pose a problem, per se. The more comfortable you are about allowing yourself to feel these feelings naturally and expressing them without judgment, the healthier (mentally, emotionally, & physically) you will become. When you become stuck in one to the exclusion of the others is when they are negative and unhealthy. Feelings are less the issue than how you cope with them, just as events are less concerning than how you handle them cognitively and behaviorally. I once had a patient tell me he didn't see the value in talking about his feelings because he said 'feelings don't solve problems', typical pragmatic problem-solving American male, be rational, not emotional. Being the budding therapist, I was eager to address the importance of emotion and we got into a debate about the importance of feelings in solving problems. The patient, reluctant to see my point of view, that dealing with feelings leads to problem solving, became more defensive (understandably so, I was most likely a little pushy with my eagerness to make my point); he couldn't see the point in talking about how he felt about something that already had happened, that simply talking about how he feels would not change his situation. Talking about how he felt would not solve his particular problem with which he was faced. At that moment, at my patient's insistence that 'feelings don't solve problems,' it hit me, 'you're right' I said, 'feelings don't actually solve problems, they alert us to problems.' But, if you don't adequately deal with them and understand them, they will get in the way of your being able to solve problems. You see it is the emotional consequences to life that we must deal with, (in part by awareness, acknowledgement, and validation of them), or these unresolved emotions will become part of the problem, or at least an added problem you'll have to deal with. So I changed my interaction with patients; after that encounter, I began discussing the issue of appropriately addressing and resolving emotional consequences to life circumstances, before solving the problem, rather than insisting that just talking about how you feel will make everything better. It doesn't, it just frees you up to begin thinking and acting differently so you can clearly address the problem. Once you acknowledge the emotional consequences, validate them as significant, appropriately express them or deal with them in some way, then you can move to specific problem solving. Remember, you are not trying to avoid negative feelings; rather you are trying to recognize them, be comfortable with them, and to let your feelings exist, as they are: important information about you and the world around you.

On the other hand, your consequent behavior can be interpreted as appropriate or inappropriate. How you choose to cope with the feelings can either be healthy or unhealthy. For example, your brother teases you about being fat, which hurts your feelings and makes you mad. You could respond in many ways: scream at him to leave you alone, punch him, throw a vase at him, ignore him (telling yourself internally it is not an accurate description), tell him that teasing hurts your feelings and you feel angry when he does it, etc. The latter two options would be considered the healthiest. You have the choice as to how you choose to respond, but remember you, not someone else, is ultimately responsible for how you feel and subsequently how you behave.

Being responsible for your own feelings is a core characteristic of Positivity. Few people realize that no one person or situation makes you feel anything. You feel they way you do as an automatic response to your interpretation of a given set of circumstances. A change in interpretation, perception, or attitude changes the feeling. Repeatedly interpreting situations as more positive, and practicing positive thoughts through *Daily Dose of Positivity*, will train your brain to automatically perceive future events as more positive and optimistic.

9

THE CARDS WE'RE DEALT

"Life is not a matter of holding the good cards, but rather in playing a poor hand well."

Robert Louis Stevenson

Because the mind can have an impact on the body does not mean your thoughts are solely responsible for disease and illness. This would be an overly simplified view that does not include the importance of environmental, socio-cultural, biological and genetic factors. However, the way you think does affect how you cope with the cards you have been dealt. Everyone gets sick or has unfortunate circumstances happen in the course of their lifetime. You have the power to choose how they will affect you. How you handle these everyday and not-so-everyday situations can be in the direction of negativity or Positivity.

When I began writing this book, John F. Kennedy, Jr., his wife, Carolyn Bessette and her sister, Lauren were killed in a plane crash while en route to his cousins wedding. No more tragedy has struck any other well-known American family than the Kennedy's. They have had two members assassinated; two killed by plane crash, one skiing accident, and the list goes on. Yet, they persevere. Why? I, although not having spoke with anyone from the family directly, speculate the answer lies in their attitude and how they handle and cope with their misfortune. While the general American point of view of the Kennedy's' circumstantial history seems to be one of a Greek tragedy interpretation, I suspect this family may view it differently. Yes, it is sad, indeed, and my heart goes out to them. But while some, if not most, people under similar circumstances would simply give up or give in to the seeming negativity, they do not. Their adversity and how they respond binds them as a family and makes them stronger. There is an old adage that "what does not kill me only makes me stronger". The Kennedy's are a very strong family indeed.

Craig S. Travis, Ph.D.

Not only does how you think affect the physiology of the body and the course of disease, but thoughts and attitude also contribute to a variety of emotional and behavioral responses as well. The science of psychology has come to accept that thoughts contribute to a variety of emotional and behavioral disorders, depression and anxiety being the most recognizable. As can be seen in the next section titled, "The Science Behind the Thought", cognitive theories of emotion and behavior suggest the importance of thinking, perception, attribution, interpretation and beliefs influencing emotions and motivating behaviors everyday.

Allow me to share a quick anecdote to illustrate this point before moving on to the next section. My grandmother died several years ago after a long and courageous battle with Alzheimer's disease. My family (myself, my wife, and newborn son) was able to attend the memorial service, but the day of her actual funeral, my 6-month-old son was still miserable from contracting his first ever virus the night before. Needless to say, no one got much sleep that night. Being new parents, my wife and I had not experienced the type of distress you feel when your helpless infant is crying miserably. Being a responsible man, good father and husband, but equally good and caring grandson, I was torn: What to do? Stay home with my wife, the inexperienced new mom, and newborn sick son, or go to my grandmother's funeral and be with the rest of my grieving family? I had an overwhelming sense of responsibility to do both. I created within myself an internal conflict of worrying about the 'right' thing to do and worrying about what other people would think, a conflict so great that I had myself in tears on the phone talking to my mother and father trying to explain that I didn't know what to do. I kept thinking, 'I need to go to the funeral, but I can't leave my wife and son alone. What kind of husband and father would I be if I did that?' Then, right back to 'what kind of son and grandson doesn't attend his grandmother's funeral? What would people think???!!!' Of course my parents could not tell me what to do, nor could my wife. Sure, they all tried to reassure me, but I had worked myself up into a frenzy with what I was thinking. What emotional agony I had put myself in with my worrying. And even though they could, and probably did, offer suggestions, I would still have to make the decision and live with the consequences of my choice of actions. And what if I make the wrong choice??!! Finally, I made a decision; I would skip the formal funeral service in the morning and attend the family and friends get-together in the afternoon at my parents' house. This was an emotionally tumultuous decision, but one that I acknowledged to myself that I had to live with. So, I reassured my wife (actually, she probably reassured me) that I wouldn't be long, and so I left to mourn with my family, my parents, and friends. No sooner did I enter my parents house, than my mother greeted me with open arms and I started sobbing again muttering something about I was sorry and what a difficult decision this was and I hoped everyone understood. Luckily, I was met with resounding support for my decision. Everyone whom I spoke with said that I had made the right decision. They all understood my predicament and supported me wholeheartedly. 'You needed to be with YOUR family at that time' they all said. Thank God for validation! I stayed a short while and then returned home. But not before I came to the following conclusion (actually, I had the insight in the car while driving over to my parents house). I was able to derive the following positive meaning from this set of life's circumstances. I am a believer that we are to learn certain messages from the situations we encounter in life. I asked myself, 'what is the message I am supposed to take from this whole thing?' I decided that my grandmother, being an elementary school teacher all her life, was teaching me a very valuable life lesson. She was teaching me that not only would my son be a source of great pleasure and joy, but he will also be a source of great pain; that we experience the good with bad, but that we must simply recognize it, understand it to the best of our ability, and move on. I have continued to be at peace with my decision about how to handle this 'problem.' Now had I had a different interaction from people, perhaps I might feel differently, but one thing I feel sure of, and that is that how I viewed the meaning of the situation, the final interpretation I came up with, that positive meaning has allowed me to move on, rather than stay stuck in the negative emotions of worry, guilt and sorrow. And so too can it be with you, for whatever emotional turmoil may come from your situation, you have the power to interpret it any way you want to. I suggest a positive one.

10

THE SCIENCE BEHIND THE THOUGHT

(Cognitive Theory Basics)

"Weakness of attitude becomes weakness of character."

Albert Einstein

"Attitude is a little thing that makes a big difference."

Winston Churchill

The following section addresses cognitive-behavioral theory (CBT) basics as applied to psychological and emotional disorders. It is believed that these principles apply to everyday emotional and behavioral reactions as well, not just to clinical syndromes such as anxiety and mood disorders. As you will see, cognition's, thoughts, attitudes, expectations, belief systems, etc., are inherently important in the nature of behavior. Never has this been more evident than in the popularity of cognitive-behavioral approaches to psychotherapy. Cognitive-behavior theorists postulate that mental events and cognitive processes (i.e., how you think) influence the nature of your emotions and behavior.

Over the past few decades, cognitive theories of personality have become a major influence in clinical psychology. These theories share an emphasis on internal, inferred mental structures, that is, your thoughts, and these are understood to be closely related to your experience and behavior. Currently, cognitive or cognitive-behavioral models of personality seem to have replaced psychoanalytic theory as the predominant theory of personality development, at least in terms of treatment for the emotional and behavioral problems that so many of us face today. The cognitive revolution that took place during the 1960's and 1970's stimulated new thinking about the nature and development of personality. This new approach has provided a basis for theorizing about personality and behavior change that is different than psychoanalytic, experiential, and trait theories. The latter three have dominated personality theory throughout the first half of the 20th century.

Although cognitive theories of personality are relatively recent, their roots can be traced throughout history. Greek and Roman Stoic philosophers believed that a *rational* principle guides the universe and that each person has a duty to follow and promote reason; passion and emotion were to be subdued. Albert Ellis indicates that the principle foundation for his Rational Emotive Behavior Theory (REBT) can be found in the Stoic philosopher Epictetus: Men are disturbed not by things but the judgments and views they take of them. Ellis even credits William Shakespeare with influencing his theory, who in Hamlet wrote: "There [exists] nothing either good or bad but thinking makes it so."

According to Aaron Beck, another pioneer in the field of cognitive-behavioral theory, an important precursor to current cognitive models of personality and emotional disturbance, was Kelly's personal construct theory, which presented the idea that individuals construe the world in relatively enduring ways and that these cognitive structures are determinants of behavior. Therefore, cognitive theories of personality are based on the assumption that there are structures of cognition that determine how an individual evaluates, interprets, and organizes the large and complex amounts of information related to self, others, and the world. In particular, cognitive theories share the idea that there are mental structures such as "scripts", "schemas", and "concepts" that organize and determine individuals' behavior, affect, and experience. Ellis refers to these constructs as beliefs. Martin Seligman, founder of the current Positive Psychology movement, emphasizes attributions in what he calls "explanatory style", that is, how you explain or make sense of your circumstances. I explain this more in another section.

Also relevant to cognitive theories of personality and cognitive therapy are attribution theory, social judgment, person perception, and implicit personality theories. Attribution theory attempts to explain the way individuals attribute causality to themselves or others, whereas social judgment, person perception, and implicit personality theory examine the ways that people look at themselves, others, and the world, and how interpersonal information is encoded, organized, and utilized.

Cognitive psychologists believe that mental events are not merely by-products of your behavior, as traditional behaviorists would have you believe, but rather cognitive processes can actually influence your behavior. Specifically, the cognitive behavioral approach contends that disordered cognitive processes cause some psychological disorders and that by changing these cognitions, the disorder can be alleviated or even cured. As mentioned, Aaron Beck and Albert Ellis were the earliest pioneers in attempting to apply cognitive concepts to clinical problems and emotional disorders. Donald Meichenbaum is also considered one of the pioneers in developing cognitive behavioral approaches to counseling and he has specifically addressed cognitive and behavioral factors in stress. For his contributions to the field of psychology, he was voted one of the ten most influential psychotherapists of the century in a survey reported in the American Psychologist. Two of his seminal works of interest are *Cognitive-behavior modification: An integrative approach* and *Stress inoculation training*.

Rational Emotive Behavior Therapy (REBT) and Cognitive Behavior Therapy (CBT) are both cognitive methods, but in the literature, REBT seems to stand alone as its own method. Interestingly, REBT often receives a detailed description in the literature, while many other specific cognitive approaches to therapy fall under the general theme of CBT, an approach attributed to Beck, and receive only general attention. This is also evident in works by Bernard who states that he is surprised by the lack of cross fertilization of REBT and CBT, two singular identities, and by providing 10 reasons why REBT will remain as a distinctive approach separate from CBT. Finally, Bernard asserts that REBT is closer to the trait rather than state end of the generality-specificity continuum of cognitive constructs. Preferential REBT is less concerned with specific behavioral change which occurs using more situationally-bound automatic thoughts and self statements. Rather, REBT searches for robust, general, underlying core beliefs and philosophical assumptions of life which elicit and influence different emotions and behaviors across time and situations. In other words, CBT seems to address situation specific disturbances, while REBT addresses more stable and pervasive general cognitive constructs. Therefore, beliefs—rational or irrational—tend to be pervasive and enduring personality characteristics. This is the premise behind *Daily Dose of Positivity*. DDP is designed to help you develop and maintain a more rational, positive outlook on life.

Daily Dose of Positivity™

RATIONAL EMOTIVE BEHAVIOR THEORY (REBT)

"Men are disturbed not by things but the judgments
and views they take of them"

Epictetus

The most popular and representative of the rational or cognitive approaches to counseling is Albert Ellis' Rational Emotive Behavior Therapy (REBT). Many counseling psychology textbooks dedicate detailed sections to REBT while only providing general descriptions of other cognitive behavioral methods showing the popularity of REBT. Although it would be inappropriate to designate any one individual as the founder of cognitive therapy, Albert Ellis has been one of the most influential theorist/practitioners in this area.

Why is REBT such an intriguing approach to the treatment of behavioral problems and emotional disturbance? There are several fundamental reasons for the widespread acceptance of REBT. First, for many practitioners, as well as laypeople, the basic assumption that what you think or say to yourself has a major bearing on the way you feel and act is irrefutable. Second, the primary method of REBT, a direct attempt by the therapist to change these mental processes, is a plausible therapeutic corollary to the first assumption. Third, in terms of both theory and practice, REBT's detailed explanation of emotional upset is clear and explicit. After merely reading some of Ellis' works, therapists (justifiably or not) can feel sufficiently knowledgeable in REBT to begin applying it to clients. Another reason REBT is so popular, although it lacks empirical justification, lies in the fact that it just makes common sense to most people.

The ABC's of REBT

The basic assumption to Rational Emotive Behavior Therapy is that emotional disturbances are caused by the individual's irrational beliefs. This basic tenet of REBT is organized and defined by using what is called the ABC theory of personality. According to the ABC theory of personality and human functioning, thinking and emotion overlap. Ellis and Harper state that:

> Human emotions do not magically exist in their own right, and do not mysteriously flow from unconscious needs and desires. Rather, they almost always directly stem from ideas, thought, attitudes, or beliefs,

and can usually get radically changed by modifying our thinking processes. (p. 11)

Therefore, thinking, a cognitive process, mediates between some stimulus event and a response. In other words, your emotional response to a situation is not caused by the situation itself, or by other people, but rather to the thoughts, beliefs and attitudes that you have about the event or persons.

The activating experience, A, refers to some real external event or stimulus, to which the individual is exposed. The belief or idea, B, refers to the chain of thoughts or self-verbalizations the individual goes through in response to the event (A). The consequences, C, symbolizes the emotional and behavioral response that result from this belief (B). So:

$$A = \text{Event or trigger}$$
$$B = \text{Belief or idea (self-talk)}$$
$$C = \text{Emotional response}$$

The assumption commonly made is that A causes C.

Remember the traffic example mentioned earlier: someone cuts you off without signaling and you get mad. The assumption is getting cut off (A) makes you mad (C).

$$\text{So it looks like this: } A \rightarrow C$$

REBT and other cognitive theories contend that an event (A) does not cause emotional upset (C), but rather, it is (B) the beliefs, ideas, or appraisal and interpretation about (A), that more directly contributes to point (C). So it often gets represented as:

$$A \rightarrow B \rightarrow C$$

This is not a linear process however. From what we are learning through scientific technology and understanding the mind body interaction, I think it is more accurate to think of this being represented like a ball of yarn; a three-dimensional diagram. Or picture a pyramid like the ones in Egypt, but suspended in space so that any point could be the top depending on how you look at it. Given the limits of the pages of a book, a two-dimensional representation of the diagram would show:

Daily Dose of Positivity™

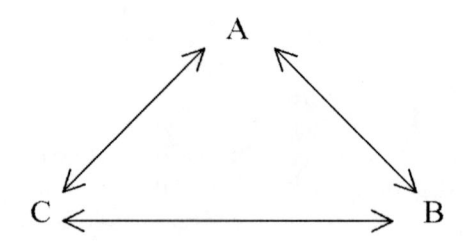

```
        A
       ↗ ↖
      ↙   ↘
    C ←――――→ B
```

And when you include recent evidence from research in psychoneuroimmunology (PNI) and nuclear imaging, you can add two other variables into the equation: your physiology (D) and subsequent behavior (E). So it looks more like this:

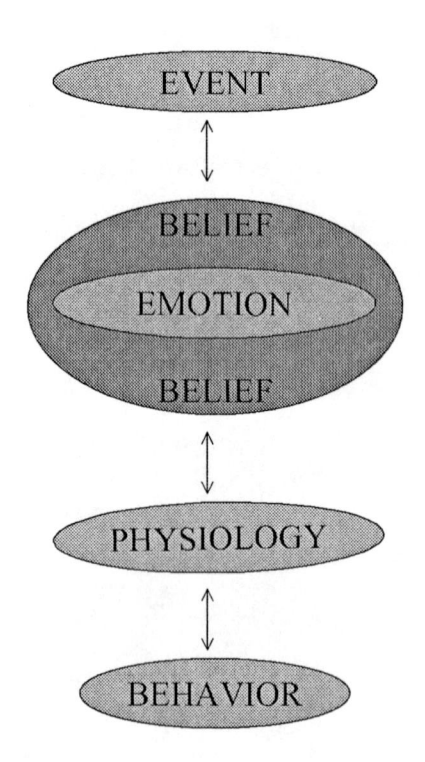

```
        EVENT
          ↕
        BELIEF
       EMOTION
        BELIEF
          ↕
      PHYSIOLOGY
          ↕
       BEHAVIOR
```

Or, perhaps more illustrative would be:

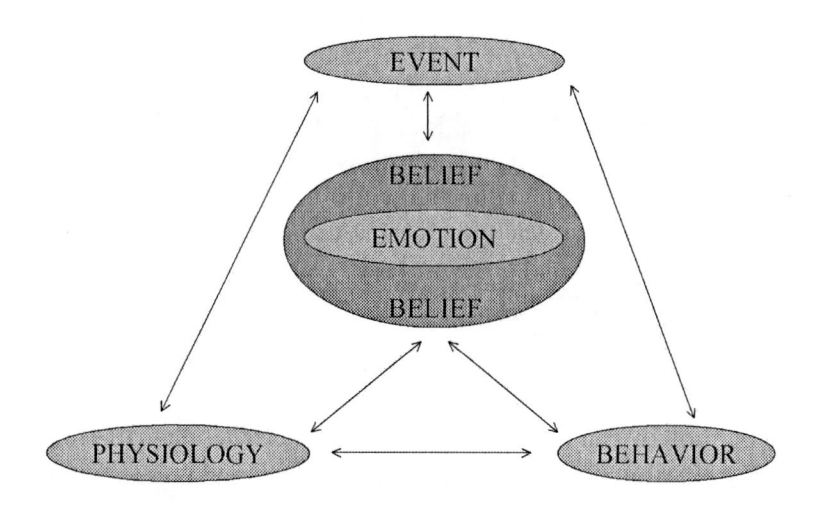

```
                    EVENT
                   ↑  ↕
                  / BELIEF \
                 / EMOTION  \
                /  BELIEF    \
               ↓  ↗      ↖   ↓
         PHYSIOLOGY ←——→ BEHAVIOR
```

So, an event or 'trigger' occurs starting the chain reaction; belief and emotion are superimposed on one another because these can co-occur with such immediacy and automation that it is often difficult to separate them, especially in the heat of the moment; your body then has physiological reactions to the thought/belief/emotion bubble and can immediately incite a behavioral response. The two-way arrows indicate these all interact with each other, thus each can have a powerful influence on the others. Generally speaking, when trying to break this chain of command, changing your thoughts or behaviors most easily does it. Sure you could attempt to try and control the events or triggers in your life, but most of what happens around you is largely out of your control. And when you try to excise control over that which you do not, the more out of control you feel, which in turn will have you reach outside of yourself and try to control others around you which you do not have control over, so you feel more out of control, so you…get the idea? What you do have control over is how <u>you</u> choose to respond to the chaos around you.

Most experts agree you cannot directly change the emotion without first changing the thought or interpretation of it. Try this and you'll see what I mean. Make yourself cry. Or, get angry, be frightened, or make yourself emote happiness, by simply feeling these feelings. That's right just feel. Pretty difficult isn't it? If you can, great! You are much more accomplished than most. Now, think of something that bothers you, when you were most recently mad or scared. Is it a little easier to feel that genuine feeling? This event is not currently happening. What is making you feel the way you feel is simply thinking about it. You can begin to see the power of your mind. Once you are good and emotional, and you can really feel that energy building and building, simply stop feeling that way! Not easy is it? Now think about that experience differently, more objectively. Put a different spin on it. What might have been going on with that other person? How can you interpret it differently, put it into perspective? Just as you can work yourself up into a frenzy similar to this, you can talk yourself into literally calming down. Congratulations, you have just engaged in a cognitive therapy strategy. There are more sophisticated methods, but this gives you the general idea of REBT-CBT. And this is the idea behind the train your brain principle of taking a *Daily Dose of Positivity*.

The semanticist, Korzybski, has had a substantial influence on the development of REBT. Semantic processes in the form of self-statements or beliefs affect your emotions, and serve to motivate your behavior. Furthermore, you can talk to yourself in optimistic, hopeful, and joyful ways inducing more positive emotions, or you can engage in self-talk that is pessimistic, hopeless, and derogatory resulting in feelings of sadness, emotional upset, anxiousness, and being depressed. Ellis also contends that this semantic labeling and self-talk can be unconscious as well as conscious. As a result, you are often unaware of the meanings or values you place onto yourself, or the attributions you make to significant other people, places and things. When you train your brain by taking a *Daily Dose of Positivity*, you are more apt to unconsciously attribute a positive slant to yourself, significant others, places and events.

REBT suggests that when you do become emotionally upset (C), that you can have either rational beliefs (rBs) and/or irrational beliefs (iBs). Rational beliefs are simply those views, philosophies, and evaluations of events (A) that help you assess whether your basic desires are being fulfilled. Rational thinking, according to Ellis, has five main characteristics: (a) thought is derived primarily from objective fact as opposed to subjective opinion; (b) thinking, if acted upon, most likely will result in preservation of your life and limb; (c) it will help define your personal life goals most quickly; (d) it will produce a minimum of inner conflict and turmoil; and (e) if acted upon, it will prevent undesirable conflict with those whom you live and associate. These beliefs (rBs) are expressed in wishes, preferences, desires and wants. For example: "I desire the approval of others for the things that I do"; "I like behaving competently and achieving things that are important to me." These types of beliefs tend to lead to appropriate emotional responses (C), such as frustration, happiness, sorrow, hope, or regret, rather than depression, rage, intense anxiety, negativity and loss of self-esteem. The former set of responses is deemed appropriate because they are much more likely to bring about constructive, goal-oriented behavior than the latter responses, which tend to produce stagnation and inertia. Ellis and Becker assert that, unlike other schools of thought, REBT clearly distinguishes between appropriate and inappropriate emotional responses (C) to activating experiences (A). Whilst the original Stoic philosophers believed passion and emotion were to be subdued, REBT merely distinguishes between appropriate and inappropriate feelings, it does not advocate eliminating emotional responses altogether. This is also the premise behind *Daily Dose of Positivity*.

When you hold rational beliefs you tend to experience less excessive and problematic emotional stress. However, as noted earlier, you can hold both rational and irrational beliefs about the same event. Irrational beliefs (iBs) are generally expressed in unquestioned absolutes, musts, shoulds, oughts, and demands. Examples include: "I should be perfect"; "I must be loved by everyone I ever meet." Irrational thoughts like these are hypothesized to generate and influence unpleasant emotional and behavioral consequences such as depression, anxiety, hostility, and chronic negativity.

At this point, I feel compelled to mention the difference between situational transient automatic thoughts and beliefs and a more enduring pervasive all-encompassing attitude. I have included beliefs with automatic thoughts even though some would argue beliefs are more enduring and pervasive than situational thoughts. Situational thoughts are immediate interpretations of your given situation, and while these may be influenced by broader beliefs about yourself, others, and the way the world works, belief systems are still more specific mental convictions or acceptance that certain things are true than your overall attitude. Attitude is more a manner of thinking, feeling, and acting in a way that shows your disposition. It is more comprehensive than automatic situational thoughts and specific beliefs. In fact attitude may be considered at the top of the hierarchy and influences situational thoughts and beliefs. It can be summed as negative or positive. To demonstrate its inclusive property, I refer to what I call the "Sphere of Attitude." This concept is further presented and elaborated in the "Combining past and present: The psychophysiology of negativity vs. positivity" section. This section includes diagrams of the psychophysiology of the mind body connection, depression, anxiety, negativity, positivity, and the sphere of attitude, all of which have developed out of my work in a medical environment.

The Original Irrational Beliefs of REBT

In their original work *A New Guide to Rational Living*, Ellis and Harper compiled a list of irrational beliefs that they believed influenced emotional and behavioral disturbance. The list is as follows:

1. The idea that you must have love and approval from all people you find significant

2. The idea that you must prove thoroughly competent, adequate, and achieving

3. The idea that when people act obnoxiously and unfairly, you should blame and damn them, and see them as bad, wicked, or rotten individuals

4. The idea that you have to view things as awful, terrible, horrible, and catastrophic when you get seriously frustrated, treated unfairly, or rejected

5. The idea that emotional misery comes from external pressures and that you have little ability to control or change your feelings

6. The idea that if something seems dangerous or fearsome, you must preoccupy yourself with and make yourself anxious about it

7. The idea that you can more easily avoid facing many life difficulties and self-responsibilities than undertake more rewarding forms of self-discipline

8. The idea that your past remains all-important and that because something once strongly influenced your life, it has to keep determining your feelings and behavior today

9. The idea that people and things should turn out better than they do and that you must view it as awful and horrible if you do not find good solutions

10. The idea that you can achieve maximum human happiness by inertia and inaction or by passively and uncommittedly "enjoying yourself"

Ellis has since revised this list to include four general assumptions or irrational beliefs.
These are discussed in the section entitled Recent Changes to REBT

Concepts of behavior change

As has already been suggested, REBT makes several assumptions about the conditions that foster behavioral change, most of which stress the importance of altering the way you think and consequently how you behave. According to Ellis, the most fundamental assumption underlying REBT is that human emotion and thinking are interconnected. In other words, you create most of your emotions by way of how you think and, conversely, create some of your thoughts by how you feel. REBT posits that humans have four basic processes: (a) perception or sensation; (b) emotion; (c) behavior; and (d) thought, and that ordinarily one does not experience these four basic processes in isolation. This interdependent principle suggests that cognitions, emotions, and behavior are parts of an interdependent system, thus, none of these elements exists independently of the others. REBT argues that changing negative or inappropriate emotions such as anxiety, guilt, or depression, requires you to identify and challenge the irrational beliefs that most likely underlie them. REBT helps you to identify and challenge the beliefs that induce absolutistic and overgeneralized demands that you place on yourself and others, and to replace them with ones that promote less self-defeating behaviors.

Rational Insight. Being trained as a psychoanalyst, Ellis values insight, however, REBT does not assume that insight will illicit spontaneous behavior change. Rather, you must actively practice rational thinking and behaving to produce healthy changes. This supports the rationale for actively taking a *Daily Dose of Positivity.*

REBT identifies three types of insight. Insight Number One implies the conventional kind of understanding postulated by Sigmund Freud: that emotional and behavioral disturbances do have antecedent causes. However, REBT argues that antecedents are not deep rooted in the past, but rather, that your existing system of beliefs constitutes the most potent antecedent of most behavior. Insight Number Two consists of recognizing that you reindoctrinate yourself with irrational and distorted ideas that originated in the past and that these continue to illicit emotional and behavioral disturbance. Essentially, you keep reinforcing dysfunction. Insight Number Three suggests that you change as a result of rational efforts consisting of steadily, persistently and vigorously working to change irrational beliefs and unhealthy behaviors. According to several authors, this is considered the most important insight of the three. This further supports the premise behind *Daily Dose of Positivity*; a steady and persistent training of the brain.

<u>Cognitive Restructuring.</u> Rational insights allow you to better position yourself to identify your rigidly held irrational beliefs that produce emotionally disturbing consequences. Once this is accomplished, you can then solidly interrupt them with strong counter-beliefs that lead to more appropriate emotional responses and desirable behavior changes.

<u>Counseling methods and techniques of REBT</u>

The major thrust of REBT is threefold. First, the therapist helps determine the activating external experiences or precipitating events (A). Second, the therapist helps determine the specific thought patterns or beliefs (iBs) that constitute the internal response to these events and give rise to inappropriate emotions (C). Third, therapists assist you in altering or modifying these beliefs and thought patterns. This is referred to as disputing irrational beliefs (D) or cognitive restructuring.

<u>Disputing Irrational Beliefs (DIBS).</u> DIBS is the most fundamental method used in REBT. DIBS begins with the ABC analysis but adds two new steps to the process, points (D) and (E). It involves logico-empirical analysis of irrational thinking. Logico-empirical methods entail applying logic, empirical observation, and testing for the purpose of achieving a more productive life. Once A, B, and C are identified you are taught at (D) to vigorously dispute your irrational thinking, and replace them with more rational ones. Point (E) refers to the effect of disputing—the relinquishing of self-destructive ideologies, the acquisition of a more rational philosophy of life, and a greater acceptance of self, others, and the frustrations of life.

Craig S. Travis, Ph.D.

RECENT CHANGES TO REBT

"Change in all things is sweet."

Aristotle

Ellis has been promoting his cognitive form of psychotherapy since 1955, and in fact, refers to it as the first cognitive or cognitive behavioral therapy. He first called this approach, Rational Therapy (RT), and then, in 1961, followed with Rational-Emotive Therapy (RET). In 1993, Ellis announced his latest revision, that Rational-Emotive Therapy would be changed to Rational-Emotive-Behavior Therapy (REBT). The inception of this modification has proven most controversial and has produced a great debate within the camp of RE(B)T, and from "other" cognitive-behavioral theorists. Following sections address the name change, additional modifications, and the name change debate.

From RET to REBT
Ellis argues that the reason he changed the name of his approach was that he was "wrong" to have omitted behavior in the first place. RET, he states, is misleading because it omits the highly behavioral aspect that he promoted from the start. Other REBT practitioners support the inclusion of behavior in the name, indicating that behavior is, always has been, and always will be an essential part of Ellis' theory. Bernard provides support for the change in the following:

> If one chooses to define a therapy by its clinical methods, then there is little doubt in my mind that the "B" in RET deserves to see the light of day. For 40 years or so, Ellis has been writing about the importance of getting clients to change their behavior both as a means to reinforce cognitive change, but also to speed up the change process (p. 79).

Of course, there are plenty of opponents to this change as will be addressed in a subsequent section.

Additional revisions beyond the "B"
In addition to the controversial and hotly debated name change, Ellis modified other aspects of his theory. Two of the more prominent changes are revisions to his ABC model and adaptations to irrational beliefs.

<u>The new ABC's of REBT.</u> ABC theory contends that strong Beliefs (B) influence emotional and behavioral Consequences (C) about Activating events (A). According to REBT, rational beliefs (rB) about A will lead to more appropriate and functional feelings (C), however, irrational beliefs (iB) lead to disturbed emotions at C. Ellis takes this a step further indicating that you can create secondary symptoms—called symptom disturbance—from the absolutistic musts you make about primary symptoms. Thus, the original disturbed feelings (C1) (i.e., depression) can become an Activating event (A2). Then, at point B2, you believe you absolutely must not be depressed, thus creating strong feelings of depression about your depression (C2). This interaction of ABC's can be circular and exponential providing additional symptoms. The argument, then, is that thoughts, feelings and behaviors can become A2's, A3's, etc. Therefore, change includes addressing symptoms about symptoms in addition to addressing your original problem.

<u>Amendment to the original Irrational Beliefs.</u> Ellis originally devised a set of 10 irrational beliefs that he hypothesized promoted problematic emotions and behaviors. He currently contends that the original beliefs can be reduced to three, which encompass all others. These 3 main beliefs include demandingness (DEM), awfulizing (AWF), and global evaluations of human worth or self-rating (SR). DiGiuseppe argues that the theory has also included low frustration tolerance (LFT), although Ellis clearly emphasizes the first three. At any rate, the emphasis of emotional disturbance lies in 4 demanding beliefs. Self-demandingness forms of irrational thinking lead to strong feelings of self-hatred, anxiety, and depression; other-demandingness leads to strong feelings of rage, jealousy, and self-pity; and world-demandingness leads to strong feelings of anger and depression. In addition, these three main beliefs may lead to destructive behaviors such as suicide, withdrawal, obsessiveness, aggression, negativity, vindictiveness, love addiction, inertia, procrastination, and phobias.

Craig S. Travis, Ph.D.

WHAT'S IN A NAME? THE NAME CHANGE DEBATE

"If nothing ever changed, there'd be no butterflies."

Unknown

In 1994, Ellis changed the name from Rational Emotive Therapy (RET) to Rational Emotive Behavior Therapy (REBT), and sparked a debate about adding the word behavior to the theory's title. Davison contends that adding the word behavior to RET is long overdue. He argues that new behavior serves primarily to change cognition, from which other constructive emotions and behaviors follow. Ellis, he states, has been advocating since the 1950's that cognitive approaches to therapeutic change are incomplete without formal attention to behavior. Woods concurs that adding behavior is appropriate stating that although it may come as a shock, classical and instrumental conditioning occur on a regular basis in daily life. Furthermore, he argues, emotions are classically conditioned to present stimuli when the emotions occur and instrumental behavior in the future will be influenced by present contingencies. This, in turn, generates cognitive changes in your expectancies. Thus, cognition's, emotions, and behaviors are all part of the domain. Corsini also favors the addition of "B" to RET. He argues that all therapy is essentially cognitive, but that without changes in behavior, assessment of therapeutic progress is difficult. He states that "in every successful therapy, the locus of change is in the mind—but for the change to be meaningful, more than just words are needed, action must take place during the process and be proved by action after the therapy" (p. 7). Finally, DiGiuseppe gives REBT high praise claiming that "it is the best system of psychotherapy ever developed" (p. 6).

Bernard explains that some of the main criticisms of adding behavior to RET regard the perceived negative effects of RET becoming associated with behavior therapy. In addition, proponents of behavior therapy contend that REBT lacks empiricism, the basic tenet of behavior therapy. In other words, opponents of REBT contend that it fails to present empirical support for its predictions. There have since been a number of studies supporting the effectiveness of REBT. In addition there is numerous research data that supports the effectiveness of general cognitive behavioral techniques for a variety of emotional and behavioral problems.

Lazarus also heavily criticizes the name change. He argues that:

Nothing is gained by fiddling with names, and by continuing to promote a school of psychotherapeutic thought…it would have been a boon and a blessing if Ellis, instead of tacking "B" for "Behavior" onto his well-known RET, had decided to change the name of his institute and his base of operation to that of *Technical Eclecticism* (original italics) (p. 100).

Wessler points out that Ellis spends most of his time writing on cognitions as causes of emotions, and that this ignores the bi-directionality of cognitions and emotions. Thereby, the result is a very linear sounding ABC theory. This implies that Ellis would have been better off leaving behavior out of the title. While you can find many critics for just about any theory, REBT and CBT are tried and true methods of successful change, and these approaches have helped millions of people live better more fulfilling lives. These basic strategies are built into each DDP and can help you achieve the same: Peak performance and optimal function on a daily basis.

Craig S. Travis, Ph.D.

BELIEFS AND PHYSICAL ILLNESS

"Belief sickens, belief kills, belief heals"

—Robert Hahn, *Sickness & Healing*, 1995

REBT has been applied to health psychology research. A brief summary is presented here.

Lichtenberg and fellow colleagues hypothesized and found a significant relationship between persons' subscription to irrational beliefs and their susceptibility to illness. Smith and Brehm found a positive relationship between irrational beliefs and Type A coronary-prone behavior pattern. In addition, Silverglade and colleagues have shown a positive relationship between irrational beliefs and disease severity in adolescent asthmatics. Finally, cognitive experiential therapy (CET) has been applied in the treatment of essential hypertension and found it to be effective in reducing several psychobiological measures of hypertension. CET is essentially the principles of REBT administered to patients while in a mildly hypnotic state. Cognitive Experiential Therapy (CET) combines cognitive restructuring, hypnosis, and developmental staging and is based upon Ellis' "ABC" theory of emotional disturbance. CET reframes the ABC model by expanding "B" (cognition) and adds "D" (physiological-biochemical responses) and "E" (behavioral responses). It is the introduction of physiological-biochemical responses that is of theoretical significance. This addition assumes that cognitions may influence physiological-biochemical responses in the body. This has since been shown to be true in the brain imaging studies that were done in the 1990's by Mark George and Daniel Amen.

Genetics and predispositions do not suffice to explain the onset of many illnesses. Conditions that initiate illness may be quite different from those that predispose them. Thus, the literature suggests that social psychological factors (i.e., anxiety and depression) are associated with the onset of disease. Therefore, arguably cognitive processes need to be recognized in the study of stress related illness. This is not to say that your thoughts are solely responsible for illness; that would be too simplified, not to mention unrealistic. But as you have seen, your thoughts will either help you or hurt you; but you get to decide which is which!

Chronic illnesses and stress related disorders have replaced infectious diseases as the major causes of death, disability, reduced quality of life, and medical expenditures. Health care experts estimate that as high as 75% of visits to primary care physicians are for stress related problems. Psychological stress and poor coping skills have been shown to be factors related to a wide variety of chronic illnesses. Although fleeting thoughts seem important in their relation to stress related disease, what may be of greater significance is the connection between a more enduring and pervasive negative "attitude" and functional health problems.

Research in health psychology suggests that cognitive processes (i.e., how people think) need to be recognized in the contribution, management and prevention of stress related illness. The placebo effect illustrates this quite well in a positive way. A placebo is generally defined as an inactive treatment (i.e., a sugar pill) that proves effective in reducing or treating symptoms of some medical illness when in fact there is no physiological data to support its efficacy. The idea of a placebo is that it doesn't actually do anything; you just think it does, so you get better. The placebo effect works because people believe they will get better. In other words, a placebo helps you harness the power of positive thinking. Just as placebo has demonstrated the positive power of expectations, belief and attitude, there are now scattered studies suggesting that negative thinking can harm patients' health. While most everyone is familiar with the term placebo effect, few are aware of its 'evil twin', the nocebo effect. Nocebo is the ability of negative beliefs and expectations to actually cause harm. Research has also shown that the nocebo effect can reverse the body's response to true medical treatment from positive to negative. That is negative attitude about treatment is powerful enough to render an otherwise effective medicine ineffective. So if the treatments actually work and people don't think they do, their effect may be reduced—they may live down to the person's expectations. Like the placebo effect, the nocebo effect is usually generated by "beliefs, attitudes and cultural factors". Herbert Benson, MD, president and founder of the Mind/Body Medical Institute at Harvard Medical School, is convinced. "The nocebo effect plays a major role in many conditions, especially stress-related problems," he says. "Skin rashes, belly aches, you name it can be made worse by worrying about it through the mind-body effect."

Whether you are suffering from a clinical syndrome, a "bad attitude", or just struggling with everyday life stress, this book will help. It is intended for the masses, not just those diagnosed with mental and emotional problems.

PART II: THE PRESENT

THE POSITIVE PSYCHOLOGY MOVEMENT

11

POSITIVE PSYCHOLOGY: WHAT IS IT AND WHY WEREN'T WE DOING IT BEFORE?

"Everything can be taken from a man but one thing:
the last of all human freedoms—to choose one's attitude
in any given set of circumstances, to choose one's own way"

Viktor Frankl, *Man's Search for Meaning*

The power of attitude is well documented in Viktor Fankl's most notable work, Man's Search for Meaning, in which he recounts his own personal experience in a Nazi concentration camp. What allowed he and millions of other Jews to survive such horrendous circumstances? Certainly, circumstance, or perhaps more descriptive, pure chance, lent itself to the fate of each survivor's existence. But how did those who were fortunate enough to escape their senseless extinction cope not only with they're own traumatic experience but also the murders of their family and friends? How were the survivors able to carry on once removed from these death camps? Frankl, in his reflection, suggests that his mental attitude is what allowed him to persevere, not only while this atrocity was occurring, but also once released. To make sense of, or create meaning out of his experience; to choose his attitude even given this horrific set of circumstances; that, according to Frankl, contributed to his ability to carry on.

I want to carefully express that I am not trivializing such an extreme event. Rather, Frankl's discovery, that regardless of the circumstances you are free to choose your attitude, seems quite fitting in regard to the concept of positive psychology. Faith, optimism, hope, perseverance, and future mindedness, combine to help develop your attitude. Research in prevention has discovered that these and other human strengths: courage, interpersonal skill, honesty, the capacity for flow and insight, etc., buffer against mental illness. So, why did Frankl and many others who experience such travesty not develop Post Traumatic Stress Disorder? The answer seems to lie in what has been labeled the positive psychology movement. While the current movement is not entirely new, Martin Seligman, former American Psychological Association president and guiding force behind the First Annual Positive Psychology Summit, suggests the time is finally right for positive psychology.

Craig S. Travis, Ph.D.

POSITIVE PSYCHOLOGY

"I would think we are more ready for positive psychology than ever before. It is there in our inheritance, as much as a predisposition for the negative."

Donald Clifton, host of the
First Annual Positive Psychology Summit

So what exactly is *positive* psychology? The aim of this movement is to shift the focus of psychology from what is wrong with you to what is right, from a disease model to one of flourishing, strength, and positivity. The overall goal is to promote human strength through a positive approach. This positive psychology movement serves to remind us that the field of psychology is not just about the study of pathology, weakness, and disease. It is also about understanding and fostering strength, virtue, healthy attitude, and developing positive character. Thus, positivity is not just about fixing what is broken, but also nurturing what is best.

Martin Seligman says positive psychology comprises three pillars. The first relating to subjective well-being—life satisfaction and contentment when about the past; happiness, joy and exuberance when about the present; and optimism, faith, and hope when about the future. The second pillar consists of positive individual traits—intimacy, integrity, leadership, altruism, vocation, and wisdom. He argues this second pillar is crucial because happiness unattached to positive character is fragile and hollow. *Daily Dose of Positivity* reflects the first two pillars and is designed to help establish this positive character. The third pillar, states Seligman, reflects the study of positive institutions.

Positive psychology is not about just trying to make you feel better. It does not solely rely on wishful thinking, self-deception, denial of circumstance, fads, or Pollyannaism. The significant message in this movement is that traits like positive attitude, strength, wisdom and morality, need to be taken seriously. There is now a scientific base for the validity of their importance to your overall health and well-being, as was demonstrated in Part I. When someone can experience what Frankl did and not only come out of it relatively unscathed, but actually be able to derive meaning from what at first glance is an apparent senseless experience, that is truly positive.

Several excellent websites have been established to provide further discussion of this forum. If you are interested in an in depth, research oriented, scientific

Daily Dose of Positivity™

presentation of what is happening in positive psychology, check out www.psych.upenn.edu/seligman; www.umich.edu/~psycdept/emotions/index.html; http://www.apa.org/releases/positivepsy.html;

Craig S. Travis, Ph.D.

THE PSYCHOLOGY OF YESTERYEAR AND REESTABLISHING THE SCIENCE OF OLD

There have been many changes for the better in recent years, and some people have been against all of them

Anonymous

Borrowing much of its philosophy from the medical model, psychology has traditionally focused on treating symptoms and disease states. As a result, the past 100 years of psychology has focused much attention on understanding and alleviating negative emotions, mental and emotional disorders, and behavioral problems. Research studies involving abuse, anxiety, depression, stress related disease and negative emotions have outnumbered those on positive emotions 14 to 1. While this has proved very fruitful, there are many effective strategies for treating such problems, positive psychology, although gaining recognition as bona fide discipline, has traditionally not been emphasized.

Why has psychology not focused on the positive aspects of human nature? University of Maryland psychologist, Lisa Aspinwall, and colleagues, provide an explanation for the unfortunate minimization of positive psychology research over the years. She states that positive psychology (i.e., the study of positive subjective experience) has suffered two unfortunate trends: the first, and perhaps most significant, is viewing positive states as trivial; the second, assuming that all positive states have the same properties and functions. Historically, the prevailing view has been that positive feelings are trivial and unworthy of scientific study. This still seems to remain true today. Even society seems to minimize the importance of positive subjective feelings, lest you be considered a narcissistic self-centered pleasure seeker and adrenaline junky. Instead we seem to focus on the negativity in the world. After-all, the drama of human suffering seems to be more newsworthy.

The second influential perspective, that all positive feelings are identical, has also minimized their importance. Perhaps common sense has swayed critical thinking in this area as well: yes positivity is good, but then we already know that, so why study it? Although it is true that there are some common properties and functions of positive states, there are also very important, intriguing, and understudied differences that we are just beginning to understand.

As indicated, the result of these two tendencies influenced the predominate study of negative feelings in psychological research. While we may know relatively little about different kinds of positive subjective experience and their relation to thinking, behavior, social interaction, and health, current research in positive psychology proves promising. But, before we move ahead, lets understand the past.

Originally, the field of psychology had three distinct missions: curing mental and emotional disorders, making the lives of all people more productive and fulfilling, and identifying and nurturing talent. So what happened? Why has psychology taken on a disease model, focusing on pathology, disease, and illness, the first of the three missions, while seemingly ignoring the other two. As with many social phenomena, the answers lie in economic events and influence. Right after World War II, The Veterans Administration (VA) was founded and soon thereafter the National Institute of Mental Health (NIMH) was established. Clinicians through the VA could make a living treating mental illness while researchers could be funded by the NIMH as long as they focused on pathology. While this arrangement brought about many benefits: better understanding of mental and emotional disorders and current effective treatment strategies, the downside was that the other two fundamental missions of psychology—facilitating human potential, and fostering personal productivity and fulfillment—fell by the wayside.

During the late 1950's and early 1960's, there was a resurgence of positive psychology in the Cognitive and Humanistic movements. Both orientations focused on the possibilities of change. While Cognitive psychology took a more directive approach and humanistic psychology adopted a more passive one, both believed in the endless possibilities of change as long as clients took themselves firmly in hand and actively got with the program. The good therapist of the 50's, 60's, and 70's was the "Coach", the can-do specialist who focused on what was changeable in the present and possible for the future; not on pathology, disease, and what was "broken".

Once again economics swayed the positive force that psychology of the time was developing. Third party payers, health insurance companies, began covering therapy visits. Although initially this may be construed as beneficial, these companies did not pay for you to achieve self-actualization or to discover your full potential. You must be ill to receive coverage. Even today, the term "medical necessity" implies coverage only if pathology or disorder exists; prevention, wellness, and developing your full potential is not a concern. While cognitive therapists were able to adapt using Beck's cognitive model of emotional disorders, humanistic therapists have all but faded away as clinicians. Until now!

Craig S. Travis, Ph.D.

As Part I stated, the science of old often recycles itself. The psychologist as Coach trend of the 50's and 60's has experienced a resurgence. This is true not only clinically ("Therapist as Coach" workshops, and life coach consultants abound), but with research as well, evidenced in the positive psychology movement. Economic institutions can no longer ignore the validity and importance of positive psychology and learning positive psychology strategies. Although learning optimistic thinking may seem like a bold new idea in clinical and research psychology, we have seen evidence for its effect in the self-help movement. Ever since Norman Vincent Peale wrote "The Power of Positive Thinking," arguably giving birth to the self-help movement, popular psychology in America has been reeling in such ideas. With positive psychology, we now stand on the brink of opportunity to develop a new discipline, a humane scientific approach, a positive psychology concerned with not only weakness and damage, but including the study and understanding of strength, character and virtue.

The remaining sections provide the "science behind this thought": Positive psychology has a solid scientific base showing the benefits of having the right attitude for your overall health and well-being.

Daily Dose of Positivity™

POSITIVE PSYCHOLOGY: FROM TREATMENT AND PREVENTION TO WELLNESS AND FULL POTENTIAL

"It is not about how to heal; it's about how to have a great life"

Martin Seligman

Positive psychology proposes that certain thought-action tendencies that produce positive emotions can help you overcome negative emotions faster and build resilience to future adversities. Barbara Fredrickson, a University of Michigan Psychologist, provides a cornerstone to positive psychology in her broaden-and-build model of positive emotion. The implications to this model suggest that positivity has the potential to counteract—both prevent and treat—individual and societal problems that stem from negativity (anxiety, depression, aggression and stress-related health problems). Your capacity for positivity, although probably a largely untapped strength, is boundless. (I assert that this is a pretty safe assumption as indicated earlier in that the science of psychology has not historically examined the positive aspects of human experience).

An important feature to your developing a more positive outlook, thus experiencing more positive emotions, is that its effect does not end once suffering is prevented or alleviated. Positivity can optimize your health, subjective well-being, and psychological resilience. So, positivity, over time and as a product of recurrence, can have the effect of building your physical, intellectual, behavioral, and social resources, essentially buffering you against the setbacks in life that can trigger psychological and emotional problems. Note that these new resources are long lasting and can be called upon later when needed. So, not only does positivity presumably prevent much emotional disturbance, given what we are learning about the effects of mental well-being on the body, positivity may also have the "side effect" of making your life physically healthier. This is the proposed view of the positive psychology movement and researchers are now examining this potential.

A wide range of research data supports the specific predictions made by the positive psychology model. This research shows the link between positive states and broadened scopes of attention, cognition, and action and enhanced physical, intellectual and social resources. For instance, Alice Isen and her colleagues have shown that positive emotions produce patterns of thought that are flexible, creative and receptive. Essentially, Isen's work suggests that tapping into positivity (i.e., positive affect) "enlarges the cognitive context," an effect that has been recently linked to increases in functional brain chemistry levels. Positive evidence for the three-dimensional circular interaction of the mind and body: your thoughts affect your feelings, but your feelings affect your thoughts, and both have a role in influencing your behavior and physiology. Consequently, your physiology and behavior have an influence on your thoughts and feelings. Research connecting thoughts to your brain chemistry is further addressed in the section: Effectiveness of Cognitive Therapy: What does research tell us?

Pioneering research by Martin Seligman has demonstrated that positive psychology is effective in treating depression. Positive psychology techniques aimed at instilling a sense of optimism cut depression in half in three studies of young adults and children that included as much as 10 years follow-up. Seligman notes that the goal of positive psychology is to enhance basic human strengths such as optimism, courage, honesty, self-understanding, and interpersonal skills, rather than focusing on what is "broken" and on repairing the damage of past traumas. This positive approach is meant to help you use inner resources as a buffer against setbacks in life and as a means to master adversity whenever it crops up so that you do not sink into depression. Similarly, participants in the workshops also had half the rates of generalized anxiety disorder. A principle skill taught at the workshop involved the cognitive therapy approach known as "disputing" addressed in Part I. This skill teaches you to recognize your own negative thoughts about yourself and then to argue against these thoughts as though you were disputing an external critic. Additional studies indicate that cognitive strategies similar to those taught in these workshops were shown to be effective in preventing depression and anxiety and that these strategies had long term effects.

Randy Larsen has also contributed significantly to the idea of a positive psychology. Using the analogy of the human mind as a mansion he equates the traditional research approach, focusing on the disease model, as spending the first century mucking around in the basement with the skeletons and rubbish. He says there is much to learn about the positive side of human nature. His research has shown that most negative emotions occur in response to threats, failures, or losses, particularly in your important relationships. He concludes that moods can be regulated by varying different coping strategies. Happiness, he says, is not tied to luck. Happy people do not have fewer negative experiences; bad things happen to all people. Instead, happy people seem to manage the bad events better. Events, situations, material objects, and money do not make you happy for as the noted 19th century philosopher Arthur Schopenhauer noted, "we come across at least as many cheerful faces among the poor as among the rich." Instead, Larsen suggests that positive upbeat people seem especially adept at overcoming negative emotions; it's not so much that happy people smile more, but they definitely frown less. His research supports other positive psychology data that suggests how you think influences your mood, and that you can change, reframe, or restructure how you think and make it more positive, often creating lasting benefits.

It bears repeating that the positive psychology model suggests that these coping strategies are not simply ways to treat and prevent disease and distress although that is certainly one benefit. Your health and well being are more than the absence of disease and distress. Positivity is perhaps best understood as optimizing health and well-being. That is to say, its effect is intended to reach beyond treating and preventing problems that result from negativity. Thus the study of positive psychology is most reflected in building your personal strength, resilience, and overall wellness.

Craig S. Travis, Ph.D.

SO, WHAT ARE WE SUPPOSED TO FEEL?

Emotion is to be used and to help one grow:
Spiritually, intellectually, in every way!

Magda B. Arnold

You have both negative and positive emotional sensations. Anger, sadness, and fear along with joy, interest, and contentment. Common sense suggests we ought to feel the positive emotions. They certainly seem more pleasant. What common sense suggests, research and clinical data now support.

First I need to clarify that the 'negative' emotions are not exclusively bad seeds. In fact they do have an evolutionary self-preservational mechanism. Your appraisal of the situation results in ensuing emotions; if threatening, unpleasant feelings follow, but, they engage your survival behavior. In Part I, I illustrated how 'negative' emotions such as fear/anxiety and anger/aggression translate into the fight-or-flight action tendencies, and that this serves as an effective survival mechanism when involving life-and-death situations. This follows the many models of emotion: that emotions by definition are associated with specific action, hence *motion* comprising most of the word. So, negative emotions seem to narrow your momentary thought-action tendencies which then direct specific action that serve the function of promoting survival. Thus, anger is linked to aggression or the impulse to attack, fear with the desire to escape or flee the situation, and so on. Thought connected to feeling connected to motion or action. Again, this makes sense from an evolutionary perspective: these are among the actions that worked best in allowing our ancestors to survive life-or-death situations. Had this thought action sequence not been adaptive, your ancestors would not have been successful in producing descendents, thus you would not be reading this book. Specific thought action tendencies are of course coupled with the idea that these promote appropriate physiological changes for survival (i.e., the emergency reaction discussed in Part I. We shall see later in this section that the literature proposes that positive emotions are evolutionary as well and thus, also are essential to survival.)

So why do negative emotions get all the bad press? After all, negative emotions (anger, fear, and sadness) can bring about anxiety, depression, aggression, and stress-related health problems. While this has been established scientifically, it does not mean that you should never experience a negative emotion. In fact, we have just evidenced their necessity for your survival. The issue at hand is to allow them to run their course naturally and then shut off, all the while finding more adaptive thought-action responses that are more acceptable given that most threatening situations today are not physical life and death battles but rather psychological ones. In today's struggles, you might get your ego damaged, but it probably won't kill you. When you allow negative emotions to continue past their usefulness by holding on to them with your thoughts, then they become destructive. Think of your emotions similar to a pot of water on the stove when you are cooking spaghetti. The pot doesn't start boiling as soon as you turn on the heat source; nor do your emotions immediately boil at the first sign of heat (or stress) in your life. Rather, they tend to build due to our thought processes about what is going on in our lives. What happens when you put a lid on the pot of boiling spaghetti? Right, it becomes a pressure cooker and if you ignore it eventually it blows its lid and spills all over the stove making a mess. Sound familiar? The same dynamic occurs with the energy of feelings. Ever keep things, your feelings, inside all bottled up, until they explode and then they appear to make a mess of things so you say to yourself, 'see feelings only create problems' so you stuff them in and start the processes all over again? The trick is to know when to let off a little steam and how long to let things cook before they burn (you).

"So what do I do?" you are saying. First take solace in the fact that this is an issue with which everyone struggles. Second, brings me to the point of this and all the DDP books: Positivity (positive emotions, learned optimism, happiness, etc. call it what you will) has an undoing effect on negative emotions.

I have discussed the specific thought action tendencies of negative emotion and their importance to survival especially from an ancestral point of view. Theory and research now indicate that positive emotions provide a distinct but complementary process. Fredrickson's *broaden-and-build model* of positive emotion provides a theoretical foundation for this hypothesis. Her theory suggests that positive emotions are the adaptive counterpart to your fight-or-flight, self-preservational defensive reaction to threats. She states that, in contrast to the momentary specific thought action tendency of negative emotions, positive emotions (joy, interest, and contentment) broaden your momentary thought action possibilities. As a result, you can build enduring personal resources that also serve the ancestral function of promoting survival. In other words, positivity can overpower negativity.

What does this all mean? Well, by broadening your momentary thought action potential, your ensuing positive emotional response loosens the hold that negative emotions gain on your mind and body. This broadening process and positive emotional experience has an undoing effect of the narrowed psychological and physiological preparation for specific action. In essence you become healthier. This happens through what I like to call the Trickle Down Process. Research has shown the effect thinking has on your brain chemistry. In essence, every experience, every thought you have is translated neurochemically in your brain, through the amygdala, neocortex, etc. These neurotransmitters are chemical messengers to the rest of your body. So what starts in the mind with a thought, interpretation, or perception, *trickles down* to the rest of your body. Neuroscientist, Candace Pert, recently made a key discovery that supports this Trickle Down Theory. She demonstrated that the chemical messengers of the brain, these neurotransmitters, are also found in the entire immune system. Pert calls these "molecules of emotion". The implications of this finding suggest that the chemical messengers, whether they be molecules of emotion, thought, or combination of both, flow throughout the body. Most important is that this chemical-molecular communication is reciprocal, thus allowing emotion to influence thought and thought to influence emotion; both of which influence your behavior. (Given the interactive nature of these thought/emotion molecules, perhaps a better moniker would be the Trickle Up & Down Process, but that is another book!)

The Trickle Down Process would then look something like the following. Your thoughts get translated into biochemical physiological messages interpreted by the body as feelings and emotions. These are then translated into action or behaviors. Perceive things as threats and you will feel threatened; your body will respond physiologically and prepare yourself for fight or flight, a narrowed thought action response. Your adrenaline and other stress hormones will kick into action to promote survival; the subsequent action or behavior, fleeing or fighting. As mentioned earlier, this is not all bad, and in fact serves a purpose. But, continued negative interpretation, distrust, perceived threats by others, hostile reactions, or essentially a negative attitude about life, and these biochemical reactions tear down your body. You literally boil in your own body's stress chemicals. When you change your thinking behavior, from negative to positive, you are reprogramming your brain chemically to imprint or blueprint positive chemical reactions-to broaden and build your coping responses. Positive thoughts bring about positive emotions which bring about positive behaviors and positive physiology. While this is not entirely linear (conscious thought does not always occur before an emotional reaction), and positive emotions can influence thinking, it is the cognitive piece or process that derives meaning. This is what I argue is crucial to the long-term benefits of positivity overcoming negativity. This is what helps broaden and build upon your positive experience. This is reflected in the second pillar of positive psychology; that positive subjective experience without positive character (which is largely determined by interpretation and meaning and subsequent behavior) is empty and hallow.

The power of changing your thinking and discovering positive meaning is well documented. Research on intervention and coping strategies have shown the benefits of both cognitive principles aimed at teaching optimism and coping strategies marked by finding positive meaning. These and other strategies optimize health and well-being by cultivating positive emotions. Not only do positive emotions counteract negative emotions, they also broaden your habitual ways of thinking and build personal resources for coping.

Let's examine this further. There is a range of intervention techniques and strategies for change. Two of the more prominent agents of change in the psychotherapy arena are cognitive or behavioral methods; often used in conjunction. Specifically, behavioral therapies are usually aimed at increasing the number of pleasant activities. Cognitive therapies often target thought processes, explanatory styles, perceptions and understandings, and teach ways of optimistic thinking or interpretation. A third style is to address coping styles marked by finding positive meaning within and despite adversity. Although this third style has been described by others as a coping strategy, I define this more as a cognitive one because meaning is largely derived from your interpretation or way of thinking and perceiving your situation. On the flip side, you could define cognitive techniques as coping strategies, but you get the point: In essence, all coping styles are thinking and behavioral responses to your environment or circumstances. You are simply trying to make sense of or find meaning to what happens in your daily world.

Most of the literature on intervention strategies comes from the treatment of depression. Behavioral interventions for depression serve to decrease the intensity and frequency of unpleasant events while increasing the amount of pleasant activities. Clinicians will often discover how depressed patients usually stop doing pleasurable activities and often "prescribe" those pleasurable activities to combat the depression. Research indicates that behavioral therapies for depression are effective: they increase engagement in pleasant activities and decrease levels of depression. However, it is important to recognize that behavioral therapies aimed at increasing pleasant activities developed within an era of psychology that largely ignored cognitive and emotion related concepts. Thoughts and emotions were not viewed as important as the stimulus that reinforced the behavior (or lack of behavior). In their minds, behaviorists viewed disorders as nothing more than a mindless emotionless stimulus response (apologies to my behavioral purist colleagues if I have offended you). Enter the cognitive era of intervention strategies.

Craig S. Travis, Ph.D.

As indicated in Part 1, cognitive strategies for treating emotional issues have dominated the last half-century. Cognition is the process of collecting, organizing and using intellectual knowledge. Cognitive strategies are mental plans you use to make sense of the world; to understand yourself and your surroundings. Cognitive theory suggests this can be done either healthily (positivity) or unhealthily (negativity) and these two are constantly battling one another. Recall the basic premise behind cognitive theory: what you think affects how you feel and this has a consequent affect on behavioral choices. There is an emphasis on thoughts and emotions. So, the theoretical focus shifted from the day-to-day events and activities to the meanings or interpretations you assign them. The reformulated learned helplessness model of depression serves as an example. This theory states that it is not bad events themselves that lead to depression, but rather the habitual style in which you explain those events. Explanations based largely on internal, stable, and global causes lead to depression. For example, if you attribute your misfortunes as being a result of personal inadequacies, that you will always be inferior, and nothing can ever change (internal, stable, and global negative attribution), you are more likely to feel depressed and hopeless/helpless about the situation. Cognitive intervention strategies focus on these pessimistic explanation styles, along with negative beliefs, and seek to change them by restructuring your explanation of bad events. Thus, your interpretation would shift to more external, unstable, and specific causes. So you would view things from a specific, temporary, external explanation that is not a character assassination of you and your abilities. This has been described as learned optimism. Similar to the learned helplessness model of depression are attribution theory and Beck's cognitive triad of depressed thinking. Attribution theory is a cognitive approach concerned with how you perceive the causes of behavior, both yours and others. Beck's cognitive therapy model suggests when you feel depressed you are probably focusing on what is wrong rather than what is right; that is you probably amplify the negativity and block out the positivity in your life. The cognitive triad that occurs consists of a negative view of yourself, negative interpretation of your experiences or events, and negative expectation of your future. You can see the similarities in each of these models. All have the goal of changing how you think to optimize your health and well-being. (If interested, see Part I summarizing Albert Ellis' REBT cognitive-behavioral model and strategies.)

Outcomes research suggests that the track record of cognitive intervention strategies (i.e., focus on explanatory styles) is better than behavioral therapies (focus on pleasant activities). This supports the crucial need for a switch in emphasis from the simple value of activities to the meanings you construct from them. As David Myers contends, the good life comes not from pleasure itself, but from kindness. This does not suggest that you do not seek out and engage in pleasant activities; it merely suggests that this alone will not bring about lasting positive change and enduring happiness. The lasting effect of these cognitive coping strategies is their connection to positive character. Positive character constitutes making lasting changes in current and future thoughts and behaviors, not just achieving immediate pleasure, which is transient and momentary. Character is the ability to find positive meaning in all events and situations. Recall that earlier I had mentioned that positive psychology had three pillars and that the DDP books address the first two: The first relating to subjective well-being—life satisfaction and contentment when about the past; happiness, joy and exuberance when about the present; and optimism, faith, and hope when about the future; the second consisting of positive individual traits—intimacy, integrity, leadership, altruism, vocation, and wisdom. Furthermore I provided the argument that this second pillar is crucial because happiness unattached to positive character is fragile and hollow. For me, this character is developed, in part, by your ability to find positive meaning. Webster's dictionary defines character as the pattern of behavior or personality found in an individual using terms such as "moral constitution, moral strength, self-discipline, fortitude, and good reputation". You can see that character in this way is reflected in such positive psychology terms as personal strength, resilience, wellness, and moral character. So, finding positive meaning is viewed as how you transcend yourself above what is happening: rising above the events. Think of someone you know whom you would consider having good character. Chances are they exhibit these characteristics and others that you probably admire. In short, they show class and are able to confidently handle life. Therefore, what appears to be more important is your *response* to life's circumstances, not the events themselves.

"How do I find positive meaning", you say. Emerging literature in positive psychology suggests ways you can find positive meaning. Holding religious or spiritual beliefs or otherwise appreciating the "meaning of life" on philosophical levels can increase your ability to find positive meaning. As research suggests, you can also find positive meaning in daily life including: Reframing adverse events in a positive light (also known as positive reappraisal); infusing ordinary events with positive value; pursuing and attaining realistic goals. The most reported forms of daily experiences of positive meaning are: feeling connected to and cared about by others; opportunity for distraction from everyday cares and woes; a sense of achievement, pride, or self-esteem; feeling optimism and hope; and receiving affirmation and validation from others. (The following section titled *In Pursuit of Happiness* addresses some ways to improve happiness. Research in the area of happiness and subjective well-being suggests there are some particular ways to increase your happiness; but remember these are suggestions and the concept of happiness is highly subjective and personal)

Research has found that daily sources of positive meaning predict not only recovery from depression but long-term psychological well-being as well. Similarly, finding positive meaning in major life events (i.e., serious medical illness or death of a loved one) also predicts long-term psychological well-being and health. Working in a medical environment, I see the significance of this everyday. Often physicians will comment that what allows someone to get well, or walk again after an accident causing paralysis, is the patient's positive mental attitude. Thus, anecdotally as well as suggested by the literature, a *Daily Dose of Positivity* can illicit positive emotions and that these needn't be either intense or prolonged to produce beneficial effects. This is the premise behind the DDP series, and while I believe this to be true, let me emphasize that you need to put continued effort into cultivating this positivity. One thing the science of psychology has learned is that when overwhelmed by stress you can easily, and rightly, revert back to defense and damage and victim mode, because, without sustained effort, negative emotions generally overpower positive emotions, as we have seen from an evolutionary perspective on survival. As with any skill (i.e., relaxation training, stress management, etc.), the time to learn them is not in the heat of battle. For example, you wouldn't wait until the moment of your piano recital to practice and learn the piece of music you are to perform. Your habit of positivity is crucially developed by practice on a daily basis in a relatively neutral calm atmosphere. This skill development is done before it is *needed*, but once developed, you can always call upon it to be there when you do need it. When you stay mindful about it, and practice it, you broaden your possibilities. This allows positivity to overpower negativity. So, you *can* choose your attitude in any set of circumstances.

It appears that Frankl was right!

12

IN PURSUIT OF HAPPINESS

"We hold these truths to be self-evident, that all men are created equal, that they are endowed by their Creator with certain unalienable Rights, that among these are Life, Liberty and the pursuit of Happiness."

Thomas Jefferson

When I began writing this section on "in pursuit of happiness," I decided to explore the Internet to see what would come up as a definition. Search engines have spaces for you to type the topic you are looking for, so the format looks something like: "Search the web for _____". I must admit, I found it amusing that I could "Search the web for happiness" as though I would actually find it. The point being when you actively pursue something intangible, such as happiness, you often cannot find it; when you stop looking for it, it often finds you. Happiness, I hope you will come to understand, is not some concrete thing; it is more an attitude, a state of mind or state of being. It starts with you and ends with you. You decide what makes you happy, not some ad agency telling you what product to buy. This section offers a summary of the research in the area of happiness, or what has empirically been called "subjective well-being." Hopefully, this section and the rest of this book series will help you come to understand how you can achieve *your* happiness. As Benjamin Franklin so wisely put it, "The U.S. Constitution doesn't guarantee happiness, only the pursuit of it, you have to catch up with it yourself."

Craig S. Travis, Ph.D.

THE EVOLUTION OF HAPPINESS

"Most people are about as happy as they make up their minds to be."

Abraham Lincoln

Evolutionary psychology provides an interesting perception on happiness or at the very least, may offer an explanation for what may prevent it.

You are an evolutionary success story. You have inherited the coping mechanisms of mind and body that allowed your ancestors to survive and thus produce descendents. Had any of them failed along the way, you would not have come to be. As their descendent, you possess the adaptive mechanisms that promote survival and success. Choose to have children and you pass these mechanisms for successful survival on to your own descendents.

But what price to pay for such success? I have addressed the idea that the fight-or-flight emergency reaction is instinctual and promotes survival. Alert individuals stayed alive to reproduce. To be alert and vigilant about impending threat, and to have the where-with-all to either fight it or flee it, allows you to "live to fight (or flee) another day." This is adaptive in that it promotes survival. Unfortunately, it often produces extremely anxious or aggressive, as well as depressed, offspring. Our society is not lacking these problems. In addition, anxiety and hostility or aggression can certainly impede your happiness. In previous sections, I have addressed that negative emotions can be adaptive. Many other findings support the notion that apparently negative emotions may in fact be quite functional for you. However, the subjective experience can be extremely painful and distressing which can interfere with happiness. Suffice to say that evolved emotions may have been well-designed to promote ancestral survival, but in some ways they also appear to disrupt your efforts to promote long-term happiness.

Tricks of the trade of yesteryear, while adaptive in the short-term, may not be health promoting in the long run, physically, emotionally, or mentally. For example, evolutionary psychologist, David Buss, provides three reasons why happiness or quality of life is so elusive. First, you live in a very different environment than your ancestors. Second, evolved distress mechanisms often serve a purpose, for instance, jealousy serves to alert the infidelity of your spouse. Finally, selection, the process by which certain characteristics are favored or perpetuated and thus passed from generation to generation, tends to be competitive. Let's examine this further.

Your environment is very different than that of your ancestors. In this case, I am talking about many generations past, not your parents. Because your current environment is very different from the ancestral environments to which their bodies and minds adapted, their form and function often don't fit in today's society. Global society is experiencing a technological explosion and we are bombarded with new information faster than we can keep up. Voice mail, pagers, cell phones, PDA's, laptops, PC's, the Internet, digital music, MP3 players, etc., all wonderful inventions but, is it any wonder that you function as though everything were urgent? A sense of urgency triggers your emergency reaction. This Digital Revolution is akin to the Industrial Revolution during the late 1800's and early 1900's, and perhaps you are experiencing similar growing pains. There has even been a recent term coined to address the stress of the Digital Revolution: digital depression. Digital depression occurs because you feel powerless over technological change. You can't keep up with the advances. Before you have even begun to master the latest technology, new equipment and software pop-up. And advertising leads you to believe you need the latest product lest you fall prey to digital Darwinism, anxiety based on the belief that technological evolution is taking place and you will survive only if you master every program, gadget, or upgrade. Your stress level skyrockets, and productivity, quality family and social time, and revitalization plummet just as quickly. You lose sight of managing your priorities, setting goals, and asking for help. You think to yourself that you just can't get a way. You take a much-needed vacation, but take along your cell phone! The Digital Revolution does indeed make it a small world after all. But, just as it is true that no one on their deathbed said, "I just wish I would have worked more," so too, is it with technology. Take the 'tombstone' test. What do you want your epitaph to say? You always answered your e-mail, and cell phone or you were a great parent, companion, and friend. Bottom line, stress causes digital (anxiety) depression. Sound familiar? I addressed the idea of anxiety and depression being signs of stress due to the inappropriate application of your normally adaptive physiobehavioral response to physical threats.

Even though technology is supposed to make your life easier, interestingly, anxiety and depression rates are increasing, especially in more economically developed countries. For instance, Americans have become the doubly affluent society—with double what money buys. While we may have doubled our income and have modern conveniences such as dishwashers, microwaves, and refrigerators, pagers and cell phones, the divorce rate has doubled, teen suicide nearly tripled, violent crime nearly quadrupled and depression is a huge concern. Americans are substantially more anxious and depressed now than in the 1950's. In one study, children in the 1990's report higher levels of anxiety than did their parents in the 1950's; depression rates have increased ten fold since World War II. Americans are not the only ones suffering the problems of anxiety and depression. The World Health Organization (WHO) lists depression as the fourth leading cause of the global disease burden, and is expected to rank second by 2020, behind ischaemic heart disease. Despite the greater number of creature comforts and technological advances, why are we more anxious and depressed than ever? Nesse and Williams, in *Why We Get Sick,* offer one possible explanation. "Mass communication, especially television and movies, effectively make us all one competitive group even as they destroy our more intimate social networks..." They continue, explaining that in ancestral times you would have had a good chance at being the best at something, and even if you weren't the best, your group would have valued your skills in some way. In today's society, you are competing with those who are the best in the world, not on your block. Being bombarded by these images of hugely successful people on television, movies, and the Internet, arouses a sense of envy. Although envy was probably useful for your ancestors to motivate them to strive for what others could obtain, it most likely does not fit in today's world. Few can achieve the goals that envy sets; none of us can achieve the fantasy lives depicted in television and movies! Hollywood has even satirically addressed this concept recently. Perhaps the following quote from the movie *Fight Club* provides a sufficient example.

> "I see all this potential—God damn it, an entire generation pumping gas and waiting tables; they're slaves with white collars. Advertisements have them chasing cars and clothes, working jobs we hate so we can buy shit they don't need. We are the middle children of history, man. No purpose or place. We have no great war, or great depression. Our great war is a spiritual war. Our great depression is our lives. We've all been raised by television to believe that one day we'll all be millionaires and movie gods and rock stars—but we won't. And we're learning slowly that fact. And we're very, very pissed off."—Tyler Durden, character in *Fight Club.*

It has been said that happiness is an agreeable sensation arising from contemplating the misery of others. As Gore Vidal noted, it is not enough to succeed; others must fail. This is evident in comedy (less fortunate individuals are often the butt of jokes), locker room talk, adolescent humor, old boys network, etc. I pointed this out in the section titled "The Functionality of Anxiety and

Depression." Seligman, who focuses on depression and believes it is a learned condition, also suggests several possible contributions to the rise of depression: too much individualism, which leads to the idea that our personal setbacks are of vast importance; the emphasis on self-esteem and the unrealistic concept that there's something fundamentally wrong if you don't feel good all the time; the 'victim' mentality that discourages people from asserting control over their psyches when in fact personal freedom has never been greater; runaway consumerism that generates unrealistic and largely unfulfilled material expectations. This supports the Nesse and Williams media argument and the issue of digital anxiety and depression.

Don't be alarmed! While evolution suggests that the proverbial cards have been stacked against your finding happiness, there are practical strategies for overcoming them. One suggestion is to close the gap between modern and ancestral conditions. For instance, David Buss, evolutionary psychologist, suggests increasing closeness of extended kin and developing deep friendships. This can be done using the technology of modern electronic communication such as e-mail and cell phones. He also suggests that reducing subjective distress (e.g., selecting a mate who is similar-reducing jealousy and infidelity; education about evolved psychological sex differences, and using extended kin vs. a closed nuclear family), managing competition and hierarchical status mechanisms (i.e., leveling the playing field), and exploiting knowledge of evolved desires (e.g., desire for health, professional success, helping others, intimacy, feeling the confidence to succeed, personal safety, and having the resources to attain all these) leads to episodes of deep happiness. But he also reminds you that, contrary to popular belief, perpetual states of happiness might be considered maladaptive. It may be more appropriate to consider that moderate levels of happiness are healthier than constant ecstasy for extreme happiness can lead to extreme depression.

I would also add the ideas contained in this book. When you follow its prescription, and you supplement your mind with DDP's, you feed a healthy attitude. This attitude then literally, biochemically, trickles down to the rest of your body promoting greater physical and emotional health and well-being. It will also infiltrate other areas of your life leading you to more healthy and happy endeavors.

Craig S. Travis, Ph.D.

THE SCIENCE OF HAPPINESS: SUBJECTIVE WELL-BEING

"People do things for one of two reasons—to gain pleasure or avoid pain."

B.F. Skinner

With the advent of the positive psychology movement in the late 1990's, research into happiness, positive emotion, subjective well-being, wellness, etc. has gained not only popularity but along with neuroscience brain imaging technology, research into this area has gained an empirical validity in the research community. Theories, and now scientific data, of happiness are now being re-explored. The Pleasure Principle probably has the longest history. The above quote by behaviorist, B.F. Skinner, sums up the Pleasure Principle quite well. Pleasure theory, which has been around since ancient Greek times and continues to abound in our society today, simply says that you are motivated to maximize your pleasure and minimize pain. Does that mean that if you experience 51% pleasure and 49% pain in your life you will be happy? Psychologist N. M. Bradburn might agree stating that the excess of positive over negative feelings can measure the quality of a person's life. While psychologist David Lykken, agrees that nature uses pleasure and pain as the stick to guide you, there is more to happiness than this simple equation. Lykken has determined that certain traits and temperaments, notably extraversion, appear to predispose you to experience happiness. In his research of twins, Lykken showed that 50% of people's overall happiness is determined genetically. So, as David Myers puts it, like cholesterol levels, happiness may be viewed as genetically influenced but not genetically fixed.

In her book *Mapping the Mind*, Rita Carter indicates that happiness is not a single, or simple, state of mind and comprises of three essential components of physical pleasure, absence of negative emotion, and meaning. Physical pleasure is the result of a rush of dopamine in the reward system part of your brain, is brought on by such things as sensory experiences like sex or eating, or the sight of someone you love, but only lasts as long as the neurotransmitters continue to flow throughout your brain. Absence of negative emotions is essential for happiness to occur because once strong fear, anger, or sadness appear, pleasure is reduced. Remember that from a survival mode, negative emotions trump positive ones. Pleasure along with absence of sorrow is not sufficient to induce an overall sense of happiness; with them you need a sense of cohesion or meaning. Psychologist Steven Reiss agrees that happiness has less to do with pleasure and pain, but more so with what he calls feel-good versus value based happiness. Feel-good happiness is sensation-based pleasure akin to Carter's physical pleasure produced by the neurotransmitter dopamine based on your current experience. Feel-good happiness is ruled by the law of diminishing returns, thus the kicks get harder to come by. This is the cornerstone problem for drug addicts. As with the addicts' 'high,' feel-good happiness rarely lasts longer than a few hours at a time. Taking an evolutionary perspective, Lykken says that it is logical that this kind of happiness is so fleeting. Feeling good is a reward system for accomplishments that make you more likely to survive, but if this kind of happiness didn't fade away, the result would be a blessed-out complacency. Again, I turn to the addiction analogy.

Value-based happiness is a sense that your life has meaning and fulfills some larger purpose. Without this cohesiveness, the world seems pointless and fragmentary. Reiss states that value-based happiness represents a spiritual source of satisfaction stemming from your deeper purpose and values and can be experienced when you satisfy any of what he calls the 16 basic desires. After a life threatening illness in which he contemplated the meaning of life and why he lived the way he lived, Reiss and his students set out to explore what really drives human behavior. He surveyed over 6,000 people from all walks and stages of life asking which values are the most significant in motivating their behavior and in contributing to their sense of overall happiness. The results of this research showed that nearly everything you experience as meaningful can be traced back to one of 16 basic desires or to some combination of these desires. The 16 basic desires are:

curiosity
acceptance
order
physical activity
honor
power
independence
social contact
family
status
idealism
vengeance
romance
eating

saving
tranquility

The extra good news, not only do you now know some of the basic ingredients to satisfy your sense of happiness, but Reiss also discovered that you do not have to satisfy all 16 to be happy, just the five or six that are most important to you. And while this kind of happiness is not governed by the law of diminishing returns, thus lending to the limitlessness of how meaningful your life can be, there is a catch. He does argue that you do have to satisfy your desires repeatedly because shortly after you satisfy a desire, it reasserts itself, motivating you to satisfy the desire all over again. So, how can you accomplish this? How do you repeatedly satisfy your most important desires and find value-based happiness? Reiss found that most people turn to relationships, careers, family, leisure and spirituality to satisfy their most important desires.

Value-based happiness tends to produce a deeper happiness than feel-good happiness. Value-based happiness is the great equalizer in life. Wealthy people are not necessarily happy, and poor people are not necessarily unhappy, for the 19th century philosopher Schopenhauer's words ring just as true today as then when he observed that "we come across as many cheerful faces among the poor as among the rich." In fact, economic growth and materialism has not provided a boost to human morale. Research shows that those who strive most for wealth tend to live with lower well-being. Those that strive for intimacy, personal growth, and contribution to community experience a higher quality of life. As you can see, value based happiness is more of an attitude than a physical or even transient emotional state. Happiness is not a matter of getting what you want but rather wanting what you have.

Daily Dose of Positivity™

HAPPY HUNTING

"Very little is needed to make life happy. It is all within yourself, and it is all in your way of thinking."

Marcus Aurelius-Roman emperor (161-180) and Stoic philosopher

Research in the area of happiness repeatedly suggests that material wealth is not the foundation for happiness. If you ask someone if money can buy happiness the resounding answer is, "No." But when asked in a slightly different way, would a little more money make you a little happier, you smirk and nod, "yes." Most of you believe that there is some connection between fiscal fitness and feeling fantastic. Okay, I admit it happens with me too, but then I remind myself of all the research I have compiled for this book and that money is not the source of happiness, but perhaps more accurately it is 'the root of all evil.' Yet financial wealth still seems to be the American dream as though somehow you can purchase happiness. Interestingly, University of Illinois psychologist Ed Diener found that even lottery winners and the Forbes' 100 wealthiest Americans expressed only slightly higher levels of happiness than the average American. Furthermore, research shows us that the relationship between income and happiness is surprisingly week; only in countries of extreme poverty is this not found. So why do we continue to pursue such materialism? Is it competition, keeping up with the Smiths and Joneses, technological advances and adaptation, (black and white TV just doesn't cut it in this electronic PDA age), and pleasure seeking as our God-given inalienable right to pursue happiness? Am I suggesting that you give up all your material possessions and settle for a less than minimum wage job? No, rather I am reminding you of what you probably already know and what formal empirically derived data from research continues to prove: there are basic ingredients for happiness, most of which stem from your relationships with other people, and all which stem from how you look at life; your attitude.

During my graduate school days I had a psychology professor who used to share his personal views as well as teach psychology. He often would remind us of *his* key ingredients to a fulfilling life. He would say that there are three important things in life: good food, good friends, and good wine! He also enjoyed jazz music accompanying the first three. 'So, what's the point, I should eat, drink, and listen to music with my friends and this will bring me happiness?' you say. Perhaps. The point is, find what makes you happy and as long as it is considered appropriately healthy, keep doing it. And as the Roman emperor, Marcus Aurelius, so succinctly put several thousand years ago, happiness is in the mind of the beholder, it is in your attitude. Be careful not to overlook your potential for happiness just because *it* didn't seem big enough.

I have often said, "it is not the big things in life that are important, for they happen too few and far between, but rather the little things in life that make you happy." Intense positive moments are rare even among the happiest people. One lesson to learn from the research on happiness is that you will likely be disappointed if, whether it be in your career or relationships, you seek ecstasy much of the time. It is important for you to understand that intense experiences are not the foundation for a happy life. As Benjamin Franklin once recognized, happiness "is produced not so much by great pieces of good fortune that seldom happen as by little advantages that occur every day." Be careful not to underestimate the power of the simple pleasures in life. In a world fixated on more is better, this is more important than ever. Stop and look around—you might just discover how happy you really are.

Daily Dose of Positivity™

SO, WHO IS HAPPY?

"A happy person is not a person in a certain set of circumstances, but rather a person with a certain set of attitudes."

Hugh Downs

So what's the conclusion regarding happiness? Perhaps you can find a lesson in the character, *Forrest Gump*; happiness is as happiness does. Happiness is largely subjective, but there are some issues that researchers and experts agree on. The term happiness is derived from a complex set of characteristics and traits, some of which are genetically predisposed, but also from primitive pleasure seeking centers in the brain. Add to this the more abstract idea of values and meaning and you pretty much get the recipe ingredients for happiness. But like, any good chef will tell you, the recipe is only a guideline to be adjusted with a pinch of this and a dash of that and each time you cook the dish comes out a little different.

13

EFFECTIVENESS OF COGNITIVE THERAPY: WHAT DOES RESEARCH TELL US?

"Wow! I never thought of it like that before"

Anonymous

There is a 'Frank & Ernest' cartoon that suggests the power of a new way of thinking. The cartoon depicts a chick breaking out of its shell, looking around and saying "Oh wow! Paradigm shift!" Not only does this free you up from the psychological barriers imposed by your rigid schemas (relax, we all have them), but research now suggests that there is a positive benefit to changing your thinking pattern from a physiological perspective as well. What you will find in the following section is evidence for the power of your mind and its ability to change your body's chemistry.

One of the more traditional methods for treating mental and emotional disorders is through the use of psychopharmacology or what I like to refer to as "medicines for the mind". Historically, this approach has been used by general practitioners and psychiatrists to treat a wide variety of conditions. Some of the more familiar, such as anxiety and depression, as well as the more complicated problems, schizophrenia and bipolar conditions, have been effectively treated with the use of medication. In fact, for some of these problems (i.e., schizophrenia, ADHD) the first-line treatment of choice is medicine. The use of medicine to treat such problems stems from research indicating that sufferers of these conditions often have chemical imbalances, too little or too much, of certain nuerotransmitters (brain chemicals). Dopamine for example is indicated in depression, mania and schizophrenia; norepinephrine is associated with anxiety, mania, depression and schizophrenia; while serotonin is involved with eating disorders, obsessive compulsive behavior, mania, depression and schizophrenia.

We all have these neurotransmitters, or brain chemistry, in our bodies. Different levels or concentrations of chemicals result in the different problems. Because we have these brain chemicals in our systems and they are implicated in the different problems, methods for changing these levels, like medicine, are effective ways for combating the problems. Different medication is designed to target specific areas of the brain and thus specific chemicals. For example, you may have heard of medicines like Paxil, Prozac, and Zoloft. These are what we call selective serotonin reuptake inhibitors (SSRI's) which are used to treat depression. Each has a different impact on the neurotransmitter, serotonin, which if you recall is indicated in depression. Thus they are referred to as antidepressants.

While medication has and continues to be effective in treating emotional problems, recent research in cognitive therapy has shown that strategies that change how you think also have a serious impact on your brains chemistry. Both the New York Times and the Washington Post have run stories reporting the effectiveness of cognitive therapy in treating anxiety and depression and that cognitive therapy is equally effective as medications. Dr. Lewis Baxter of the U.C.L.A. School of Medicine compared SSRI's to cognitive behavior therapy for a particular type of anxiety. The results showed virtually the same changes in patients' brains, decreases in the activities of the caudate nucleus, changes toward normal functioning. PET scans showed patient improvement via changes in their brains that looked the same regardless of whether they received medication or psychotherapy. Furthermore, a recent article in the *American Journal of Psychiatry* compared psychotherapy to pharmacotherapy in the treatment of depression and concluded that both achieved equal remission rates. They further stated that both methods could be considered first-line treatments for mild to moderately depressed individuals. Another study reported at the 2002 American Psychiatric Association's annual meeting indicated that cognitive therapy was as effective as medicine in treating mental and emotional disorders. The study presented indicated that cognitive therapy held its own with medication in treating even severe depression and that the relapse rate for those receiving psychotherapy was lower than for those on medication. As Robert Leahy, a psychologist who heads the American Institute for Cognitive Therapy in New York, says, "pills don't give you the skills." Psychotherapy helps you develop skills and a healthy attitude for living. These studies show that changing how you think can have the same effectiveness as medication. Let me clearly state that if you are on such medication this is not permission to stop that prescription; you should consult a physician about this. Rather, these studies simply serve as evidence for the power of your mind and how you can develop strategies for effectively coping with life's struggles and push yourself beyond treatment, healing, and "dealing with problems" and into what flourishes and blossoms, into a world filled with positivity, so that you may have a great life.

14

COMBINING PAST AND PRESENT: THE PSYCHOPHYSIOLOGY OF NEGATIVITY VS. POSITIVITY

"What's with them negative ways?
Always with the negative waves, Moriarty, always with the negative waves."

Odd Ball—Character in *Kelly's Heroes*

In earlier sections, I mentioned how powerful your mind is; that it can work for you or against you. This section further explains the research showing that your thought processes have an impact on your physiology and provides a diagram model for understanding this mechanism. We still don't know the specific pathways of the mind body interaction; so the model(s) is a conceptual representation of what we do know and should help you better understand the relationship between the mind and body, between psychological and physical phenomena.

Intuitively, there is an indirect influence of mind over body through feelings and behavior. When you have stressed-out thoughts, you have a stressed out-body, as evidenced through your emotional and behavioral consequences, such as anxiety, depression, overeating, hostility, alcohol and substance abuse, relationship difficulties, muscular tension, headaches, etc. Over the years, research in stress and health psychology has repeatedly shown this indirect psychophysical relationship connection with these types of variables. In essence, what you think affects how you feel and how you feel impacts your behavior and all three have bearing on your physical health. The research community has been able to consistently show a relationship between emotional distress, unhealthy behavioral patterns and physical health problems. But, until recently, scientists haven't focused much on thinking, most likely, in part, due to the difficulty in measuring thought processes. You might be able to infer a person is in deep thought through their behavior or expression on their face, but you can't literally see what they are thinking. Cognitive processes are very abstract things that you can't see, until now. Technology now allows us to take both structural and functional images of your brain. Think of these as comparable to still and moving pictures of your brain, respectively. With technology like MRI, fMRI, CAT, PET, and SPECT scans, neuroscientists can now see how you think. We still can't see exactly what you think (i.e., we can't literally create images of the scene you remember from your last birthday), but we can see how your brain functions while you are thinking. Because of this technology, researchers now have evidence that thoughts have direct influence over physiology through your brain's chemistry, through neurotransmitters. And as Candace Pert discovered, these brain chemicals, or what she refers to as molecules of emotion, are not just in your brain, they flow throughout your body (recall the Trickle Down process mentioned earlier). What you think has a direct bearing on your body's chemistry. Basically, the research in brain neuroimaging studies can be summed up as follows:

Negative thoughts lead to negative physiology and positive thoughts lead to positive physiology.

Yes, this is an overly simplified version of what happens that doesn't describe the specific mechanisms or structures, or chemicals, or amounts of chemicals involved, but the basics that apply are: thought processes influence your biology, and negativity alters brain chemistry negatively and positivity alters it positively. And chronic negativity is far worse than transient situational negative thinking, which we are all capable of doing, and as described earlier is probably done out of an evolutionary need for survival. But a chronic negative attitude has far-reaching, all encompassing detrimental effects on your health: physical, psychological, and social.

I know it sounds too simple (or perhaps too good) to be true, but it is true. Recall the research by Mark George, who asked women to think about positive things, negative things, or neutral things while he took functional pictures of their brains? And the results were that positive thoughts had a positive impact on physiology, and negative thoughts had a negative impact, while neutral thoughts had no influence. Your brain produces chemicals, various neurotransmitters, in response to thinking processes. These chemicals affect your immune system, endocrine system, cardiovascular system and other functions. From a biological point of view, every cell in your body has receptors for these molecules in these chemicals. Each system communicates with the others passing information back and forth. Perhaps the following series of diagrams will help you picture this in your mind.

Below is a conceptual representation and general overview of the psychophysiology of the mind-body connection. There are five total components, four (4) of which are housed within your person, and one (1) that represents outside events and is labeled as environment, which is either stimulating (growth enhancing) or stressful (tearing down). In reality, the three arrows that are labeled Thoughts/Feelings, Physical, and Behavioral, depending on what form they take, can also be considered stimulation or stress, as you will see with each new diagram.

Starting at what would be the 12:00 O'clock position, *Environment* represents the events, circumstances, people, situations, etc., in your life. *Physical* would consist of various structural systems within your physical body like your muscular system, skeletal system, cardiovascular system, and so on. I also include genetic make up in the physical category. *Behavior* describes your actions in the world. *Thoughts/Feelings* represents your cognitive processes, like perception, interpretation, belief systems, assumptions, attitude, and your emotional experience, like the 4 primal feelings of anger, joy, sadness and fear. At the center is labeled, *Biology* and represents the biochemical make-up of neurology, immune system, and electrical impulses of the chemical messengers generated by your brain. While the immune system extends throughout your body and is not 'housed' in the brain, I have included it with the *Biology* bubble because research in health and stress psychology has shown that depression decreases important brain chemicals and reduces immune system function. Each system has subcomponents that are in part shared by the others. For example, electrical impulses and nerves extend into the muscular system and cardiovascular system and your blood flows throughout all these systems carrying various molecular messengers to each other. As you can see by the arrows, this process is multi-directional and highly interactive. What is of particular importance is the impact these all have on the center *Biology* bubble. And what I will focus on is the particular interaction between the psychological aspects of *Thought/Feelings* arrow and the positivity vs. negativity mind set and their impact on your overall health as they relate to the key concepts of stress, anxiety, and depression that I have addressed throughout the book.

Craig S. Travis, Ph.D.

Psychophysiology of Mind Body Interaction

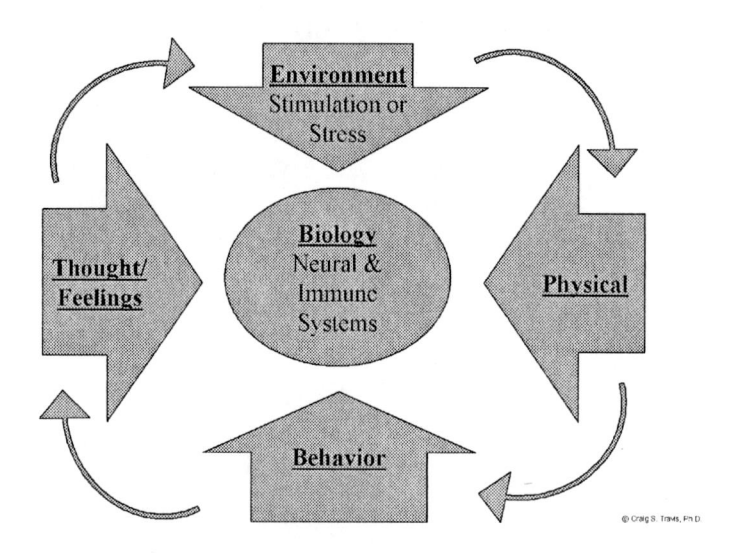

[Diagram: A cyclical diagram showing the interaction between **Environment** (Stimulation or Stress), **Thought/Feelings**, **Physical**, and **Behavior**, all surrounding a central **Biology** (Neural & Immune Systems). © Craig S. Travis, Ph.D.]

Most of what we know about the mind-body connection comes from research in stress and the effect depression has on various systems, most importantly the neural and immune systems (brain chemistry, immune (dys)function and illness/disease). The following diagram depicts the psychophysiology of the mind body connection from a depression explanation. Key stressors for depression are commonly depicted as loss of some sort. This may be connected with loss of physical health through disease, illness, medical problems and symptoms. Recall the dynamics of the Inverted Triangle Stress Response and that with added stress you tend to regress biologically and decrease activity and withdraw and go into shutdown mode. Contributing to all of this of course is what and how you are thinking, what is the attitude you are taking regarding what is happening around you and with you. If it is negative, it leads to decreased self-esteem, worries, hopelessness, helplessness, and continued negativity, which is perceived as added stress and you start the vicious cycle of negativity infection and ego wound. All of which contribute to negative changes in your brain's chemistry and immune function, which results in poor health.

Daily Dose of Positivity™

Depression Model
Psychophysiology of Mind Body Interaction

Stressors
Triggering events
(Loss),
work/family

Think/Feel
Negativity,
worries,
↓ self-esteem,
hopeless

– change in brain chemicals & immunity

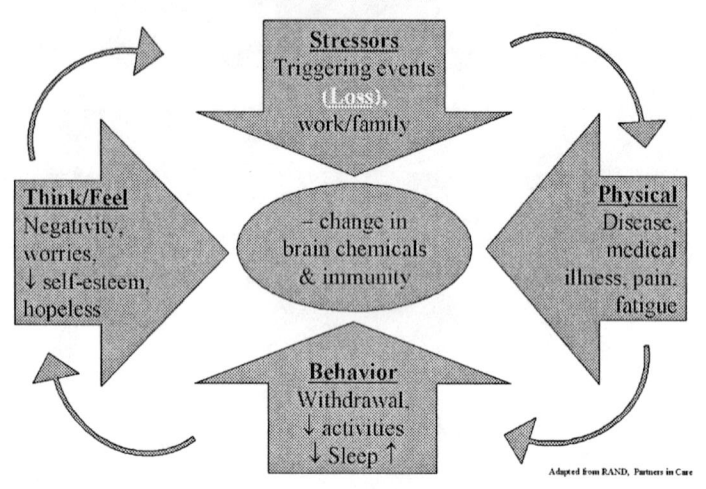

Physical
Disease,
medical
illness, pain,
fatigue

Behavior
Withdrawal,
↓ activities
↓ Sleep ↑

Adapted from RAND, Partners in Care

Based on the Depression Model of the Psychophysiology of Mind Body Interaction, and while I was playing with the ideas of ego wound damage control and functionality of anxiety and depression, I thought to myself "how might this look if we plugged in anxiety?" Since anxiety and depression share so many characteristics (recall the 50% to 90% symptom overlap), I thought the anxiety model might look very similar to the depression model. So I applied this to the formulation and came up with the Anxiety Model version below.

Craig S. Travis, Ph.D.

<u>Anxiety Model</u>
Psychophysiology of Mind Body Interaction

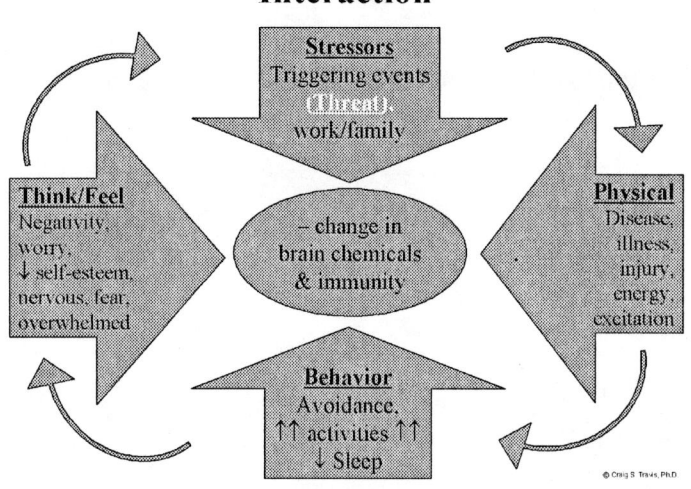

Stressors
Triggering events (Threat), work/family

Think/Feel
Negativity, worry, ↓ self-esteem, nervous, fear, overwhelmed

– change in brain chemicals & immunity

Physical
Disease, illness, injury, energy, excitation

Behavior
Avoidance, ↑↑ activities ↑↑, ↓ Sleep

© Craig S. Travis, Ph.D.

The main difference here is that stressors with anxiety are usually associated with a threat of some sort (as you learned earlier, they are often psychological threats to your ego and fear of ego damage). Anxiety shares similar *Physical* problems as depression (in disease, illness, and injury), but there would be an increased physical energy and excitation through feeling agitated, largely due to the activation of your body's emergency reaction, fight or flight response. *Behaviorally*, anxiety is coupled with increasing activity (thus creating a perpetual feeling of stress and feeling overwhelmed, which is threatening to your sense of competence, ability and hence potentially ego damaging) and is often dealt with by avoidance. *Thought/Feelings* include worry, nervous, fear, overwhelmed, which leads to lowered self-esteem and an overall negativity infection, which becomes contagious to all other aspects and systems and has a negative impact on brain chemicals and immunity. Examples of negativity self-talk or thoughts might be: "I am overwhelmed, this is too much, I can't handle it." The thought, "I can't_____" (fill in the blank) is inherently threatening to your ego, self confidence, competence, etc. and fuels a vicious cycle of negativity infection that infiltrates/impacts thoughts, behavior and physiology, and probably indirectly your environment based upon your behavior.

I then thought to myself, if this depression model and anxiety model were truly representative of the mind body interaction, why not combine them and create a *Negativity* model that would simplify the conceptualization and further help explain the functionality of anxiety and depression along with the ego wound damage control model. So below is the resulting combination of the anxiety and depression models into the *Negativity* Model.

Psychophysiology of Negativity

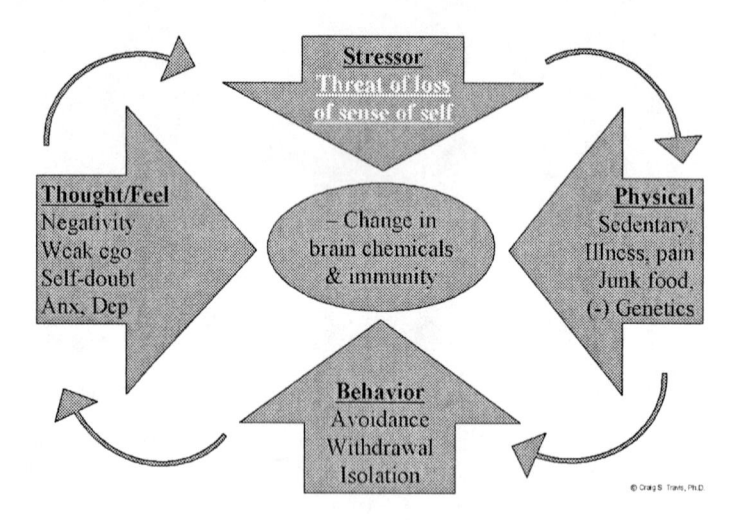

Stressor
Threat of loss of sense of self

Thought/Feel
Negativity
Weak ego
Self-doubt
Anx, Dep

– Change in brain chemicals & immunity

Physical
Sedentary,
Illness, pain
Junk food,
(-) Genetics

Behavior
Avoidance
Withdrawal
Isolation

© Craig S. Travis, Ph.D.

Combining the main stress themes for anxiety and depression, you get a '*threat of loss* of sense of self'. This fits into the ego wound damage control model described earlier. *Thought/Feel, Physical,* and *Behavioral* responses become negative and have a negative impact on brain chemistry and immunity. This infection of negativity feeds on itself and eats you up and leads to poor health, illness, and disease.

After educating and presenting on this process for a while, I ran across some Positive Psychology articles and research and I started thinking that if this model accurately depicts what happens with negativity, then couldn't it be applied in the opposite direction. That is if this was true for negativity, that it would also be true for positivity, but positivity would have a positive influence over physiology and body chemistry. So, I developed a model to depict that process.

Craig S. Travis, Ph.D.

Psychophysiology of <u>Positivity</u>

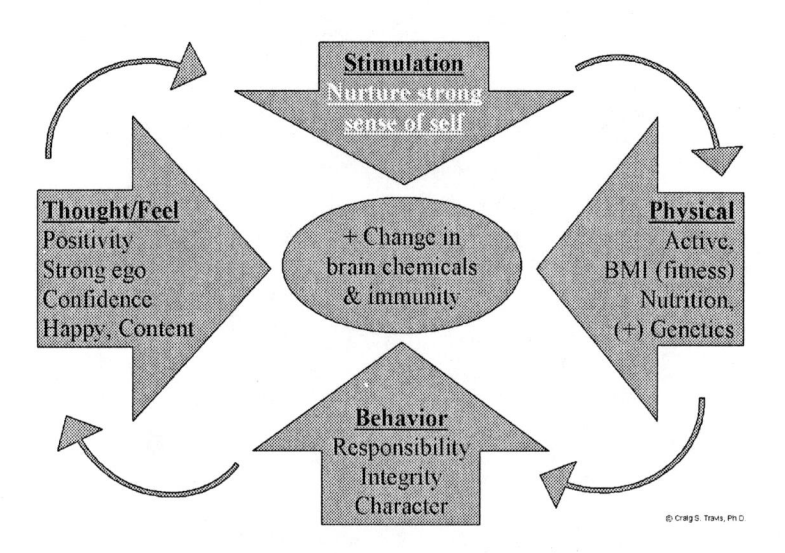

Stimulation
<u>Nurture strong sense of self</u>

Thought/Feel
Positivity
Strong ego
Confidence
Happy, Content

+ Change in brain chemicals & immunity

Physical
Active,
BMI (fitness)
Nutrition,
(+) Genetics

Behavior
Responsibility
Integrity
Character

© Craig S. Travis, Ph.D.

In the case of the *Positivity Model*, your *Environment* arrow would be stimulating rather than distressful, *Physically* you would be active, be blessed with good genes, eat well and use proper nutrition, and be physically fit, *Behaviorally* you would exhibit responsibility, integrity, character, etc., and *Thought/Feelings* would be confidence, happy, content, a strong ego and an overall sense of positivity. The variables of each arrow of course would be both transient or circumstantial and more encompassing, long term, habitual ways of functioning. What is important from a health psychology perspective is establishing these longer habitual lifestyle changes. This model does not mean there is never anything negative that happens in your life, but rather, that the positive outweighs the negative, and one key aspect you all have control over to ensure this happens, is based in your attitude. Your attitude is a mediator to all the other arrows. Positivity is a grander philosophical belief, an ever-powerful attitude that has an all-encompassing effect on everything within you and around you. More so than the transient automatic thoughts that occur as result from the events in your life. I call this the Sphere of Attitude. As shown below, your attitude impacts your immediate interpretation or belief and subsequent emotions, behavioral, and physical responses about life events and circumstances. Positivity is more than just thinking happy thoughts, it is how you think, how you feel, your behavior, what you do, they way you handle and conduct yourself; it is a way of life.

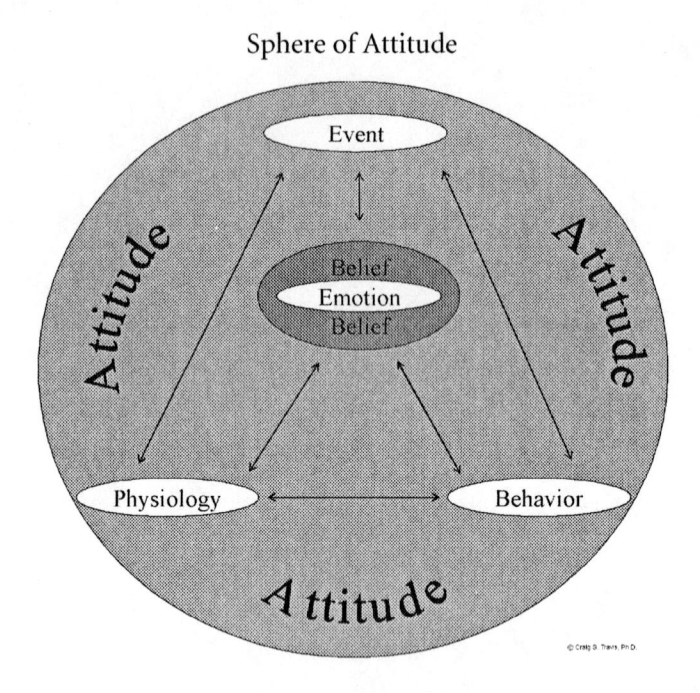

Sphere of Attitude

The mind is a glorious and wonderful, yet tricky entity; it can work for you or work against you. The beautiful thing is that you get to put into it exactly what you want to get out of it! You have the power to think whatever you want. Make your mind work for you or make it work against you. It's your choice!

PART III: THE FUTURE
DAILY DOSE OF POSITIVITY™

The remainder of this book is designed to train your brain for Positivity. You are provided with 202 sources for a *Daily Dose of Positivity* so that you may continue to train your brain every day of the year…

It is important for you to understand the effect of each *Daily Dose of Positivity* is cumulative. To receive the maximum benefit, read them, but more importantly, believe them, everyday. You cannot wait until the end of the year to do 3,650 sit-ups in one day and expect to trim your waistline. The same is true for waiting until the end of the year and then reading all the DDP's in this book. Reading all the DDP's in one day won't bring about the lasting change you desire. The principles for DDP's are similar to those regarding healthy physical exercise; a little each day is what brings about lasting and cumulative results to changes in your body. The same principle is true for the mental training exercises provided in each DDP. Each DDP builds upon the last when used daily to create a result where the whole is greater than the sum of its parts. In addition, each DDP can be used more than once. The cognitive "medicine" here is for chronic and acute negative thinking; you could take two DDP's, one in the morning and one at night, for prevention of chronic negative thinking patterns, and you can use them acutely for situational negativity, as you might take aspirin for a headache. Keep the medicine handy by keeping your DDP source handy while you train your brain for Positivity. You can even take a double dose when necessary. You can even memorize a few for maximum efficiency as coping strategies for every day stress.

DDP1

DAILY DOSE OF POSITIVITY™

EACH DAILY JOURNEY BEGINS WITH ATTITUDE

Every morning we wake up, we choose the path we want to follow. Do you embark down the dark, dangerous, narrow road of negativity? Or, do you choose your destiny to be filled with travels of prosperity and positivity?

You decide.

Even rough roads and unfortunate circumstances have value for it is true that adversity builds character. "What does not kill me makes me stronger." It is attitude such as this that determines not only the mood of your journey, but also your final destination.

Begin your journey today by asking yourself what path do you want to travel?

©Craig S. Travis, Ph.D.

DDP2

DAILY DOSE OF POSITIVITY™

CHANGING YOUR BEHAVIOR STARTS WITH CHANGING YOUR THOUGHTS

Before you can change your behavior you must first change how you think. If you do not think you can change, you won't. If you do, you will.

And you *can* change it.

You are not powerless to control yourself. Do not box yourself in because you were just "born that way." You do not have to succumb to your family's behavioral history.

Think this way and you will remain stagnated.

Learn from but overcome your past. Triumph over any misfortunes. We all have something from our past that we need to overcome. What often gets in the way of being able to move on is the idea that we can't. Entertain the possibility of moving forward and your opportunities are endless.

If you think it, you can be it.

©Craig S. Travis, Ph.D.

DDP3

DAILY DOSE OF POSITIVITY™

AWARENESS IS THE KEY TO ALL CHANGE

Before you can make anything different, you must first be aware of what you want changed. If you do not put an effort into paying attention to what is happening in your life, then you will not be able to change anything in your life.

Self-awareness brings personal power.

Increasing your awareness of how your life is marks the beginning of change to how you want your life to be.
Know how you think, know how you feel, and know how you behave. If any of these needs changed, you will only know it once you become aware of it.

You cannot change what you cannot see

©Craig S. Travis, Ph.D.

DDP4

DAILY DOSE OF POSITIVITY™

REACH FOR YOUR DREAMS

The only one who can make your dreams a reality is you. No one else knows your true dreams and goals better than you.

Your dreams are up to you.

Ask for someone else to fulfill them and you might be disappointed. Rely on your self to achieve them and two possibilities emerge: You most likely will achieve them, and you feel accomplished in achieving them on your own.

Your dreams are your dreams alone.

Sure you can talk with people who are supportive and may share in your vision, but you ultimately have to know what you want to make it happen. You do not need others to clarify your dreams. You only need to look within yourself.

After-all, who better to understand you, than you?

©Craig S. Travis, Ph.D.

DDP5

DAILY DOSE OF POSITIVITY™

ATTITUDE IS WHAT MAKES YOU SUCCESSFUL

Your success is determined by how you view yourself. People will judge you by your attitude, not your accomplishments.

Who you are is more important than what you do.

It does not matter what you do for a living, it does not matter how big your house is, it does not matter how much money you make. What matters is who you are, and how you see yourself.

Who do you want to be?

View yourself as successful and you will be successful. See your self as competent and you will achieve what you set out to accomplish. Believe in yourself and you will be inspired to face life's next challenge.

Become what you envision for yourself.

©Craig S. Travis, Ph.D.

Daily Dose of Positivity™

DDP6

DAILY DOSE OF POSITIVITY™

YOU ARE WHAT YOU THINK

Everyone has the potential to do great things, but only if you think you are capable. Your destiny lies in your belief in yourself. Who you think you are is important in establishing who you really are.

Your belief in yourself brings power and self-confidence.

Believe in yourself and others will believe in you also.
Think you are worthwhile and you will be; think of yourself as insignificant and you will continue to be uninspired.

Think of whom you want to be and actively strive to be that.

To paraphrase Rene Descartes: I think, therefore, I am; therefore I am what I think.

©Craig S. Travis, Ph.D.

DDP7

DAILY DOSE OF POSITIVITY™

DON'T GIVE UP, DON'T EVER GIVE UP

No matter what life throws at you, don't give up. You only triumph if you keep pursuing what you want.

Perseverance leads to success.

Find solace in the fact that to be successful at anything, you must continue. Believe in yourself and your abilities; keep struggling and eventually you will accomplish the things in life you desire most.

Remember the motto of the *Little Engine that Could:* "I think I can, I think I can, I think I can."

Thinking you can leads to knowing you can. Faith in knowing you can stems from convicted action and the sense of accomplishment that you never gave up.

Keep on keeping on.

©Craig S. Travis, Ph.D.

DDP8

DAILY DOSE OF POSITIVITY™

SUCCESS IS YOUR RESPONSIBILITY

You already have everything you need to be successful.
Just look deep within yourself and you will find it.

The answers are there, but you must take the first step to look.

What you accomplish in life will come from your desires deep within you. True happiness is yours if you look for it, but you must actively search your soul.

Keep looking until you find what's right for you.

Do not rely on others for your success, or you may be disappointed. No one else can determine your success for you. Know that you are ultimately responsible for your own success and happiness and you have already become successful.

Growth, change and fulfillment lie within you.

©Craig S. Travis, Ph.D.

DDP9

DAILY DOSE OF POSITIVITY™

ACTION IS FUNDAMENTAL FOR SUCCESSFUL ACCOMPLISHMENT

Few people are lucky enough to have success drop in their laps. Attainment of your goals depends on your action.

To accomplish anything you must put forth effort.

Ambition is what allows conquest; action is what achieves it. Although dreams are vital blueprints for reward, no amount of dreaming alone will make a thing a reality without hard work.

Keep dreaming AND keep doing.

Inspiration is the fruit of creativity, but without action your dreams will remain unmaterialized. People with ideas are a dime a dozen; people who put those ideas into action are priceless. You can be one of those people.

Faith alone does not bring about success; faith with convicted action is what triumphs.

©Craig S. Travis, Ph.D.

DDP10

DAILY DOSE OF POSITIVITY™

HAPPINESS IS JUST A THOUGHT AWAY

Think happy and you will be happy. Your moods are largely controlled by how you think. Control your thoughts and you can manage your mood.

Determine what you want your mood to be.

Become aware of your self talk, that internal dialogue you have as you observe your world. Once you begin to control this language, then you can control your emotions.

Control your moods or have your moods control you; you choose.

Talk negatively to yourself and you will be miserable; think positivity and you will be happier. Learn the language of success and your life will be successful.

Think happy and you will be happy.

©Craig S. Travis, Ph.D.

DDP11

DAILY DOSE OF POSITIVITY™

LIFE IS ONE BIG CHOICE

Everyone makes choices everyday. What to wear, what to eat, what job to do, what to do on the weekend...

But the *internal* choices are often neglected.

Choose to feel good about yourself, choose to have self-esteem, choose to define your success, choose how you will feel, choose to be angry, but understand it is your choice, not something or someone else making you feel that way.

The idea that we are powerless to choose our emotions is a lie! You control how you think and feel.

You always have a choice.

You can choose to move forward or choose to remain stuck, but the choice is still yours.

©Craig S. Travis, Ph.D.

DDP12

DAILY DOSE OF POSITIVITY™

MOTIVATION IS THAT DEEP DESIRE WITHIN

Search within your soul and you will find what you desire. This is what will motivate you to accomplish what you want in life.

The only obstacle standing in your way is yourself.

Remove the barriers that you have put up in front of you and you will move forward. Stop telling yourself you can't. Stop saying I will do it tomorrow.

Start today.

If you desire happiness and success, tell yourself to begin thinking and acting happier and more successful. Eventually you will become more motivated to achieve this. Once you ingrain this into your thoughts, it will become habit.

You cannot motivate yourself without first knowing what you want. What you want is found by looking within.

Start looking today.

©Craig S. Travis, Ph.D.

DDP13

DAILY DOSE OF POSITIVITY™

START LITTLE, BUT THINK BIG

You cannot climb a mountain in one giant step. First you must start with a single step. Know that each movement progresses you forward to your ultimate goal.

Take one step at a time.

Each step builds upon the last to make a journey as you travel through life. Growth is that journey. Achievement is the success of finally reaching your goal.

You can conquer your big goals by mastering the small details.

©Craig S. Travis, Ph.D.

DDP14

DAILY DOSE OF POSITIVITY™

POSITIVE BEHAVIOR BEGINS WITH POSITIVE THOUGHTS

If you want to behave healthily you must think positivity. Positive thinking leads to optimism and prosperity. Negative thinking results in bad attitudes, pessimism, and poor physical health.

The power to change is within you.

You have the power to change by changing the way you think.
The messages you send to yourself daily will translate to behavior. Think poorly of yourself and your abilities, and you will fail. Think today what you can accomplish today; do tomorrow, what you think today.

Believe in yourself and you will succeed.

©Craig S. Travis, Ph.D.

DDP15

DAILY DOSE OF POSITIVITY™

ATTITUDE IS THE ONLY THING

It doesn't matter what happens in life. What matters is your attitude. How do you perceive life, how do you interpret the events and circumstances?

What do you see?

You can either give up power by giving into external forces and allowing them to dictate your attitude, or you can decide your own mood destiny.

It is not the things in life that make us happy or unhappy. It is our perceptive attitude that dictates this feeling.

So, what's your attitude going to be?

©Craig S. Travis, Ph.D.

DDP16

DAILY DOSE OF POSITIVITY™

ADVERSITY MAKES US STRONGER

Life is filled with struggles and challenges. Sometimes even tragedy. Those who are successful do not succumb to life's adversity. Rather, those who succeed learn from their misfortunes.

You can rise above it.

Everyone faces challenges everyday. How you respond to those challenges is truly a gift. The power to overcome is yours if you want it.

It is only during difficult times that you truly discover what your capabilities are.

©Craig S. Travis, Ph.D.

DDP17

DAILY DOSE OF POSITIVITY™

LIFE IS A JOURNEY

Everyday that you get up, you embark on a new journey. You travel through the day affected by the circumstances you face, but destined by the choices you make.

Travel each day as if it were a new adventure, for in fact it is.

Sometimes the trek may by long and arduous, but the outcome will be prosperous as long as you view it as positive; a valuable lesson to be learned.

It is true that challenging situations build character.

Sometimes the road may be rough, sometimes it may be smooth, but remember; never traveling down a rough path lacks adventure.

And sometimes, getting there can be half the fun.

What road are you traveling?

©Craig S. Travis, Ph.D.

DDP18

DAILY DOSE OF POSITIVITY™

MAKE YOUR GOALS CLEAR

Clear objectives are what propel you toward your dreams. Without knowing what you want to accomplish you have nothing by which to gauge your progress.

Set measurable goals.

Clear intentions allow you to determine how far you have traveled and how far you must continue to go until you reach your destination. Once you know what it is that you want actively pursue it until you reach it.

You can't hit the bulls-eye without aiming at the target.

©Craig S. Travis, Ph.D.

DDP19

DAILY DOSE OF POSITIVITY™

WHAT YOU SEE IS WHAT YOU GET

We determine what we get out of life by the attitude that we take. There is an old adage that says we tend to find what we are looking for. If your mind set is focused on negative, then that is all you will tend to see happening around you.

Your point of view is very influential.

If all you ever see is negative, then that is what you get. You will miss the opportunity to see what is really happening around you because your mind will allow you to see only what it is being told by you.

A negative mind set overlooks the good and only notices the flaws.

Open your mind to the possibilities of optimism and hope and life will seem more positive and pleasant, even in the unfortunate circumstances that can occur everyday. When you continually welcome the vision of prosperity, then this positive surge will overpower negative forces.

What you get in the future is determined by what you see today.

©Craig S. Travis, Ph.D.

DDP20

DAILY DOSE OF POSITIVITY™

YOU SET YOUR OWN DESTINY

You and only you are in control of your life. You have the power to choose the path that marks your destiny. You will be faced with many choices along the way, some may be pleasant others not so, but you always have a choice.

You can choose to do nothing, but remember that is still a choice.

The realization that you have choices in your life brings with it a sense of power. Thinking your life is run by outside circumstances will give others power and render you powerless. Take back the reigns by making choices. Steer yourself in the right direction by making the right choices.

Choose your path wisely and you will find success and happiness.

©Craig S. Travis, Ph.D.

DDP21

DAILY DOSE OF POSITIVITY™

YOUR FUTURE LIES IN WHAT YOU ENVISION TODAY

The destiny that your future brings is determined by your actions today. You cannot assuredly predict the future anymore than you can change the past. The only power you have is over the present. Your attitude today determines how you feel about the past; your actions today best control your future tomorrow.

Too often we are consumed by the horrors of the past or worried about what awful thing might happen in the future. These are things over which we have no power aside from how we think about them and what we do about them today.

The more you envision what might happen ahead and what your best options and responses are, the more you are able to allay your fears about the future. Your future is controlled by the power of your actions in the present.

What you see and do today is what you get tomorrow.

©Craig S. Travis, Ph.D.

DDP22

DAILY DOSE OF POSITIVITY™

IDENTIFY YOUR DREAMS AND GOALS

How will you know when you have reached your destination if you don't know where you are going in the first place? Without direction, you will feel lost. Your life will seem to run in circles and you will remain unfulfilled until you determine your destination.

You cannot become successful without first setting goals.

You will become successful and fulfilled only when you truly know what it is that you desire. Determining your goals will help you measure your accomplishments.

Be specific, be realistic; start small but reach high.

How will you know when the race is over if there is no finish line?

©Craig S. Travis, Ph.D.

DDP23

DAILY DOSE OF POSITIVITY™

HAPPINESS IS A CHOICE

Happiness is not a mythical entity that you must seek outside of yourself from other people. How you feel is solely your choice. You can choose to be miserable or you can choose to be enthused.

True happiness comes from within each individual.

Your happiness is your responsibility and yours alone. It is determined by how you think about yourself and by your perception and attitude about your self-image. It is determined by how you view yourself and what you say to yourself.

View yourself favorably and you will be happy.

Rely on others for fulfillment and you will remain unfulfilled.
Rely on yourself for your own happiness, and you will always know where to look to find it.

Seek happiness within yourself and you will find it.

©Craig S. Travis, Ph.D.

DDP24

DAILY DOSE OF POSITIVITY™

CHALLENGE YOURSELF EVERYDAY

Give yourself something challenging to accomplish everyday. It doesn't need to be a monumental thing. The little things in life that we can accomplish give us a sense of achievement. By accomplishing these little things everyday, you stay motivated and keep growing.

Each little step combined together creates a greater whole and instills a sense of hope.

Without challenges life becomes boring and stagnated. So embrace each challenge with fervor and set goals daily. Celebrate each minor triumph, for the pathway of your journey is marked more often by single steps than giant leaps.

Challenge yourself and the possibilities are endless.

©Craig S. Travis, Ph.D.

DDP25

DAILY DOSE OF POSITIVITY™

PERSONAL GROWTH MEANS LEARNING FROM YOUR MISTAKES

It is incredibly helpful to remember that no one is perfect. You will not always successfully accomplish everything you do the first time you try it.

Do not give up.

It is the pain of our mistakes that is a valuable teacher. It teaches us to do something different the next time a similar situation arises. We make mistakes everyday, but those who can learn from their mistakes are not destined to repeat them. If you do not repeat mistakes, then you will be successful.

Learn from your mistakes in life.

Understanding your errors will make you wiser. This leads to better choices; better choices lead to better outcomes. Better outcomes lead to a greater sense of accomplishment and fulfillment.

The seed of every failure germinates the work of new art.

©Craig S. Travis, Ph.D.

DDP26

DAILY DOSE OF POSITIVITY™

PERSISTANCE IS WHAT MAKES PEOPLE SUCCESSFUL

Benjamin Franklin said that success is 5 percent inspiration and 95 percent perspiration. Many people have wonderful ideas. Not many people pursue them until they are realized.

Continue to act on your ideas.

Success comes from pursuing your dreams until they become your realities. You cannot accomplish your goals if you give up on them. Set realistic goals and pursue them. Pursue them long enough and with appropriate ambition and you will be able to accomplish them.

Quitters never succeed, success never quits.

©Craig S. Travis, Ph.D.

Craig S. Travis, Ph.D.

DDP27

DAILY DOSE OF POSITIVITY™

WORDS ARE TOOLS OF POWER

The words we use can carry a lot of weight. You can make them your friend, or you can make them your enemy. They can build you up, or they can tear you down.

What you say to yourself is up to you.

The words you use in your thoughts about yourself and others make your destiny. Your words build your character and they shape your identity. How you choose to use them is up to you. Choose the language of positivity and success and this will reflect in your life.

The word is mightier than the sword.

©Craig S. Travis, Ph.D.

DDP28

DAILY DOSE OF POSITIVITY™

ENTHUSIASM IS A CHARACTERISTIC OF SUCCESS

If you have a zest for life, then you can be successful at anything. Success is determined more by attitude than anything else. Be enthusiastic in everything you do and you will reap what you sow.

Continually seek knowledge about yourself.

Maintain your desire for personal growth and life will become more fulfilled. Wake up each day and embrace life with new abandon. Savor every moment for the treasure it is. Open your eyes to new experiences. See the mundane as though it were being seen from fresh eyes.

Your attitude will carry you through the day.

©Craig S. Travis, Ph.D.

DDP29

DAILY DOSE OF POSITIVITY™

LIFE IS WHAT YOU MAKE IT

When you change your interpretation of something you've changed the meaning. Change the meaning and you've changed the impact of that set of circumstances.

There is tremendous power in the words "I never looked at it like that before."

View your life how you want to view it. You needn't succumb to the negativity of others. Life and other people cannot make you feel bad without your permission.

You have a choice about how you view life. You can go from bad to worse or bad to good.

It's your choice.

©Craig S. Travis, Ph.D.

DDP30

DAILY DOSE OF POSITIVITY™

ACTION AND THINKING ARE CONNECTED

What you think impacts how you feel and in turn dictates how you act. Consequently, how you act influences how you think and feel.

Few things in life function in isolation.

Acting incompetently will lead to incompetence. Act with an air of confidence and you will begin to feel capable. Thought, feeling, and behavior are interdependent principles.
You cannot have one without it impacting the others.

Truly thinking one way and acting in another cannot be.

Even when you know you are acting unhealthily, you have convinced yourself on some level that it is ok. Positivity is removing the denial and rationalization.

What you say to yourself, is what you end up doing.

©Craig S. Travis, Ph.D.

Craig S. Travis, Ph.D.

DDP31

DAILY DOSE OF POSITIVITY™

YOU DETERMINE YOUR OWN DESTINY

The direction you travel in life is not set in stone. It is not predetermined by someone else. You have free will; the path you choose is yours to choose.

Your choices become your destiny.

You may run into obstacles that gently nudge you into a different direction than your ultimate goal, but you do not have to stay on this alternate course for eternity.

Steer yourself back into the direction you desire.

Believe in the power of freedom of choice. Choose your direction based on your deepest desires. Your goals will light your way.

Have faith in yourself and destiny will show you the way.

©Craig S. Travis, Ph.D.

DDP32

DAILY DOSE OF POSITIVITY™

HAVE FAITH IN YOURSELF

Believe that you have the knowledge and power within you to make the right decisions. Look within yourself and you will discover the answer that is right for you.

You really do know better.

Who better to know what is right for you than you? You've just got to believe it to be true. See life how you want to see it. Make it positive by seeing it positive.

Confidence in yourself enhances your abilities.

Yes, there are always new worries that seemingly will not go away. You can constantly let this affect your state of mind or have your state of mind affect your worries. Trust in your ability to competently handle life's daily challenges.

Believe in yourself and the world is yours.

©Craig S. Travis, Ph.D.

DDP33

DAILY DOSE OF POSITIVITY™

DON'T JUST DREAM IT, BE IT

Dreams are extremely important to attaining success. They guide your life in the direction you want to go. However, you will never reach your goals if all you only do is dream.

You must act upon your dreams to make them realities.

We would not have computers; we would not have cars, nor would we have any of the luxuries we have come to rely on everyday had the inventors left their dreams on the drawing board. Theirs, and your success, lies in the implementation of dreams.

Dare to be what you dream.

Don't just wish your life was different, make it different. Act differently and you will become who you aspire to be. Dreams are mere stepping stones to greatness; acting upon dreams is what makes you successful.

If you can dream it, you can be it.

©Craig S. Travis, Ph.D.

DDP34

DAILY DOSE OF POSITIVITY™

IMAGINATION IS THE SEED OF SUCCESS

Your minds ability is limitless. You have the power to conceive and create anything in your minds eye. Broaden your boundaries and expand your horizon. Set forth your journey into the possibilities of what lie ahead.

Use your imagination.

Imagine yourself successful. Envision triumph over life's obstacles. See this to be true and it will become true, but only if you act upon this vision. When you act on your imagination, the possibilities are endless.

Creativity costs nothing, but it is priceless.

©Craig S. Travis, Ph.D.

DDP35

DAILY DOSE OF POSITIVITY™

DON'T LET FEAR BE THE MASTER OF YOUR LIFE

If you want to succeed in life, then do not allow fear to rule it. There will always be new worries that present themselves to you; how you face them will determine your future. Successful people acknowledge their concerns then, systematically approach them until they are no longer a problem.

Your fear promotes inaction.

Fear is what prevents you from taking that first step. Wait until you feel 100 percent comfortable with any decision and you may never start.

If you allow your fears to rule your life, then you will remain stuck where you are. Face your fears; bring them out of the shadows. Shed light on your fears and you will make them smaller.

Remove you fears and you remove your obstacles.

©Craig S. Travis, Ph.D.

DDP36

DAILY DOSE OF POSITIVITY™

DON'T WAIT UNTIL TOMORROW, START TODAY

Don't say, "I'll start tomorrow" for tomorrow never really comes. Instead take that first step toward your goals today. Tomorrow is always in the future, something you can only control by what you choose to do today.

Today is where the action is.

Take responsibility for changing your life right now for there is no better time than the present. When you say you'll do it later, you are only postponing your success.

Do it now.

Take charge of your future by taking that first step today. You will not move toward your goals if you continually wait until later.

Don't put off until tomorrow what you can accomplish today.

©Craig S. Travis, Ph.D.

DDP37

DAILY DOSE OF POSITIVITY™

CHANGE IS ALL AROUND YOU

People who cannot accept change, who remain rigid and stuck in their ways, are people who are never happy. Stability is one thing; rigidity is something completely different.

Adaptation is the key to success.

You cannot control all of life's circumstances, but you can choose to adapt to these changes. Learn to adapt to your ever-changing environment and you will achieve success in life.

Rigidity is the stagnation of life while flexibility is the spice.

©Craig S. Travis, Ph.D.

DDP38

DAILY DOSE OF POSITIVITY™

YOU MUST SEE IT, TO BE IT

Whatever you want to accomplish in life, you must first be able to visualize it. Understanding where you want to go, points you in the right direction.

You must see it before you can be it.

Create in your mind's eye your vision of success. Once you establish this image, you can call upon all forces to realize that dream. Clear goals and dreams are the building blocks for accomplishment.

Methodically build upon what you have visualized.

Painstaking work and effort to make your dreams a reality are necessary ingredients for success. But you must have a map to work from. Hard work with no blue print doesn't allow you to build the future you want. Make sure you chart the territory you intend to go.

Remember, lack of vision is lack of direction.

©Craig S. Travis, Ph.D.

DDP39

DAILY DOSE OF POSITIVITY™

IF YOU PUT YOUR MIND TO IT, YOU CAN ACCOMPLISH ANYTHING

Life is a maze; each new wall a challenge. See no way over, under, around or through and you will remain confined. What you accomplish in life is limited only by the obstacles that you set forth in your own mind.

There are no problems, only solutions yet to be discovered.

The only barrier is the barrier your mind has set by limiting your options. Expand your horizons outside of the box. Move beyond the walls created by the messages from others and perpetuated by your own mind.

Break free and the world outside is yours.

If you let negativity affect you, then you will never know how successful you can be. To make an attempt is to set forth on your journey to success. Even monumental accomplishments start with small steps. But you must step.

You won't know what you can accomplish if you never try.

©Craig S. Travis, Ph.D.

DDP40

DAILY DOSE OF POSITIVITY™

BE FULL OF HOPES ABOUT YOUR FUTURE

If you do not see prosperity in your future, then you will not move in that direction. Envision your tomorrows as though they can be, not what they cannot be.

Your destiny lies in your own hands.

No matter what life throws at you, be hopeful about what lies ahead. If there is one thing certain, it is that you don't know what the future brings.

Your future is unwritten.

You can only prepare for the future by what you choose to do today. Choose to be healthy, upbeat, and positive and prosperity is destined to come your way.

There is always hope if you believe.

©Craig S. Travis, Ph.D.

DDP41

DAILY DOSE OF POSITIVITY™

REPETETIVE ACTION PAVES THE ROAD TO SUCCESS
___

Few if any things are accomplished with great success the very first time you try. You did not walk successfully, nor did you ride a bike successfully, the very first time you tried.

But you did not give up.

The way you become successful is to understand what you want to accomplish, then continuously engage in action that brings about that accomplishment.

Practice makes perfect.

The more you do something over and over again, the more skilled you become at it, and the easier it gets. A little each day is all it takes. This adds up over time and the effects can have lasting impact.

Even sports superstars practice the basic skills everyday.
___
©Craig S. Travis, Ph.D.

DDP42

DAILY DOSE OF POSITIVITY™

SUCCESS IS A MATTER OF EXPECTATION

Your expectations about life are influential to your actions. Expect to fail and you will. Expect to succeed and you will rise to the top.

Expectation is a power to behold and use wisely.

Your mind is an extremely powerful tool. It can point you in the right direction or take you down a dead end road. The beautiful thing is that you get to tell your mind what to think.

Life is not a one way street.

Decide where you want to go. Choose the actions and behaviors that will get you there. Expect the positive and you will be amazed at what you can accomplish.

What are your current expectations?

©Craig S. Travis, Ph.D.

DDP43

DAILY DOSE OF POSITIVITY™

THERE IS NO FINISH LINE WHEN IT COMES TO PERSONAL GROWTH

Personal growth is an ever-changing constant process. It does not stop just because you've reached a particular goal. It is the process, not the destination that brings about reward.

Keep striving for personal development.

Set new goals for yourself to accomplish and you will continue to grow. Strive to be better each and everyday. Be a better parent, be a better neighbor, a better brother or sister, lover, and friend.

Just make sure you do something.

No matter what you choose to do for continued growth, put forth the effort to do it well. Action is the key to a healthy life, stagnation the end to it.

There is always room for improvement.

©Craig S. Travis, Ph.D.

DDP44

DAILY DOSE OF POSITIVITY™

YOU HAVE WHAT IT TAKES TO BE SUCCESSFUL

You have everything that you need to be successful right at your fingertips. All you need to do is look deep inside yourself. Call upon what strengths you do have, all your positive qualities, and allow them to overshadow your limitations.

It is helpful to understand what you can and can't do. You can acknowledge your weaknesses yet strive to make them strengths.

Successful people are not perfect. They just know how to use their abilities to get what they want. Look inside yourself to find the light that will guide your way.

It's in there, if you look for it.

©Craig S. Travis, Ph.D.

DDP45

DAILY DOSE OF POSITIVITY™

FEEL THE POWER OF YOUR MIND

The thoughts in your mind are what compel you. They can either push negativity or positivity. What direction you go is up to you.

Determine a positive direction.

Your mind is vast thus your possibilities expansive. There are no limits to what you can accomplish if you believe that nothing will stand in your way.

Commit to move past any mental barriers.

Set forth upon your journey of accomplishments by pledging to yourself beliefs about your abilities. Your positive beliefs in yourself will reinforce your strengths so that you may act accordingly.

Your actions are your commitment to your mind.

©Craig S. Travis, Ph.D.

DDP46

DAILY DOSE OF POSITIVITY™

TRAIN YOUR BRAIN FOR SUCCESS

Your body and your behavior respond to what you think. You have the power to be as accomplished as you want to be. But you have to believe in your self and your abilities.

Know the talent that lies within you.

Peak performers, whether they are great athletes, musicians, or entrepreneurs, all understand the monumental importance of mental training. Successful accomplishment lies in your minds eye.

Imagine your success.

If you want to be successful at something, then see it in your mind first. Mental rehearsal is what sets apart the superstar performers from the ordinary.

What the mind believes, you can achieve.

©Craig S. Travis, Ph.D.

DDP47

DAILY DOSE OF POSITIVITY™

MOVEMENT MAKES YOU HEALTHY

The human body was not designed to sit still. Even when we are still, are bodies are in constant motion.

So too is your mind; put it to good use.

Life is about movement; movement from one thing to the next, from one phase to another. Moving on, moving up, and moving out. We are not meant to be still, not physically, not emotionally, and not spiritually.

Let your mind flow.

No movement literally and metaphorically results in stagnation. Stagnation is the poison of life. You cannot achieve your goals without moving toward them by your own thoughts and actions. At the very least, movement guarantees a change of scenery.

Even if you are on the right track, you will eventually get run over by the train if you just sit there.

©Craig S. Travis, Ph.D.

DDP48

DAILY DOSE OF POSITIVITY™

IT'S THE THOUGHT THAT COUNTS

What happens in life is less important than your view of what happened. You can assign any meaning you want to anything you want. The choice is yours and yours alone.

You decide what is significant to you.

Most of our daily nuisances are just that, nuisances. But we make them bigger than they need to be. If you let it, your mind can runaway with negative imagination.

Think what happens as awful and it will be.

This does not mean that there are no unfortunate circumstances in life. It just means it's helpful to interpret life's events realistically without blowing them out of proportion.

Do not make mountains out of molehills.

©Craig S. Travis, Ph.D.

DDP49

DAILY DOSE OF POSITIVITY™

HAPPINESS IS NOT AS ELUSIVE AS YOU THINK

Happiness is not some tangible thing. It is a more abstract sensation. You cannot expect to find it somewhere without looking inside yourself.

You are responsible for your own happiness.

Your ultimate happiness stems from your comfort with yourself. It is derived from your self-acceptance. You are a special and unique individual. All you need to feel good is to believe you are worthy of your own happiness.

And you are worthy of happiness.

Think and act how you deem morally responsible and you will be healthy and happy. Chances are that you already are if you truly know where to look.

Let yourself slow down and recognize it before it passes by.

©Craig S. Travis, Ph.D.

DDP50

DAILY DOSE OF POSITIVITY™

PUSH IT TO THE LIMIT

If you want to be successful at anything you have to push yourself. Do not let ordinary limitations stand in your way.

Overcome your obstacles.

Remove all barriers and you can accomplish anything in life you want. What stops most people from true happiness and success is the belief that outside forces prevent it.

Don't let daily minor obstacles stand in your way.

Push yourself to the limit and you will be surprised how much farther you can actually go. You can be successful at anything you put your mind to.

Believe it!

©Craig S. Travis, Ph.D.

DDP51

DAILY DOSE OF POSITIVITY™

UNLEASH YOUR POTENTIAL BY UNLEASHING YOUR PASSION

You can accomplish more than you ever dreamed possible as long as you passionately engage yourself in life. Commit yourself fully and you will be rewarded greatly.

All that life offers is to be savored.

Your motivation to achieve any endeavor is proportional to your intensity of action. Work hard and your motivations increase. Work little and you care less.

Motivation dies without passion.

The harder you work the harder it is to surrender to your demons of futility. You get out of life exactly what you put into it. The benefits you receive are determined by you.

Find your intensity for life.

©Craig S. Travis, Ph.D.

Daily Dose of Positivity™

DDP52

DAILY DOSE OF POSITIVITY™

KEEP MOVING FORWARD AND YOU WILL MEET YOUR DREAMS

You will not accomplish your goals if you just sit there and wait for them to come to you.

A body at rest tends to stay at rest.

If you want to achieve your goals then you have to actively pursue them. You get out of life just what you put into it. Do nothing and you will get nothing. Give nothing and you will receive nothing in return.

What do you want?

Actively seek out what it is that you desire. You will achieve what you set out to accomplish only if you commit to it in your mind; and only if you pursue it in your actions.

Don't just sit there and watch the world pass you by.

©Craig S. Travis, Ph.D.

DDP53

DAILY DOSE OF POSITIVITY™

STICK TO IT
___

Whatever you decide you want to accomplish, stick to it until you accomplish it. You cannot complete anything if you do not stick to the activity.

You will not reach your destination if you do not travel the road.

Engage yourself in what you set out to do and you will be amazed at how easily you may accomplish it. Encourage yourself by committing to act on it a little each and every day.

Perseverance is what allows accomplishment.

You may not be able to run a marathon under three hours but you can travel 26 miles by running a little bit everyday. And when you keep training, you can eventually complete it successfully at one time.

A single swing of the axe does not fell the tree.
___
©Craig S. Travis, Ph.D.

DDP54

DAILY DOSE OF POSITIVITY™

SET YOUR MIND TO IT AND YOU'LL DO IT

True success at anything comes with conviction. You've got to believe it possible for it to be possible.

Convince yourself of the possibilities.

Commit your mind to achieving what you desire to accomplish and you have already accomplished half of what you need to achieve that goal. Failure to see it brings failure to do it.

What you cannot see in your minds eye, you will not accomplish.

©Craig S. Travis, Ph.D.

DDP55

DAILY DOSE OF POSITIVITY™

KEEP MOVING FORWARD NO MATTER WHAT

Whatever life throws at you keep pushing ahead. Do not let life's obstacles discourage you. Your journey will often be filled with trials and tribulations. You may feel like quitting but keep pushing ahead.

Life is filled with many ups and downs.

Rather than focusing on the barrier, focus on a way around, over, under or through it. If all you see is a blockade, then you fail to see the solution.

Find perspective.

Sometimes we need to travel sideways to get ahead. Or, even take a step back, but follow that by foraging two steps forward. Whatever direction you need to go, keep moving.

Standing in the doorway of success does not mean you've entered the room.

©Craig S. Travis, Ph.D.

DDP56

DAILY DOSE OF POSITIVITY™

DARE TO PAVE A NEW PATH

You do not have to follow another's path in order to be successful. Do not be afraid to blaze your own trail. Pioneers in any endeavor may start out on the same path but those who are successful dare to be different.

If you aren't the lead dog, the view never changes.

Don't be afraid to lead yourself in a new direction. Take a small step followed by another, and soon your new trail will seem as easy to navigate as the already worn path.

Carve your own path to your destiny.

©Craig S. Travis, Ph.D.

DDP57

DAILY DOSE OF POSITIVITY™

HAVE FAITH IN YOUR ABILITIES

Start believing in yourself and you've taken a step in the direction of Positivity. Each thought, each action you have will reinforce that direction.

Motivation comes with belief.

Do not be discouraged if you are only taking small steps. Inching forward is still progress. Celebrate it as such. For each movement forward is a success that can be built upon.

You have what it takes to be fulfilled.

Call upon your capacity to fulfill your life with emotional success. To be an MVP, you do not need to do extraordinary things, rather do ordinary things extraordinarily.

Believe in yourself and you just may surprise yourself with what you can do.

©Craig S. Travis, Ph.D.

DDP58

DAILY DOSE OF POSITIVITY™

DO A LITTLE EACH AND EVERY DAY

If you want to accomplish great feats, you have to accomplish things on a smaller scale first. No one expected you to walk across the room the very first time you ever took a step.

Be excited by the first movement.

Each day you achieve something little you achieve something greater. The whole is greater than the sum of its parts. Each action builds upon the last until you have completed what you set out to accomplish.

To move mountains, move one pebble at a time.

©Craig S. Travis, Ph.D.

DDP59

DAILY DOSE OF POSITIVITY™

YOUR EMOTIONS ARE TO BE MANAGED, NOT FEARED

You emotions are precious. They bring with them life's passion. They are energy that can be used to dictate your direction in life.

Do not judge them, understand them.

Emotions are simply information about your perception of your world. They tell you whether you like what is happening or that you don't.

If judgement, judge your thoughts and actions, not emotions.

Your emotions are neither appropriate nor inappropriate. They simply exist. What can be judged is your attitude, your thoughts and consequent behavior. Thoughts and actions are deemed healthy or unhealthy, your emotions responses to them.

Manage your moods, have your moods manage you; it's up to you which it will be.

©Craig S. Travis, Ph.D.

DDP60

DAILY DOSE OF POSITIVITY™

GOOD HABITS COME FROM REPETITIVE BEHAVIOR

You will not succeed in changing over night. You must decide what you want to be different and then continue to act that way over and over again before it becomes a habit.

Start first by thinking it in your minds eye.

If you think it, you can become it. Think about this every day. Envision yourself successfully acting the way you want to be. Once you have ingrained that habit you will keep it until you actively do something different to change it.

Success is marked by those who practice, practice, practice...

©Craig S. Travis, Ph.D.

Craig S. Travis, Ph.D.

DDP61

DAILY DOSE OF POSITIVITY™

YOU SHAPE YOUR DESTINY BY THE CHOICES YOU MAKE

You are in control of your life. No one is running your life but you. You may have numerous outside influences but the direction of your path is ultimately up to you.

Every set of circumstances involves choice.

You can choose to do nothing but understand that that is still your choice. The journey toward enlightenment and true happiness is filled with many options. This destiny is determined by your choices.

Choose your destiny by making your choices.

Choosing what is easy, is easy. Choosing what is difficult takes character. Difficult choices are often the healthiest ones.
These kinds of choices take discipline, focus, and intensity. Integrity is a choice like anything else.

You hold in your own hands your future. What do you want that future to be?

©Craig S. Travis, Ph.D.

DDP62

DAILY DOSE OF POSITIVITY™

YOU DETERMINE WHAT WILL BE

Whatever happens down the road is largely determined by the choices you make today. Your thoughts will encourage your actions. Your actions will determine the course you take.

The future is uncertain and cannot be predicted.

You can determine how you will respond to what the future brings by affirming your actions today. Decide to be prepared and you will be. Choose to have positivity today and it will remain with you into tomorrow.

You control your response to the future.

©Craig S. Travis, Ph.D.

DDP63

DAILY DOSE OF POSITIVITY™

YOU HAVE THE KEYS TO OPEN THE DOOR TO YOUR FUTURE

You have all that is necessary to accomplish your goals. Make the commitment to get there. Clearly identify those goals and know that opportunity to get them lies everywhere.

Behind the door of success is everything you've ever dreamed.

To open it, call upon all your resources. A well developed mind, a passion to live and learn about life, the ability to put your knowledge to work for you, these are the keys to your future.

Use the tools that you have.

Know that you have what it takes as long as you take what you have and put it to good use. Be ready to open the door when opportunity knocks.

Unlock the mysteries of your mind, and you open the door to your future.

©Craig S. Travis, Ph.D.

DDP64

DAILY DOSE OF POSITIVITY™

HAPPINESS IS YOURS FOR THE TAKING

You are in charge of how you feel. Pleasure in life comes from pleasurable things. Think pleasant thoughts and engage in pleasurable activities and you will begin to feel happiness.

Be happy with who you are.

Your attitude manages your mood. You determine what your outlook on life will be. Be grateful for the things in your life. Honor what you already have rather than taking them for granted.

Happiness comes to those who realize their riches.

Notice all the things you have rather than all that you have not. Seek what it is that you are looking for within yourself. Look for happiness in external material things and you only chase misery.

Dare to look internally.

Deep within you lies the secret to your goal of happiness. Embrace and accept who you are while allowing yourself to continue to grow and you will find the happiness that you seek.

You will find what you are looking for, if you look for it.

©Craig S. Travis, Ph.D.

Craig S. Travis, Ph.D.

DDP65

DAILY DOSE OF POSITIVITY™

INVENT YOUR OWN FUTURE

Your destiny is not set in stone. Give up control of your life and you give up control of your future. Choose your future by choosing your actions.

If you think you can or think you can't, you're probably right.

What sets apart achievers from dreamers is the courage to act upon their visions. Your actions depict your character.

What does your behavior say about you?

Choose to take responsibility for your future for no one better than you can determine what you want from life. Don't just say you'll do something, do it.

Your actions speak louder than words.

©Craig S. Travis, Ph.D.

DDP66

DAILY DOSE OF POSITIVITY™

SEEING IS BELIEVING

Visualize in your mind how you want to be. See your self as accomplishing many things. Know it is possible to accomplish that which you desire.

If you can see it, you can believe it.

One thing in life is certain; what you tell yourself about yourself will result in your self-image. It is a simple yet effective truth that works both ways, negative or positive.

What do you want to see in yourself?

When you see yourself as unable you will not perform to the best of your abilities. See your potential so that you may realize your potential.

Inside you is a world of possibilities. Let them out.

©Craig S. Travis, Ph.D.

DDP67

DAILY DOSE OF POSITIVITY™

THE MOST VALUABLE ASSET YOU CAN POSSESS IS A POSITIVE ATTITUDE

Nothing else in life matters more than your attitude. How you perceive the world is fundamental to your well-being. No matter what happens in life, you still control your own attitude. The power of interpretation is yours.

Make it work in your favor.

What goes on around you is often chaotic. It is largely out of your control. However, what you do have control over is how you choose to interpret what happens around you.

You do not control life, you control _your_ life.

You determine how you view things. No one can tell you how to think anymore than they can tell you what to do.

Just ask the parent of a two year old.

©Craig S. Travis, Ph.D.

DDP68

DAILY DOSE OF POSITIVITY™

BEHOLD THE POWER OF YOUR MIND

Everything you need to be successful resides in your mind. You have the power to accomplish things you never dreamed possible once you put your mind to it.

You'd be amazed at what you can do with the right attitude.

Accomplishing anything starts with the right attitude. If you do not believe you can do it then you won't even try.

Try not and you will do not.

Believe in yourself and the faith in your abilities grows. You will risk trying more new things when you believe there is value in doing so. As a result you will accomplish more.

Make no attempt and you will accomplish nothing.

©Craig S. Travis, Ph.D.

DDP69

DAILY DOSE OF POSITIVITY™

CHANGING YOUR LIFE STARTS WITH CHANGING YOUR MIND

The beginning step to making your life different starts with changing how you think.

Healthy change results from healthy thinking.

You will continue to keep doing the same thing until you change your thinking habits. It is very difficult to change if you do not know what it is that needs changing.

Know the thoughts that perpetuate your behavior. Become aware of them; understand them, so you can do something about them.

In physics, electrical current takes the path of least resistance. So too, can it be true for human behavior. The path of behavioral least resistance results in a rut. No resistance means no change, no change in terms of human behavior leads to boredom.

Doing what is right for you is not necessarily what is always easy.

©Craig S. Travis, Ph.D.

Daily Dose of Positivity™

DDP70

DAILY DOSE OF POSITIVITY™

YOU CAN IF YOU THINK YOU CAN

You have no limitations other than the ones you impose upon yourself in your mind.

Think you can and you will; think you can't and you won't.

You have everything that it takes to be successful. Just conjure up all your mental abilities and apply them to the challenges in your life.

Success is about trying, not quitting.

It's about using what you have to overcome what you don't.
Your strength lies in knowing your weakness, but not letting them prevent you from accomplishing that which you desire.

Success is mind over matter.

©Craig S. Travis, Ph.D.

DDP71

DAILY DOSE OF POSITIVITY™

POSITIVE THOUGHTS AND ACTIONS BRING POSITIVE RESULTS

You have been blessed with one of nature's greatest gifts. You have the choice to decide what thoughts and attitudes you put into your mind.

And your thoughts permeate your actions.

What you think filters down into action. When you think positivity you begin to act in positive ways. If you see yourself negatively you will act accordingly.

Think positive so you can act accordingly.

If you want to make lasting positive changes then dedicate yourself to thinking this way everyday. Stop thinking about what you can't do and start focusing on what you can do.

Envision making positive changes for yourself.

Positively visualize your success in each step of the process. Favorable outcomes in any endeavor result from constructive thinking.

Your success depends on what you think.

©Craig S. Travis, Ph.D.

DDP72

DAILY DOSE OF POSITIVITY™

HEALTHY CHOICES ARE NOT ALWAYS EASY

No one ever said life was going to be easy. Expect it to be fair and you will no doubt be disappointed. Understand that life is filled with trials and tribulations and you understand the ingredients necessary to successfully accept what challenges life gives you.

Accept the tests gracefully and understand you have the power to rise above them.

Many times you will be faced with options. Many times you will be asked to make a choice. Do you take the smaller reward now or take the steps to accumulate greater wealth for tomorrow?

A choice only you can make.

Some may encourage participation in indulgence while others suggest no risk, safety at all cost. Follow the pack or dare to blaze a new trail? The decision is yours to make.

Choosing to stand alone for what you believe takes courage.

©Craig S. Travis, Ph.D.

DDP73

DAILY DOSE OF POSITIVITY™

YOUR ATTITUDE IS ALL THAT MATTERS

What more powerful concept is there in human dynamics than the force around ones attitude? Your attitude permeates just about everything about you and around you.

Attitude really is everything.

You hear reference to it just about everyday, albeit it is usually in a sarcastic critical way. For instance, he has a bad attitude; or she needs an attitude adjustment.

Attitude is a driving force behind one's personality.

Your attitude is the reference point from which you interact with the world. Have a positive attitude and you tend to have positive outcomes.

Your attitude also determines how you feel about what is going on around you. Circumstances themselves are less important in how they impact you than your perception.

If you don't mind, it doesn't matter.

©Craig S. Travis, Ph.D.

DDP74

DAILY DOSE OF POSITIVITY™

AVOID YOUR RESPONSIBILITIES AND SUCCESS WILL AVOID YOU

Success is a multidimensional concept. It's achievement in one area depends on its achievement in another. Nothing in this world works in isolation and neither do your successes or failures.

Neglect your responsibilities and success will remain out of reach.

Success is a hierarchy of accomplishment. What you accomplish at the bottom determines how far up you can go. Attending to the basic building blocks now, ensures success later. But you must keep building and pursuing.

Groundwork is fundamental for success down the road.

Successfully attending to your responsibilities frees you up to pursue your dreams. Cheat life and it cheats you.

Accountability has a way of tracking you down.

©Craig S. Travis, Ph.D.

DDP75

DAILY DOSE OF POSITIVITY™

GIVE IT YOUR BEST SHOT

You have choices in life. You can do nothing, you can do things half-heartedly, or you can put effort into everything you do.

Make no attempt and you guarantee lack of success.

When you try and fail you can at least find solace in your trying. The human mind finds comfort in knowing that at least it tried for the uncertainty of not knowing is answered.
Do nothing and your mind is left wondering what could have been.

Regrets are what you are left with when you do not try.

©Craig S. Travis, Ph.D.

DDP76

DAILY DOSE OF POSITIVITY™

SUCCESS IN LIFE INVOLVES RISK

Success in any endeavor does not just fall in your lap.
Even behind those who seem to be "overnight sensations" there is a story of belief, determination, action, perseverance, and risk.

Often *your* success will involve risk.

You risk trust when you take a chance on someone. You risk being hurt when you share how you feel. You risk rejection when you express your opinions.

But you must risk if you want to move forward.

Without such risks, you miss out on life fulfillment. Without such risk, you will not know love. Without such risk, you will miss opportunities to be successful in the meaningful areas in your life. As you travel life's journey, you will discover that there are healthy risks and there are foolish ones.

It pays to know the difference.

©Craig S. Travis, Ph.D.

DDP77

DAILY DOSE OF POSITIVITY™

SUCCESS DEPENDS ON ACTION

Success comes to those who wait only when they prepare to seize opportunity when it presents itself. Opportunity is everywhere, but you must grab it when it presents itself.

Do nothing and that is exactly what you will get.

Even if you want to successfully achieve peace and harmony, you need to do what will bring that about. Most notably, think it, believe it, act it.

Be careful not to confuse peaceful action and relaxation as doing nothing. Sometimes less is more.

You can accomplish a lot with your mind while your body is still.

©Craig S. Travis, Ph.D.

Daily Dose of Positivity™

DDP78

DAILY DOSE OF POSITIVITY™

NO AMOUNT OF BELIEF WILL OVERRIDE INACTION

What you think and believe is inherently important to what you can accomplish. Thinking you can't do something will keep you from the attempt.

Without action your dreams remain out of reach.

No matter how much you believe something merely believing it, won't accomplish it. Acting upon that thought transforms your ideas into realities.

Accomplishment starts with thought and ends with action.

©Craig S. Travis, Ph.D.

DDP79

DAILY DOSE OF POSITIVITY™

BELIEVE IN YOUR ABILITIES AND YOU CAN CONQUER YOUR GOALS

What you believe has substantial influence on what you can achieve. Think you can and you will desire to try. Think you can't and you are already defeated.

Don't quit before you even start.

What prevents most people from accomplishing anything is their belief that they can't. When you allow your mind to defeat yourself before you even begin, you start a chain reaction of negativity.

Break the chain by believing in yourself.

Even when you fail, you at least succeeded in trying. Build on your courage to attempt. Without attempt there is no success. Attempt begins with it the belief that you have some bearing on the outcome; when you try, you will make an impact of some sort.

Achieving your goals starts with your belief.

©Craig S. Travis, Ph.D.

DDP80

DAILY DOSE OF POSITIVITY™

IT PAYS TO KNOW YOUR LIMITATIONS

Know your limits so that you may compensate for them. When you know the reality of your obstacles you will know what you are up against. Face your challenges with courage and conviction and you are likely to overcome them.

Challenging your limits takes courage.

The way to breakthrough your barriers is to know their boundaries. Knowing when to give that extra little effort is often what enables you to reach your goal.

You can move beyond perceived limits.

Breaking through to the other side results from knowing where to invest your energy. Choose your battles wisely by knowing when it is worth the struggle.

You win the battles of life with strategy, not brute force.

©Craig S. Travis, Ph.D.

DDP81

DAILY DOSE OF POSITIVITY™

YOUR POSSIBILITIES ARE ENDLESS

What is possible depends on what you think is possible. When something is inconceivable to you, you won't even think to accomplish it.

Thinking you can't, leads to the reality that you won't.

Your mind can be a powerful ally or it can be a cruel enemy. The beauty is that you get to choose which direction to lead your mind. Which would you rather have, friend or foe?

Where your mind leads, behavior follows.

©Craig S. Travis, Ph.D.

DDP82

DAILY DOSE OF POSITIVITY™

FOR FUTURE DREAMS TO BE POSSIBLE, PLAN TODAY

What you do today determines what you get from tomorrow. Your actions today are the best way to prepare for what lies ahead.

To be certain of where you are going, know where you are.

The way to achieve your dreams is to know what to do right now. Begin by understanding that any achievement requires action and hard work.

Determine where you want to go.

Prepare a clear road map by establishing a clear set of goals. Impose upon yourself a firm devotion to strive for your objectives each and everyday.

When it comes to achievement, preparation is your friend, idleness your enemy.

©Craig S. Travis, Ph.D.

DDP83

DAILY DOSE OF POSITIVITY™

MOVE BEYOND MENTAL BARRIERS
___

There are physical limitations and then there are limitations of the mind. What keeps most people from accomplishing things are the mental barriers they place upon themselves.

Test your mental obstacles.

What allows those with physical limitations to rise above those obstacles is the attitude they have toward their life.
In their mind, they believe they can.

You can too, when you believe in yourself.

Believe you can overcome self-imposed barriers and you will find a way to remove those obstacles. You can go anywhere and do anything in your own mind, if you let it. See what happens when you push your mind. Take the risk and believe in yourself.

Use your attitude to rise above.
___
©Craig S. Travis, Ph.D.

DDP84

DAILY DOSE OF POSITIVITY™

LIFE IS FILLED WITH OPTIONS

You have choices everyday. You may not like your choices, but rejoice in the fact that you at least have them.

Choice, even when limited, brings with it power.

There are always at least two possibilities: you can do something, or you can do nothing. Understand that this is still a choice. Even having to choose the lesser of two evils is still a choice.

Know that ultimately the choice is yours, and you will come to understand the power that choice has over your life.

You do not control life; you control your response to life.

You control *your* life by what you choose. Each choice bears outcomes. Choose to affect outcomes or have outcomes affect you.

The choice is yours to make.

©Craig S. Travis, Ph.D.

DDP85

DAILY DOSE OF POSITIVITY™

EXPECTATIONS ARE POWERFUL

You tend to get out of life exactly what you expect from life. Our tendency is to repeatedly behave in ways that reinforce our expectations, and in turn, those expectations propel the same behavior to continue. This can be positive or negative.

You get what you think you deserve.

If you think you don't deserve any better, then you will not act in ways that will bring about better outcomes. Your expectations dictate your behavior and your behavior reinforces what you expect.

Your expectations are powerful forces.

Expect something different, something more positive and you have introduced a new variable into life's equation. As a result, you often will get different outcomes. You tend to find what you are looking for in life.

What do you want to find?

©Craig S. Travis, Ph.D.

DDP86

DAILY DOSE OF POSITIVITY™

SUCCESS CAN BE FOUND IN MANY THINGS

Success comes in many different forms not just how much money you make. Success is found in a love for life and the people in it.

Define success in your own terms.

You are the one who has to live your life. You live with the consequences of the choices you make everyday. Yes, there are universal truths that govern right and wrong, but what dictates day to day action is much more subtle.

Obvious right and wrong is obvious.

What is less obvious are the choices that you need to make to determine what is right for you. What you consider to be successful may be entirely different to someone else. Do what you choose as long as it isn't harmful to others.

Stand firm in your beliefs.

©Craig S. Travis, Ph.D.

DDP87

DAILY DOSE OF POSITIVITY™

IT PAYS TO BE PREPARED

Opportunity is everywhere. You just need to be prepared to look for it. Missed chances stem from not being ready. Having a positive attitude enables you to be ready.

Opportunity is having a chance; success comes from acting on that chance.

It is better to miss chances because life does not present them, rather than to miss them because you were not prepared to act upon them.

Regret is fueled by inaction.

See opportunity in everything that life presents. Seize your opportunities with action. Capture accomplishment by being prepared.

Life's success tends to present itself to those whom are ready.

If you are ready when opportunity presents itself, you are more likely to grab it then if you weren't prepared.

Preparation breeds success.

©Craig S. Travis, Ph.D.

DDP88

DAILY DOSE OF POSITIVITY™

IT PAYS TO THINK THINGS THROUGH

All choice results in consequence. Everything we choose to do brings about repercussion. It is a law of nature that for every action there is reaction.

Think before you act.

Giving thought to action before the action tends to lead to better outcomes. Planning for potential consequences before they occur will help you determine which choice is right for you.

You have the ability to make the right choices.

Listen to your self-talk; your internal dialogue will help guide you, if you listen to its wisdom. When it comes to important life decisions, think it through.

Your inner voice has something important to say.

©Craig S. Travis, Ph.D.

DDP89

DAILY DOSE OF POSITIVITY™

HOW YOU THINK DETERMINES YOUR SUCCESS IN LIFE

You have within you the ability to accomplish many things. But, you will only do so when you believe in yourself. Faith in your abilities is crucial to your accomplishment.

When you think you can, you will.

Fan the flames of desire with more belief. Build upon the tiniest of encouragement and you will amaze yourself with the things that you can accomplish.

The power of doing is in your power of thinking.

Truly believing that you are capable of accomplishing great things marks the beginning of your achieving your goals. Set forth upon that journey.

Believe in yourself and the possibilities are bountiful.

©Craig S. Travis, Ph.D.

Daily Dose of Positivity™

DDP90

DAILY DOSE OF POSITIVITY™

ATTITUDE MAKES THE DIFFERENCE

What sets your destiny apart from others is the attitude you take toward life. You alone determine that mind-set. And you have the ability to control what you think.

Influence your attitude.

Your attitude is a powerful motivator. It will encourage you to move forward or it will encourage you to remain where you are. It might even hold you back. You choose which one you want.

Choose an attitude that motivates you.

Understand that your attitude is essential to your behavior.
Think a certain way and you will act a certain way. A life of positivity is one option. It's all in the way you think.

Your destiny lies in your attitude.

©Craig S. Travis, Ph.D.

DDP91

DAILY DOSE OF POSITIVITY™

BELIEVE IN FAITH, NOT LUCK

Everyone gets lucky every now and then. The problem with luck is that it eventually runs out. And when it comes and how long it lasts is unpredictable.

Faith is forever when you believe.

Have faith in your abilities. Don't just attribute your accomplishments to luck without also knowing that your actions had some influence on the outcome.

Faith is different from luck.

Believe in your self and your abilities. You possess many positive qualities. All you need to do is nurture them and let them shine. Faith is trust that you have control of your outcomes. Faith is that glowing ember inside you that believes you can accomplish anything.

Faith is forever, luck is circumstantial.

©Craig S. Travis, Ph.D.

DDP92

DAILY DOSE OF POSITIVITY™

SPEAK YOUR MIND, YOUR BODY WILL FOLLOW

You create a greater sense of commitment when you externalize your thoughts. Write down your goals or say them out loud. This is the beginning step to taking action and making your life different.

Say how you want to live, live what you say.

Once you externalize your dreams you will begin to feel compelled to achieve their realization. Many people talk the talk, without backing it up. Be one of the few who follows through on your dreams.

Talk is cheap without the intention for action.

©Craig S. Travis, Ph.D.

DDP93

DAILY DOSE OF POSITIVITY™

CHANGE HAPPENS EVERYDAY

The paradox to life is that the only constant to life is change. You may not want things to change but you cannot keep things from changing. The sooner you realize this the sooner you give up unnecessary struggles.

What happens around you is less important than your adaptability.

Your flexibility around change will determine how successfully you adapt to what life presents you. The greater your willingness to adjust creates greater opportunity for success.

Stay rigid and you stay unhappy.

Don't continue to resist change that is a battle you won't win.
Instead, begin to accept its inevitability. When you do, a softness within you begins to emerge.

Acceptance brings with it a sense of peace.

©Craig S. Travis, Ph.D.

DDP94

DAILY DOSE OF POSITIVITY™

SET GOALS FOR YOURSELF, NOT OTHERS

You will find that in your lifetime there will be many people who tell you what to do. Some may have good intention, others not. You need to determine your own goals and pathways in life.

Advice is worth the respect you give the source.

Those who aren't successful running their own life are the ones who most likely will tell you how to run yours. You can decide the value that you place on the advice. Are you living their life or yours?

Choose your own priorities.

Don't set your goals by what other people deem important. No one else has to live your life but you. Discover what it is that you regard as important and commit yourself to stand by your convictions.

Know what you want to do, not what others tell you.

©Craig S. Travis, Ph.D.

DDP95

DAILY DOSE OF POSITIVITY™

YOUR ATTITUDE IS A GIFT

Positivity is one of the best free gifts you can receive. It is a gift you give yourself and others. It is the kind of gift that gives back the more you give it away.

There is no cost but a lot of reward.

What goes on in your mind shapes your overall happiness and influences your sense of well-being. That in turn impacts your life around you. Notice what happens around you when you focus on having a positive attitude.

Change inside you impacts change outside you.

At this very moment you have the ability to make lasting changes. Changes that are powerful and will significantly enhance your life. It all starts in the power of your mind.

Your attitude is the gift that keeps on giving.

©Craig S. Travis, Ph.D.

DDP96

DAILY DOSE OF POSITIVITY™

YOUR VALUE AS A PERSON IS IMMEASURABLE

Don't undermine your sense of worth by comparing yourself with others. Your differences are what make you special.

You have an inherent self-worth as a human being.

Believe you can contribute something of value and you will. Your opinion is equally important as that of others. Do not let anyone tell you any different.

You have value simply because you exist.

Your strength and your ability come from your belief that you matter. Be less concerned with what others think of you and more concerned with how you view yourself.

Your vote holds just as much weight as everyone else's.

©Craig S. Travis, Ph.D.

DDP97

DAILY DOSE OF POSITIVITY™

KNOW WHAT IS IMPORTANT TO YOUR HEART

Do not take for granted the things closest to your heart. Cling to them as you would your life, for without them, life is meaningless.

Remember what is important.

That which you already have, remains to this day, as important as when you first discovered it. Keep this in mind the next time you think there is something missing in your life. Chances are you already have what you need, what you are looking for is merely what you want.

Recognize the value of what you have, even if it appears small.

Small things are often more important to happiness than big things. Overlooking the small things in life can lead to the misperception that you don't have what you need.

Don't confuse luxuries with needs.

Simple pleasures, although simple, often bring the greatest reward. Know what is of value to you. Worry about what others think is valuable and you will miss the treasures you already have.

Good things often come in small packages; that's why children are small.

©Craig S. Travis, Ph.D.

Daily Dose of Positivity™

DDP98

DAILY DOSE OF POSITIVITY™

IT AIN'T OVER UNTIL (UNLESS) YOU GIVE UP

Don't give up when you still have something to give. Nothing is really over until the moment you stop trying. Often you can do more than you think you can do.

Allow your momentum to carry you to your goals.

Those who lose opportunity for success are those who give up not knowing how close they were to achieving their goal. The time at which you want to quit is the time to give a little extra effort. Even when you think you can't, you can go farther.

Very often success finds us at our most desperate hour.

Give up and you will never know what you could have accomplished. Give yourself another chance for often your second effort, not your first attempt is the one that is successful. This is what is meant by mental toughness.

Success comes to those who want it most.

©Craig S. Travis, Ph.D.

DDP99

DAILY DOSE OF POSITIVITY™

BRAVERY INVOLVES RISK

Don't be afraid to take risks. When you refuse to take risks in life, you never get anywhere. Movement forward, venturing into the unknown is a healthy risk. This type of risk propels you further toward your goals and dreams.

Know that great achievement involves great risk.

Take risk and you can achieve what you desire to accomplish. Take that first step into your brave new world of courage. Make the effort to try new things and grow into the person you want to be.

Life is full of risks; be brave and take one.

Mind you, this is not permission to do foolish things. It simply means risk in the right proportion can be healthy to life's journey, for risk involves growth.

Without risk, you will not dare to spread your wings to fly.

©Craig S. Travis, Ph.D.

DDP100

DAILY DOSE OF POSITIVITY™

INTERPRETATION REFLECTS ATTITUDE

William Shakespeare once wrote: There [exists] nothing either good or bad but thinking makes it so. It is your interpretation of the world and the events in it that determine where you go.

Your interpretation is influenced by your attitude.

Life presents to you many unfortunate experiences. You and you alone determine your responses. You create your own feeling, positive or negative given the circumstances presented to you.

How you think is important to how you respond.

You will discover that much of life's circumstances are beyond your control. But, you have control over how you choose to respond to the chaos around you. How you look at life will guide your interpretation of it. The destiny of your mood depends on you and how you think.

What will it be? Positive or negative?

©Craig S. Travis, Ph.D.

DDP101

DAILY DOSE OF POSITIVITY™

YOUR MIND IS POWERFUL

Your mind is a very powerful influence. It can take you places that you haven't yet dreamed. It can also prevent you from your greatest accomplishments.

Defeat yourself in your mind, and you defeat yourself at life.

You set forth to accomplish things, only when you believe in your mind that you can. If you think you can't you won't even make an attempt.

Your mind tells you what to do.

The beautiful thing is that you get to tell your mind *what* it tells you. Your accomplishments start with your belief; belief in yourself and your abilities. Think you can and you initiate a desire to try. Your mind can help you or hurt you. It's up to you.

Don't let your mind defeat you.

©Craig S. Travis, Ph.D.

DDP102

DAILY DOSE OF POSITIVITY™

HONESTY AND INTEGRITY ARE AMONG YOUR BEST ATTRIBUTES

Think of the people who have been the greatest influence in your life. Chances are they were influential not for what they did for you, but for who they were to you.

You see, your character has far reaching impact.

So, show class, have pride, and display character. For if you do, success takes care of itself. Treat those around you with honesty and integrity and *you* will become the influence.

Allow these attributes to shine on others.

Your influence is reflected in your actions. Your actions reflect your attitude. Your attitude displays your character and that is what others will remember.

Show the positive nature of who you are.

©Craig S. Travis, Ph.D.

DDP103

DAILY DOSE OF POSITIVITY™

TRUST YOUR INTUITION

Knowledge not only comes from others, it also comes from within. Trust in your feelings. Know what they are telling you. They are there for a reason; nurture them as you would any other valuable asset that you posses.

Your body has a lot of valuable information if you listen to it.

Understand your emotions about your circumstances and they will lead you in the right directions. Believe what your "gut" is telling you.

To thine own self be true.

Your sense of intuition culminates from many sources. Past experience brings with it wisdom. Know this may influence your situation. Reflect on your thoughts and emotions and let them guide you.

Listen to your wisdom.

©Craig S. Travis, Ph.D.

DDP104

DAILY DOSE OF POSITIVITY™

EXPECT THE UNEXPECTED

Know that life is unpredictable. You never know what will happen next. Be confident in your ability to handle unexpected things.

Uncertainty is your adventure in life.

You cannot tame life but you can train your response to it. Stay grounded and centered in who you are and your belief in your abilities.

Know your control lies in controlling your self, not others.

Choose how you wish to respond rather than simply reacting. This implies greater sense of control. With greater control comes greater predictability and increased optimism.

You are capable when you believe so.

©Craig S. Travis, Ph.D.

DDP105

DAILY DOSE OF POSITIVITY™

WHATEVER YOU DO, BE SECURE IN YOURSELF

No matter where you are, even if it is a new uncomfortable experience, be secure in yourself and your abilities. New experiences are opportunities that take you out of your comfort zone and into areas of growth.

You can handle each new situation competently.

What makes you nervous or anxious about any given situation, is the unexpected. And the concern you will not handle the situation well or somehow embarrass yourself.

Believe in your ability and you are destined with competence.

You cannot predict life's circumstances and usually you cannot control them. But, you can be prepared for them by believing in yourself and your ability to act competently no matter what cards you're dealt.

Know you've done your best and you will be satisfied with what you've done.

©Craig S. Travis, Ph.D.

DDP106

DAILY DOSE OF POSITIVITY™

ATTITUDE IS WHAT GETS YOU THROUGH LIFE

It's less about what happens in life than your response to it that matters. Many unfortunate things will occur, but you have the power to choose how you will handle them.

Choose your attitude.

Select one of grace, dignity, and confidence, or be overwhelmed by inferiority, doubt, and fear. You decide your mind-set in life, not your circumstances.

Accept the power of your mind.

Wealth and power do not make you happy for you will come across as many cheerful faces among the poor as among the rich. What determines your success in life is your approach to life.

Make your attitude work for you.

©Craig S. Travis, Ph.D.

Craig S. Travis, Ph.D.

DDP107

DAILY DOSE OF POSITIVITY™

SUCCESS IS BUILT ON UNITY

Life is not about opposition. It is not about looking for a fight to prove you are better than someone else. Being proud of your accomplishments is one thing reveling in your power over another something else.

Embrace others and you will know the power of Positivity.

Life is about coming together. It is about belief and trust. Trusting that others have good intentions and sharing these with each other.

Your connection to others is favorable.

Surround yourself with those who are successful at caring and you will find success too. Show your care for others and your compassion will breed.

Selfishness leads to isolation, selflessness to harmony.

©Craig S. Travis, Ph.D.

DDP108

DAILY DOSE OF POSITIVITY™

BECOME THE PERSON YOU DREAM TO BE

Even successful people strive for growth for growth is what makes you feel alive. And opportunities for personal growth are around every corner.

Seize these opportunities of change.

You see, change is movement, and movement means development. Continue to develop who you are for without this you will become stagnated.

Growth is movement toward your future and dreams.

Visualize the kind of person whom you want to be. Know what it is that you want and take action to move in that direction. Your success is marked by stepping towards your dreams.

Dare to be what you have always dreamed.

©Craig S. Travis, Ph.D.

DDP109

DAILY DOSE OF POSITIVITY™

TRUST IN YOUR FEELINGS

Feelings can sometimes be uncomfortable, many of which you may not want to experience. It is natural to want to wish them away. But be cautious in your desire to judge and avoid them for they are simply information.

Judge your behavior not your feelings.

Thinking Positivity doesn't mean not experiencing your feelings. It means making the best of the situation. Acknowledge how you feel and choose a healthy response.

Cherish the validity of your feelings.

Simply put, your feelings are valuable information that are telling you one of two things. They tell you that you either like what is happening or that you don't.

You can use the information in your emotions positively.

©Craig S. Travis, Ph.D.

DDP110

DAILY DOSE OF POSITIVITY™

DON'T WAIT, START NOW

If you want to change your life you can begin at any time. But you must begin. Simply wait for things to change and you will remain discouraged.

Change your life by changing yourself.

You can continue to improve and grow. Even experts strive for growth and change for that is what makes them successful.

Start today and you approach your dreams.

Take the step to achieve your goals. Make a small change today. See that your success is a series of small triumphs everyday.

Today sets the tone for tomorrow; make it count.

©Craig S. Travis, Ph.D.

DDP111

DAILY DOSE OF POSITIVITY™

CALL UPON YOUR STRENGTH

You have both strength and weakness. Know what your limitations are but do not dwell on them. Focus instead on your strengths and nurture their growth.

Allow your assets to outshine your faults.

You have the ability to choose your destiny. Defeat yourself in weakness or celebrate your power. The path is yours to decide.

Be your best by doing your best.

©Craig S. Travis, Ph.D.

DDP112

DAILY DOSE OF POSITIVITY™

POSITIVITY MEANS REACTING POSITIVELY TO A NEGATIVE SITUATION

Life's circumstances are largely out of your control. But your thoughts and actions you do control. The impact of your situation depends on your interpretation.

Things in life are neither good nor bad, but your thinking makes it so.

Optimism is a phenomenon where things turn out best for those who make the best out of every situation. Your situation is less important than your reaction to the situation.

Your response to circumstance is what matters most.

Your life is influenced by many factors. Many occur externally and are not directly within your control. However, your attitude reflects your response to what is happening. You have control over your attitude. Life can be difficult or life can be easy.

It all depends on your attitude.

©Craig S. Travis, Ph.D.

DDP113

DAILY DOSE OF POSITIVITY™

HAPPINESS STARTS WITH BELIEVING IN YOURSELF

If you want to be happy, start by accepting who you are. Your happiness depends on your acceptance of self. Self satisfaction is the seed from which your happiness will grow. Before you can be happy, you need to first have this foundation.

Happiness comes from within.

This does not mean you have to settle for mediocrity. You can strive to improve yourself. But remember to look at the good in yourself and happiness will follow you wherever you go.

Erase any deep seeded self-doubt.

You can begin to believe in yourself at anytime, but you must put forth a conscious effort to do so. Happiness stems from liking yourself and appreciating your abilities.

Look deep within yourself and ask, "What's not to like?"

©Craig S. Travis, Ph.D.

DDP114

DAILY DOSE OF POSITIVITY™

KEEP YOUR GOALS IN MIND AND YOU WILL BE SURPRISED

Know what it is that you wish to accomplish and you will bring about the results that you want. Stay committed and you will surprise yourself at how quickly you can achieve what it is that you set out to do.

Stay focused on your desire.

When you keep your goals in mind you feed your motivation. Your goals provide the direction and energy that propel you along the path to your dreams.

You can accomplish whatever you commit your mind to.

©Craig S. Travis, Ph.D.

DDP115

DAILY DOSE OF POSITIVITY™

DISCOVER A PASSION FOR WHAT'S POSSIBLE

You can be anything you dream to be and do anything you dream to do. Understand your ambitions and dreams and be passionate in your pursuit of them.

Believe in the possibilities.

Know that you can accomplish whatever you set your mind to do. Have faith in your ability to achieve the things that you want. It takes strong effort and conviction, but it is possible.

Success is waiting for you.

Triumph in knowing you can find it. Do not think it impossible for if that is what you think, that is what you'll get. Imagine that it can't be done and you won't see the possibilities. Instead, dream of what might be and then go find it.

Your success is out there but you have to look for it.

©Craig S. Travis, Ph.D.

DDP116

DAILY DOSE OF POSITIVITY™

WHEN FACED WITH ADVERSITY, STILL BELIEVE

Life is filled with all kinds of heartache. Know that you can live through all the pain and grief. Through all the tears you can still believe in yourself.

There is power in belief.

Everyday there are new challenges. Through all the adversity and negativity put trust in your belief that you can survive it all. Believe you have the ability to persevere.

Hope is there when you believe.

Know that good fortune will eventually come your way. Through your belief you create the opportunity for such success. Without your hope you will not recognize it when it passes your way.

Put your trust in the power of hope.

Given that life is filled with many challenges, you need all the hope that you can get. Look upon others for hope in trying times. Although hope may start with others, know that it spreads in you.

Through it all, still believe in hope and prosperity.

©Craig S. Travis, Ph.D.

Craig S. Travis, Ph.D.

DDP117

DAILY DOSE OF POSITIVITY™

INTENSITY, FORSIGHT, AND ACTION ARE ESSENTIAL FOR SUCCESS

You possess the necessary ingredients for winning. Search your soul to find them. Understand the elements for success and the world is yours to conquer.

Posses with conviction these qualities that will determine your future.

Have no passion and motivation dwindles. Lack vision and your roadmap is left unfolded. Do not act and your final destination will be where you already are.

See things not as they are and ask why, rather, dream of things that never were and ask why not?

©Craig S. Travis, Ph.D.

DDP118

DAILY DOSE OF POSITIVITY™

SATISFACTION COMES WITH A JOB WELL DONE

You may accomplish many things in life, but to feel pride in whatever you do, you must put forth an effort to do it well. True satisfaction does not come just with the completion of some task. Satisfaction comes from the amount of effort put forth in the process.

You may not do great things, but you can do things greatly.

You get a sense of pride and worth out of the amount of desire you put into something. See how much more fulfilling your accomplishments are when you fill them with desire to begin with.

What you ultimately get out of something is what you are willing to put into it.

Whatever you do, do it well.

©Craig S. Travis, Ph.D.

DDP119

DAILY DOSE OF POSITIVITY™

SUCCESS IS A WAY OF LIFE

Success is not some final goal whereupon once you arrive you quit doing what got you there. Success is the means rather than the end. There is no rest for the weary traveler for to truly be accomplished, you must continue to forge ahead.

However, you can make a pit stop along your journey to refuel.

While the road to success is paved with effort, dedication, and hard work, so too should it be balanced with peace, tranquility and relaxation. Taking a moment to recharge your batteries will allow you more energy to faithfully commit your success.

You define how this will be.

How you choose to live your life determines how successful you are. Continue life with enthusiasm. Embrace each obstacle as a challenge to overcome. Stay motivated to remain positive and life will feel fulfilled.

Just because you've arrived doesn't mean the journey's over.

©Craig S. Travis, Ph.D.

Daily Dose of Positivity™

DDP120

DAILY DOSE OF POSITIVITY™

ORGANIZED PEOPLE ARE SUCCESSFUL

If you want to be successful, then you must first get organized. Organization and preparation are the fertile ground for success and happiness.

Clarity does not come with clutter.

Many people spend a significant amount of time looking for things rather than doing what they want to be doing. Looking for keys, looking for tools, looking for happiness…

Everything has its place.

Organize and structure your day according to how you want to live. Find a place for your things, your happiness, your spirit, and you will always know where to look when you need them.

Start simple, but set your goals high.

©Craig S. Travis, Ph.D.

DDP121

DAILY DOSE OF POSITIVITY™

SUCCESS IS MARKED BY EACH SMALL ACCOMPLISHMENT

Success is not measured by monetary gain. Or how much "stuff" you have accumulated. It is not a competition to see who can accumulate the greatest net worth.

It is measured by smaller more subtle definitions.

Success is measured each day by how you choose to interact with others. Smile and say hello to each passerby. Treat others as you would have them treat you. Respect each person you meet, and consider their feelings.

Connection with others is what makes you successful.

Think of others you consider successful. Aren't they usually well respected for how they treat other people? If you only define success as financial rewards, then you have missed one of life's greatest riches:

Friendships.

©Craig S. Travis, Ph.D.

DDP122

DAILY DOSE OF POSITIVITY™

POLITENESS NEVER GOES OUT OF STYLE

Treat people nicely and you will be rewarded. Treat others with respect and you yourself will be respected. How you relate to others has a direct bearing on your happiness and future success.

Your future is anchored in your manners toward others.

Success in life is marked by the quality of your relationships with others. If you want to be successful in this area of your life then you must consider the well-being of others.

Remember the golden rule we learned as children;
Do unto others as you would have them do unto you.

Be nice; think nice thoughts, do nice things, and people will look upon you in a positive favorable way. The world is like a mirror; what do you want reflected back to you?

Remember, what goes around eventually comes around.

©Craig S. Travis, Ph.D.

Craig S. Travis, Ph.D.

DDP123

DAILY DOSE OF POSITIVITY™

WORTHWHILE THINGS ARE WORTH THE EFFORT

Effort is directly proportional to satisfaction. Your sense of accomplishment will only come with hard work. Those things in life that are worthwhile are worth working for.

Do not expect to be handed things on a silver platter.

Strive hard to achieve your best each and every day and you will find yourself accomplishing more and more. Continue to work hard and put effort into everything that you do and you will be successful.

A hard job well-done is truly rewarding.

While the resulting accomplishment may be your ultimate goal, your effort will be its own reward. You get out of life exactly what you put into it. Your resulting investment depends on your effort.

Remember, there ain't no such thing as a free lunch.

©Craig S. Travis, Ph.D.

DDP124

DAILY DOSE OF POSITIVITY™

YOU CANNOT GET AHEAD IF YOU ONLY LOOK BACK

If you want to get ahead in this world, do not live in the past. Learn from your past, but know that you have the power to overcome it and break free.

Choose to let go of what holds you back.

Holding onto the past and wanting things to remain the same is a futile effort. The only constant in life is change. Live your life in the past and life will pass you by. Embrace your life today while preparing for tomorrow and you will achieve satisfaction in your life.

Look back and you will slip backwards, look forward and you will move forward.

Your future is yet to be determined. You possess what is necessary to move forward, but you must look up ahead. If you do not know where you are going, how will you get there?

You cannot safely move up when you are looking down.

©Craig S. Travis, Ph.D.

Craig S. Travis, Ph.D.

DDP125

DAILY DOSE OF POSITIVITY™

DON'T JUST THINK IT, DO IT

If you want to accomplish anything in life then act upon that thought. Set forth a logical course of action in order to realize that dream.

No one ever got anywhere only thinking about it.

A well thought-out plan is just that: only a well thought-out plan. Without implementing action, that thought cannot be realized. Think of what you what to accomplish and then actively go after it.

Seize the opportunity provided by thought with a course of action.

©Craig S. Travis, Ph.D.

DDP126

DAILY DOSE OF POSITIVITY™

LIFE IS AN ADVENTURE

Life is a delicious potion; a magic elixir that is to be gobbled up. It is to be savored, not wasted. Enjoy the variability that it brings for this is the spice of life.

Do not settle for the mundane, or life will swallow you whole.

Life is supposed to be adventurous. It is contagious, a feast to be enjoyed. It is not supposed to be boring. Engage life with abandon and you will see how happy you can be. When you are happy, you are successful.

Celebrate the magic of this creation.

©Craig S. Travis, Ph.D.

DDP127

DAILY DOSE OF POSITIVITY™

A KIND THOUGHT GOES ALONG WAY

Doing nice things, good deeds for people, transcends time. Caring and sharing with others is what makes your relationships healthy.

Think of others as well as your self and see what happens.

Successful people do not only do for themselves, they also commit to others. Life is not only about what you can do for you. Your compassion for others is what makes you successful.

After-all, we reap what we sow.

©Craig S. Travis, Ph.D.

DDP128

DAILY DOSE OF POSITIVITY™

GENEROSITY IS A GESTURE OF SUCCESS

Success comes from your ability to give not from your ability to take. Spread your happiness with a smile. Share your thoughts with a friend.

Your success is marked by friendship.

If you only take and never give, then you will end up alone. When you are selfish, people will no longer want to be around you.

Giving happiness and joy brings happiness and joy.

Successful people are successful not necessarily because of what they do but because of their relationships. You are a reflection of your associations. If you give, you are more likely to receive.

Be not afraid to share the wealth of your knowledge and happiness.

©Craig S. Travis, Ph.D.

DDP129

DAILY DOSE OF POSITIVITY™

PUT YOUR THOUGHTS OF POVERTY BEHIND YOU

In order to feel fulfilled, you need to make lasting changes. Significant change does not happen overnight. You will need to put forth effort into establishing your riches.

That which is accomplished quickly can be lost just as fast.

Permanent change begins in tiny increments; a day, an hour, a minute, a heartbeat. Encourage yourself to become an optimist and you will begin to see the possibilities.

Invest in a positive future by seeing it for what it is.

See the forest through the trees and you embark on the journey into the bigger picture of Positivity. Start with a deep breath, take a step forward and lasting change will begin. What lies ahead is up to you.

The riches of optimism can be learned.

©Craig S. Travis, Ph.D.

DDP130

DAILY DOSE OF POSITIVITY™

YOU CAN ACHIEVE HARMONY IN YOUR LIFE

Take time to listen to all the songs in your life; the song of family, the song of friendship, and so on. Your harmony and contentment reside in the inner cadence you feel when the melody of your life is in tune.

Does your song ring true?

What you might find upon looking deeply enough is that you already have what it takes to make beautiful music. Ask yourself; are your songs in tune? If not, perhaps it is time to change your music.

What beat do you want to dance to?

©Craig S. Travis, Ph.D.

DDP131

DAILY DOSE OF POSITIVITY™

DARE TO BE DIFFERENT

Marching to the beat of a different drummer doesn't make you oppositional, it makes you unique. Everyone is weird in their own way. Remain comfortable in your individuality.

Your difference is a gift.

Rebels with a cause are people who can successfully change the world for the better. If you want to make your world a better place, you can start by leading yourself down a different course. You need not be a follower if only you choose to lead.

Be who you want to be, not what others expect you to be.

©Craig S. Travis, Ph.D.

DDP132

DAILY DOSE OF POSITIVITY™

LIFE'S ADVENTURE AWAITS YOU

Many people travel the world only to find that life's true adventure awaits them at home with each new day. How you view life, determines how you live it. Embrace life for what it can be.

To truly live, now that is an adventure.

The journey of each new rising sun culminates with your voyage into tomorrow. Each new dawn brings upon it a new adventure. Live life's adventure like you mean it.

Embrace the adventure of life with full abandon.

Fully engaging in life is a choice; a choice that brings with it many opportunities for growth and fulfillment. What a better thrill ride than life, filled with ups and downs, not knowing what to expect next.

Isn't that why we ride roller coasters?

©Craig S. Travis, Ph.D.

Craig S. Travis, Ph.D.

DDP133

DAILY DOSE OF POSITIVITY™

LIFE IS NOT A ONE WAY STREET

You can choose the direction you take in life. You do not have to blindly continue to travel down your current path, unless you want to; or perhaps you are too afraid to change. Break free from this one way thinking.

You decide where you want to go.

If you do not like the path you are traveling or do not like the final destination of where you seem to be heading, change the course.

Navigate yourself in the direction you want to go.

When you are driving the freeway and notice you are travelling the wrong way, you do not simply keep going. You exit and turn around going in the direction you wanted. Life can be that simple too. Recognize what direction you are traveling.

You are your own copilot.

©Craig S. Travis, Ph.D.

DDP134

DAILY DOSE OF POSITIVITY™

GET IN THE GAME

No one accomplished anything by just sitting there. Take the risk to participate. You will not know what you are capable of accomplishing unless you involve yourself.

Don't be afraid to fail.

Don't be left wondering what might have been, thinking, "If only I had done this". Make the possibilities realities by engaging in life. You can accomplish just about anything if you put your mind to it.

You cannot score unless you're on the field.

©Craig S. Travis, Ph.D.

DDP135

DAILY DOSE OF POSITIVITY™

THERE ARE NO SHORTCUTS TO HONOR

Honor is not something bestowed upon you. You have to earn it. You pay for it by how you think, perhaps more importantly, by your actions.

Act honorably and people will respect you.

Success in relationships depends on your actions. Treat others how you want to be remembered. Others will define you by your behavior. To them, what they see becomes who you are in their mind.

How do you want others to define you?

Everyone knows the ultimate truth. It is deep inside you if you look hard enough. Actions do very often speak louder than words. Set your goal of integrity by showing others you can be trusted.

Trust is a foundation for honor.

©Craig S. Travis, Ph.D.

DDP136

DAILY DOSE OF POSITIVITY™

VOW TO ACCOMPLISH ONE GOAL A DAY

You do not have to always accomplish great things. Celebrate the little things in life. Each minor success builds upon itself and becomes the foundation for future success. Be proud of what you accomplish as long as you are moving toward your dreams.

Sometimes the small stuff gives us the most pleasure.

Accomplishing something little everyday reinforces your ability to accomplish great things down the road. Every achievement is contagious. It brings about the desire for more accomplishment. Set and celebrate little goals each day and you will stay motivated.

Do not miss the beauty of one tree by only seeing the forest.

©Craig S. Travis, Ph.D.

DDP137

DAILY DOSE OF POSITIVITY™

WHEN YOU GIVE UP, YOU MISS OPPORTUNITIES

It has been said that many of life's failures come from people who did not realize how close they were to success when they gave up.

Opportunity often presents itself when we are not looking.

Be alert to what happens around you and you will see opportunity in abundance. What appears at first to be a problem may in fact be opportunity. Once you recognize it, you need to seize it for it may not come your way again soon.

Don't be left out in the cold.

Open the door to opportunity and go inside. Enter through the world of your imagination. Open up the possibilities with your perseverance. Your attitude is what defines opportunity; you have found it when you can see more than what is actually there. Obstacles are merely unrecognized opportunity.

Keep forging ahead and you are bound to succeed.

©Craig S. Travis, Ph.D.

DDP138

DAILY DOSE OF POSITIVITY™

CHEERFUL DISPOSITION IS A GIFT

One of the easiest ways to feel good is to extend a kind word to someone. Compliments are powerful mood boosters. And the effects are mutually beneficial.

Positivity rubs off on those around you.

Give the gift of love by showing you care for others. Acknowledge others feelings. Listen; really listen, to what they have to say. Tell them you understand before you have the urge to tell them what to do.

Consideration toward others goes a long way.

Being kind is its own reward, if you let it be. Others will appreciate your consideration and shower you with the same. Positive energy is a funny thing, by giving it away you get more in return.

Really, it's not that difficult to say "thank you", and mean it.

©Craig S. Travis, Ph.D.

Craig S. Travis, Ph.D.

DDP139

DAILY DOSE OF POSITIVITY™

GENUINE VISION MAKES YOU EXCEL

Your aspiration for success is what moves you closer to your goals. When your dreams are clear, they will shed light on your path and guide your way to your destiny.

Visualize your dreams and you will shine.

Darkness does not mean nothing is there. You simply need to shed light on whatever it is you are looking for. Goals will light a path to your final destination.

Excellence happens when your visions are ambitious.

©Craig S. Travis, Ph.D.

DDP140

DAILY DOSE OF POSITIVITY™

A TASTE OF SUCCESS LEADS TO MORE SUCCESS

Once you have accomplished something of importance you will want to enjoy that feeling again. It feels good when you accomplish what you set out to do.

Success is contagious.

Build upon prior successes and you will continue to be successful. Each step builds upon the last until you reach exactly what it is that you desire.

Continue to inch toward your goals.

Along the way, you will find that the process of accomplishment itself is what becomes rewarding, not just the end result. Your journey, what you had to do to achieve your dreams, reinforces your ability to accomplish them.

Motivation skyrockets as you approach your goals.

The closer you get, the more you've accomplished. The more you've accomplished means your almost there. Reach for your success by building upon your past success.

The top is not as far away when it is only at arms length.

©Craig S. Travis, Ph.D.

DDP141

DAILY DOSE OF POSITIVITY™

PUT FAITH IN YOUR ABILITY TO DO ORDINARY THINGS EXTRA-ORDINARILY

What you do is less important than how you do it. How you treat the mundane reflects your outlook on life.

Whatever you are doing, strive to do it well.

You can derive a great sense of satisfaction from life by doing ordinary tasks with passion and fervor. Your energy toward daily responsibilities spills into other arenas of your life.

Passion in practice leads to greater accomplishment.

When it comes time to get in the game you'll play the way you've practiced. Make a zest for life a habit, and when you are called upon to do something extraordinary, you will find that ability to be routine.

In life, it is not whether you win or lose; it's how you play the game that counts.

©Craig S. Travis, Ph.D.

DDP142

DAILY DOSE OF POSITIVITY™

FAVORABLE RESULTS START WITH A GOOD PLAN

You accomplish in life, what you set out to accomplish not by waiting for fortune to fall in your lap. Rather, a clearly defined set of goals provide the road map to establish positive results.

It is difficult to find your way when you can't see.

Without clearly defined objectives you won't know which direction to go. Goals are the instruction booklet for success.
When all else fails, read those instructions.

Know how many times you're spun, and you can pin the tail on the donkey.

©Craig S. Travis, Ph.D.

DDP143

DAILY DOSE OF POSITIVITY™

THAT WHICH TAKES NO EFFORT TO ACHIEVE REWARDS AS MUCH

Pride in your accomplishments is directly proportional to your effort. Put nothing in and you get nothing in return. Investment in your actions leads to greater return in results.

You really do get what you pay for.

Reward comes from knowing that you put as much into accomplishing something as you possibly could. If you want to receive great reward, then you have to achieve great effort.

There is success in every attempt.

Effort brings with it a sense of accomplishment even if you do not successfully achieve your ultimate goal. Knowing you tried somehow makes a difference.

You get out of life exactly what you put into it.

©Craig S. Travis, Ph.D.

DDP144

DAILY DOSE OF POSITIVITY™

FRIENDSHIP MAKES YOU SUCCESSFUL

Friends are a very rare jewel indeed. They make you smile and encourage you to succeed. They lend an ear, they share words of praise and they open their hearts to you.

Your friends define who you are.

Look around at the people with whom you associate. Do they support and encourage you? Do they stay positive and make you feel good when you don't?

True friends stick with you through good times and bad.

Success is so much more than how much stuff you accumulate. Without people to enjoy it with you, what importance is monetary success?

Money and things don't make you happy; people do.

Chase success in things and you will run yourself ragged looking for something you can't possibly find. Look to your relationships and you needn't look any further. You may accumulate great wealth in your lifetime, but neglect your relationships and you will never be wealthy.

People matter more than things do.

©Craig S. Travis, Ph.D.

DDP145

DAILY DOSE OF POSITIVITY™

ACTION ENABLES ACHIEVEMENT

Your success depends on your actions. Whether or not you accomplish something depends on whether or not you do something. Sit watching the world pass you by and you miss opportunities.

Take the risk to do something.

Opportunity to accomplish things is all around you. This does not mean you have to kill yourself working to accomplish it. Mental training, the principle behind peak performance psychology, allows you to work smarter, not harder.

Use the power of your mind.

The reason you set goals, define a clear plan, visualize, dream, and such, is to achieve peak performance. When you work smarter not harder you have more time to enjoy life's riches.

If you think it, you can act on it; act on it and you can achieve it.

©Craig S. Travis, Ph.D.

DDP146

DAILY DOSE OF POSITIVITY™

FOOLISH ACTS COME FROM FOOLISH THOUGHTS

Doing something foolish because you tell yourself it isn't, is still foolish. Convincing yourself that unhealthy behavior is healthy does not magically make that behavior healthy. Merely believing you don't have a disease does not cure that disease.

Your beliefs do not overrule reality.

No matter how much you believe something it will not change the laws of physics. You do not posses the magic to change the laws of nature. Try as you might, you cannot walk through walls.

No amount of belief will override a foolish act.

When you continue to act the part of a fool by disbelieving reality, you remain foolish to others. However this is not permission to blindly accept things in life without examining them first. The world is what it is; how you handle the world is up to you.

You may not be able to change the reality of nature's laws, but you can change the reality of your own life.

©Craig S. Travis, Ph.D.

Craig S. Travis, Ph.D.

DDP147

DAILY DOSE OF POSITIVITY™

YOUR ACTIONS DETERMINE WHO YOU ARE

You are not successful without acting successful. You will not be happy without acting happy. You are not trusted without acting trustworthy.

Whether you like it or not, others judge you by your actions.

You determine how others view you more by your actions than your words. If you want respect, then act in a respectful manner. Tell people you will do something, and you don't, and people will lose faith in you.

You are accountable for your actions. If you think you can cheat life you are mistaken.

©Craig S. Travis, Ph.D.

DDP148

DAILY DOSE OF POSITIVITY™

IF IT WORKS, KEEP DOING IT

There is an old saying, "if it ain't broke, don't fix it". If what you are doing brings you true happiness and doesn't hurt anyone, then by all means continue what you are doing.

There is no need to abandon a strategy that works.

Success at anything is determined by the plan of action that you implement. When your behavior is successful, you are successful, no matter what someone else tells you.

There is more than one right way.

People who insist that you do something their way and only their way, are not paying attention to your results. As long as it's healthy, do what works for you.

Do what works and you will be successful.

©Craig S. Travis, Ph.D.

DDP149

DAILY DOSE OF POSITIVITY™

HAPPINESS IS A JOURNEY NOT A DESTINATION

The truth is, there is no better time to be happy than right now. If not now, when? Now is the only time that you have any control over. The present moment is the path on your journey in life.

The path traveled is often more adventurous than the destination.

Your life will be filled with many challenges. It is beneficial to admit this to yourself and decide to be happy anyway. What does and does not make you happy is up to you.

You do have a choice.

Treasure every moment that you have on life's path. Treasure it more because you shared it with someone special; special enough to spend your time with you. The way to happiness is to know that happiness is the way, not the journey's end. Spend your time with someone special. Don't wait.

Time waits for no one. Find your happiness today.

©Craig S. Travis, Ph.D.

DDP150

DAILY DOSE OF POSITIVITY™

KEEP LIFE'S SIMPLE PLEASURES IN MIND

You are wealthier than you realize even though your bank account may say otherwise. Lose sight of simple pleasures and you miss opportunity for happiness.

There is more to life than money.

Wealth comes in all shapes and sizes. It is determined by family and friends. Take pleasure in a child's smile, and enjoy the riches in little things.

See the joy in all that you have and do.

The little things in life are what tend to bring the most pleasure when you let them. Added up, they amount to greater pleasure than most major accomplishments by themselves.

Acknowledge only big things and you miss lots of celebrations.

©Craig S. Travis, Ph.D.

DDP151

DAILY DOSE OF POSITIVITY™

ENJOY LIFE BY ENGAGING IN LIFE

Life is meant to be lived, to be experienced with connected passion. Life truly is a gift. To fully appreciate its beauty, you need to unwrap it.

Don't leave it in the box.

Everyday, vow to be involved in life with enthusiasm. Passion and Positivity are contagious. Once you've tasted them, you want more. The more involved you get in something, the more you tend to appreciate it.

You miss the joys of life when you don't actively participate.

©Craig S. Travis, Ph.D.

DDP152

DAILY DOSE OF POSITIVITY™

COMPASSION IS NEVER OUT OF STYLE

One of our greatest emotional needs is to feel appreciated. To know you are accepted, leads to a sense of belonging. Compassion is what allows you to feel comfortable and to feel like you fit in.

Do unto others what is compassionate.

Compassion for others not only leads to their sense of appreciation, but brings to you a sense of pride and accomplishment. When you give of yourself emotionally, you receive so much more in return. Your compassion is what maintains the connectedness in your relationships.

Show others you care.

©Craig S. Travis, Ph.D.

DDP153

DAILY DOSE OF POSITIVITY™

SUCCESS IS YOURS IF YOU WANT IT

Success does not discriminate. It offers itself to those who are willing to strive for it. It does not come cheaply for we often have to pay it our dues before we are its recipient.

What are you willing to pay for your success?

Sometimes we have to make sacrifices now to accomplish what we want in the long run. For true success, you need to be in it for the long haul. To ensure that you get what you want from life tomorrow, you have to take care of your responsibilities today.

There is often a bigger picture in life.

Take what you can today and you have it for today. Learn what you can and that lesson lasts well into tomorrow. As the old saying goes, "Give a man a fish and you feed him for a day; teach a man to fish, and you feed him for a lifetime."

What is easy is not always what is best.

©Craig S. Travis, Ph.D.

DDP154

DAILY DOSE OF POSITIVITY™

MAKE NO EXCUSES

Do not wait until tomorrow to embark upon your journey to accomplish your dreams. Fear does not allow for successful accomplishments. Success comes from breaking through your fears, not in making excuses.

Excuses are for those whom have no sense of adventure.

Do not let fear rule your life. The limits you impose upon yourself are probably most likely the wounds that are kept in your heart; wounds from past hurts. To move beyond your limits, you need to risk opening your heart. It is a risk, but success is built on risk, and so is life and what it has to offer.

Be willing to take risks in life and you more likely achieve that which you desire most.

Know that truly living involves taking risk. Without risk, you will not know love. Your life's dreams are just beyond risks door. Engage life by opening that door and stepping through.

Make excuses and you miss out on life.

©Craig S. Travis, Ph.D.

Craig S. Travis, Ph.D.

DDP155

DAILY DOSE OF POSITIVITY™

FIND SUCCESS YOUR OWN WAY

Just because something worked for one person doesn't mean it will be right for you. It might be, but there are many formulas for success.

Find what is right for you.

You determine your own success by finding and doing what you are comfortable with. Find your own style and your success will fit you rather than you trying to fit someone else's success.

Success is a custom fit.

©Craig S. Travis, Ph.D.

DDP156

DAILY DOSE OF POSITIVITY™

EMBRACE YOUR DIFFERENCES

Your differences make you unique. Rejoice in the fact that this makes you special. Celebrate your differences for life would be boring if we were all the same.

The most valuable gems are the ones unlike any other.

Your differences make you charismatic. See your differences not as flaws but rather as rare and cherished gifts. Gifts that are to be shared with others.

You are different so you can be a difference-maker.

©Craig S. Travis, Ph.D.

DDP157

DAILY DOSE OF POSITIVITY™

MASTERY COMES FROM PRACTICE

Talent is raw natural ability and we all have talent to some degree. But, rarely are we so naturally gifted with talent that all we have to do is show up and we will be consistently successful.

Skill for most comes from practice.

Successful individuals know that accomplishment comes from hard work. If you want to get better at something, you have to practice to refine that skill.

Practice is what separates achievers from dreamers.

Your ability to improve your life stems from your commitment to rehearsing the skills you want to have. Know what you want to be different. Continue practicing until it becomes second nature.

You become successful with lots of practice.

©Craig S. Travis, Ph.D.

DDP158

DAILY DOSE OF POSITIVITY™

LIFE IS TOO SHORT NOT TO HAVE FUN

Life is supposed to be fun; A celebration of joy each and every day. Live each day by vowing to experience something pleasurable each day.

All work with no play makes you dull.

Work is important and gives you a sense of accomplishment and purpose. But, when you take life too seriously you tend to miss out on the joys that life brings.

Life is a treasure to be enjoyed, not buried.

©Craig S. Travis, Ph.D.

DDP159

DAILY DOSE OF POSITIVITY™

ENJOY WHAT YOU ALREADY HAVE

Life brings with it change and unforeseen circumstance. There will always be something else trying to grab your attention. Allow this to occur and you miss what is important. The answer to truly enjoying how you live is to take the time to know what you love.

Enjoy what you have; don't dwell on what you have not.

How can you reasonably expect more from life if you aren't grateful for the gifts you already have. To start living the life you deserve, see what you have right now and start enjoying it today.

Often the simplicities in life are the most enjoyable.

©Craig S. Travis, Ph.D.

DDP160

DAILY DOSE OF POSITIVITY™

ADMIT YOUR VULNERABILITIES

Don't be afraid to admit that you are less than perfect. It is this fragile thread that bonds us to each other. We connect with others at this emotional level. It is this thread of insecurity that makes us human, so embrace your humanity.

In showing weakness there is strength.

It takes tremendous courage to share your vulnerabilities with others. Being vulnerable enables closeness. If you do not let others past your wall you will not know the true meaning of intimacy.

Being comfortable in your discomfort, that is strength.

Being vulnerable and admitting that you are not perfect does not make you inferior. It makes you human. The reality is that you share this commonality with everyone else. And this makes you stronger than you can ever measure.

Your strength lies in understanding your imperfections.

©Craig S. Travis, Ph.D.

DDP161

DAILY DOSE OF POSITIVITY™

YOUR LIFE IS FILLED WITH LESSONS

There are all kinds of lessons in life. When you lose at something there too are lessons to be learned. Lessons in poise, lessons in grace, lessons in dignity.

When you lose, don't lose the lesson.

It takes class to acknowledge your loss and admit that someone else was better that day. Hang your head high, not low. Be proud of your effort, and learn from your loss. Sometimes not getting what you want is a wonderful stroke of luck.

Failure at something often has more valuable information than winning.

©Craig S. Travis, Ph.D.

DDP162

DAILY DOSE OF POSITIVITY™

THERE IS MORE TO SUCCESS THAN REACHING A GOAL

Achievement has relative value. It means as much as the energy and enthusiasm you've invested.

The return on your success depends on what you invest.

Do little to obtain something and it has little value. The more you have invested in your goal the more meaning it has for you. This is true for business, relationships, and life.

Know what you are willing to sacrifice.

You see, success is often about sacrifice. Concentrate your energies too much in one area and you are bound to lose some focus in another. Be aware of the sacrifices you choose to make.

Know what's involved for your success.

Success is more than just getting what you want. Success is also about how you achieve what you want. Your behavior toward others on the journey toward your goals will be remembered.

Judge your success by what you had to do in order to get it.

©Craig S. Travis, Ph.D.

DDP163

DAILY DOSE OF POSITIVITY™

PURSUE YOUR DREAMS

Define your goals in life. Know exactly what it is that you want and then go get it. The only thing holding you back is yourself.
Loosen the fear that binds you.

The barrier to your dreams is your disbelief.

Have the courage to pursue your dreams and you are one step closer to them. Believe in yourself and in your dreams and your journey will bring that which you aspire.

Don't limit your quest by doubt.

Be afraid to try and you have already failed to achieve them. When you keep yourself from your dreams, you live with regret. Regret is not necessary when you have the courage to act.

Success of dreams lies in active pursuit.

©Craig S. Travis, Ph.D.

DDP164

DAILY DOSE OF POSITIVITY™

IT'S NOT ABOUT WHAT HAPPENS, BUT RATHER YOUR RESPONSE TO IT THAT MATTERS

You cannot control everything that happens in life. In fact, some days are just better than others. Understand that unfortunate things can occur at anytime.

Be prepared by believing in your ability to cope.

Know that bad things will happen. If they didn't, how would you know when the good things did? Everything is relative and depends on your interpretation.

Set-backs are momentary.

There is a balance to life; Good and bad, Positive and negative. Each flows in and out of your life. Acknowledge that both can occur and learn to focus on the Positivity in your life, not the negativity. You may not be able to choose what happens but you can choose what you do when it does.

Your response is your choice. Make it a good one.

©Craig S. Travis, Ph.D.

Craig S. Travis, Ph.D.

DDP165

DAILY DOSE OF POSITIVITY™

CHANGE STARTS WITH YOUR ATTITUDE

If you want things to be different change your attitude. How you interpret things mentally determines your satisfaction in all areas of life.

Your perception persuades your mood.

The way you approach life is governed by what you think, by how you see every situation. You have the control to view life anyway that you want.

Get what you want by thinking what you want.

Choose to take the challenge by choosing to see the Positivity. That is the power of attitude, use it. You have the power and ability inside you.

Your mind is waiting.

©Craig S. Travis, Ph.D.

DDP166

DAILY DOSE OF POSITIVITY™

KNOWLEDGE IS POWER

Self-knowledge is the catalyst for change. With this knowledge comes power. Power to see things differently and power to act differently. For when you truly understand yourself then you are truly powerful. Powerful enough to make lasting changes.

There is empowerment through self-awareness.

Know your limitations, faults and weaknesses. For without this knowledge, you will not know what you need to change. Turn this knowledge into strength.

Make the change that you seek by knowing yourself.

Know what you want to be different by knowing what you don't like. Understanding what you don't like allows you to know what you need to change.

The power of change is simply choosing to do so.

©Craig S. Travis, Ph.D.

DDP167

DAILY DOSE OF POSITIVITY™

EXPERIENCE CAN BE A GREAT TEACHER

Your life is filled with many different experiences; some pleasant others not so. Each of these can shape who you are. But it is your attitude toward your experiences not the events themselves that defines them as valuable or not.

Positive attitude is what makes you rise above.

How you view your experience guides your direction. Don't be quick to judge the unfortunate as solely negative and valueless. There is often more than meets the eye.

See the lesson in your misfortunes.

Experience is not so much what happens to you as it is what you choose to do with it. Learn nothing from it and it remains meaningless. Understand it, and you become wiser. Wisdom is nothing more than learning from experience.

Experience is a valuable lesson, if you let it be.

©Craig S. Travis, Ph.D.

DDP168

DAILY DOSE OF POSITIVITY™

WHAT IS, IS NOT ALWAYS WHAT MUST BE

You do not have to stay stuck in the same established routine. Especially if you think it not helpful. Habit is one thing, rigidity something entirely different.

You have the power to change.

If you do not like the path that you are traveling in life, then change the course of your direction. No one else but you determines your destiny.

Break through your pattern and move beyond your barriers.

Nothing is set in stone unless you limit yourself with this belief. Set forth the course you desire by establishing the right attitude. Believe you can change your reality and you <u>can</u> change your reality.

Expand your horizons by expanding your attitude.

©Craig S. Travis, Ph.D.

Craig S. Travis, Ph.D.

DDP169

DAILY DOSE OF POSITIVITY™

LIFES MEANING IS SET BY YOUR ATTITUDE

Your frame of mind is extremely important to healthy daily functioning. It can either lead you into a world of optimism and hope or drive you down a dark path of despair and desperation.

What do you choose?

View your life as joyful and joy is what you shall have. Your happiness and satisfaction with life is not determined by external possessions. Know the difference between necessities and luxuries.

A healthy attitude is both necessary and luxurious.

Your peace is ultimately set by the attitude that you possess. Money cannot buy happiness. That is why you cannot put a price on attitude.

Positivity costs nothing; not using it is costly.

©Craig S. Travis, Ph.D.

Daily Dose of Positivity™

DDP170

DAILY DOSE OF POSITIVITY™

YOUR GREATEST ACHIEVEMENT IS A POSITIVITE ATTITUDE

You have the power to view the world in any way that you choose. See the tranquility and beauty in life or attend to the chaos and turmoil.

The power of your attitude lies in you.

Maintain a negative attitude and you will always be miserable.
Take a more positive approach and chances are you will find happiness.

What you see truly is what you get.

Your potential success in all your endeavors is directly proportional to your attitude. Seek to achieve a positive attitude and it will infiltrate your entire life.

Give yourself the gift of a positive attitude.

©Craig S. Travis, Ph.D.

DDP171

DAILY DOSE OF POSITIVITY™

BE THE CHANGE YOU WANT TO SEE IN THE WORLD

A popular song sings, "if you want to make the world a better place, take a look at yourself and make a change". If you want things in your life to be different, then start with yourself.

Change what you can by changing yourself.

Do not focus your energies on what you want others to do for the only control you have is over you. Know that what you do not like in others is often what you see in yourself.

You can change what you do not like.

Inherent in you is the ability to make your corner of the world more peaceful. Make an effort to engage those around you. Be pleasant and smile more. You just might be surprised at what a positive effect this can have on you as well as those around you.

You can, if you really want to.

©Craig S. Travis, Ph.D.

DDP172

DAILY DOSE OF POSITIVITY™

DISCOVER PEACE OF MIND

You can achieve success in any area you choose. Visualize your accomplishment and savor those details. The more vivid the image the greater your chances for success.

Peace of mind is believing you can.

Don't' wait for obstacles. For when you consider them now, you increase your ability to conquer them later.

Visualize yourself overcoming them.

Picture the end result in your mind then go live that dream.
When you want it intensely enough you'll know you will succeed. You can overcome incredible challenges by conquering them one step at a time.

Your success is mind over matter.

©Craig S. Travis, Ph.D.

DDP173

DAILY DOSE OF POSITIVITY™

DELVE INTO YOUR DREAMS

Whatever your goals may be, develop a plan for achieving them. Your potential to make a significant difference in your life is governed by your choice and your commitment to do so.

Choose it or lose it.

You can choose to pursue your dreams or leave them unreachable by your inaction. If you do not have the courage to try you are left with regret. The challenge of risk is there so that when you attempt to reach your dreams you feel good about yourself and what you did, even if you do not succeed.

It is better to try and fail, then not try at all.

When you try but fail take comfort in your action. If you don't try, you will be left wondering. Fear of taking a healthy calculated risk because you might fail is what fuels regret.

See the possibility of your dreams.

©Craig S. Travis, Ph.D.

DDP174

DAILY DOSE OF POSITIVITY™

YOUR SUCCESS LIES IN YOUR GROWTH

Bad things happen to everyone. Your success depends on your response to life's unpleasantries. Learn nothing from your misfortunes and you will not move forward in life.

Do not stay stuck in circumstance.

Valuable lessons are often learned as a result of unfortunate experience. Personal growth occurs when you discover the lesson from your circumstances. Experience does teach you wisdom, if you let it.

Wisdom often comes from pain.

Discomfort, growing pains, stretching out of your comfort zone, this is what allows you to grow into a better person. Emotional pain will never feel good, physically. The more you accept its inevitability rather than attempting to avoid it at all costs, the less control it has over you. Move beyond your pain and into your growth.

When you aspire for personal growth you are already successful.

©Craig S. Travis, Ph.D.

DDP175

DAILY DOSE OF POSITIVITY™

CHANGE YOUR ATTITUDE AND YOU CHANGE YOUR WORLD

Open up your world of potential by recognizing that how you see things has bearing on your success in life. There is power in your attitude to make it good or bad.

Paint the picture you want to see.

Your possibilities emerge when you open yourself to the flexibility and creativity that exists in your mind. Your vision of potential will result in achievement.

See what is and what can be.

You are where you are today because your thoughts have brought you. You will be tomorrow where your thoughts take you.

Where do you want to go?

©Craig S. Travis, Ph.D.

DDP176

DAILY DOSE OF POSITIVITY™

CHOOSE APPROPRIATE COURSE OF ACTION

No one thing or person has control over your thoughts more than you do. The thoughts you chose drive your actions. Your actions determine and display your character to those around you.

If you want integrity choose to be honorable.

How you conduct yourself in daily life is up to you. You are the master and gardener of your destiny. Good thoughts bear good fruit, bad thoughts bear bad fruit.

You reap what your thoughts sow.

You choose your own direction in life so choose this wisely for all choices, both good and bad, result in consequent forces. You have control over those forces by how you think and what you choose to do.

Choose what brings the results that you desire.

©Craig S. Travis, Ph.D.

Craig S. Travis, Ph.D.

DDP177

DAILY DOSE OF POSITIVITY™

THERE IS STRENGTH IN ACKNOWLEDGING WEAKNESS

Show your confidence by acknowledging your weakness. There is tremendous power in your comfort with vulnerability. The ultimate control is when you recognize weakness in you and not having a problem with that.

What makes you strong is your comfort with times of weakness.

Weakness and vulnerability are part of you, we all have them. Know that you can visit weakness, but you do not have to live there. Strive to turn failings into triumphs. By understanding it, you can turn weakness into strength.

All you need is the right attitude.

©Craig S. Travis, Ph.D.

DDP178

DAILY DOSE OF POSITIVITY™

SET YOUR MIND ON YOUR GOALS AND THEY CAN BE ACHIEVED.

Your success at anything is determined by the amount of effort that you put forth toward your goals. Simply think of them in passing and they will pass you by.

When you actively think about it, success is waiting to happen.

Don't miss the opportunity to realize your dreams by not focusing on accomplishing them. Dreams don't just happen, you make them happen. Dedicate your mind to successful goals by setting aside time every day to think about how to accomplish your dreams.

Effort can reward more than skill.

Effort more than skill is often the key ingredient to successfully attaining your dreams. Behind every successful story there is hard work, motivation and dedication. Think about what you want, set your mind on it and actively pursue it.

Think what you can accomplish; accomplish what you think.

©Craig S. Travis, Ph.D.

Craig S. Travis, Ph.D.

DDP179

DAILY DOSE OF POSITIVITY™

DARE TO CHASE YOUR DREAMS

Do not be afraid to seek what it is that you desire. You will not accomplish things without taking that first step. No one ever reached the finish line standing still.

Take a risk and venture into the unknown.

You will not discover the wondrous possibilities without first having the courage to try. Daring to leave your zone of comfort brings with it a world of new promise.

Embark on that journey.

Taking the risk to step into new situations, to think differently and try new behaviors is the beginning to making your dreams a reality. The first step is often the hardest for fear is what drives it away. Be bold, break through your apprehension and take that step; the step into your future where the possibilities are endless.

Your dreams are within reach when you dare to chase after them.

©Craig S. Travis, Ph.D.

DDP180

DAILY DOSE OF POSITIVITY™

SUCCESSFUL CHANGE IS MIND OVER MATTER

You can change your life at any time that you want. Simply put your mind to it. Your success at anything is directly proportional to the commitment you make to your mind.

Use the power of your mind.

The company of thoughts you keep will determine your accomplishments. Think you can and you will strive to do it. Think you can't and you defeat yourself.

Let your mind lead your motivation.

Remind yourself everyday how badly you want the change to which you have committed yourself. In your minds eye, visualize your achievement. The more you think about it the more likely you'll do it.

The surest way not to fail is to be determined to succeed.

©Craig S. Travis, Ph.D.

Craig S. Travis, Ph.D.

DDP181

DAILY DOSE OF POSITIVITY™

YOU CAN CHANGE YOUR LIFE IN AN INSTANT

You can make your life better. Simply make the decision to commit to it now. You have the power to choose continued self-improvement. Understand that this change starts with your choice of attitude.

Make the choice to be in control of your life.

Recognize that your happiness and wellness is a choice you make by the frame of mind you keep. Know you have the power to choose your attitude no matter what happens around you.

Choose to maintain Positivity.

Continue to increase your awareness about how you live your life. Persist in cultivating your own personal growth for what you get out of life is determined by what you put into it.

Keep on doing what you have always done, and you will keep on getting what you have always got.

©Craig S. Travis, Ph.D.

Daily Dose of Positivity™

DDP182

DAILY DOSE OF POSITIVITY™

PICTURE YOUR SUCCESS IN YOUR MIND

See what it is that you desire and actively pursue it. Stay focused on your goals and commit yourself to their accomplishment.

Imagine your success.

See yourself as successful by picturing how you will be once you have accomplished it. What are you doing? What are your thoughts, your actions? How do you feel?

Establish a clear vision of these things.

Once you see these in your mind, your successful accomplishment of them will not be far behind. Make the commitment to yourself by establishing a clear picture in your mind of what you want to accomplish and achievement is yours.

You've got to dream it before you can be it.

©Craig S. Travis, Ph.D.

DDP183

DAILY DOSE OF POSITIVITY™

KNOW YOUR DREAMS; SEEK YOUR VISION

If you want to achieve your goals set forth upon that journey. Travel the road to your dreams by following the course that you set. You will accomplish your goals by knowing what they are.

Clear vision paves the path to success.

Knowing what you want to accomplish is only half the battle. Actively seeking what it is that you envision increases your likelihood for success.

Determined effort will allow you to reach your dreams.

Take a step in the direction of your dreams everyday. What often appears to be one small step may in fact be a giant leap of effort. The amount of effort you put into accomplishing your dreams and reaching your vision will determine the amount of your success.

Put forth half the effort and you'll only achieve half the success.

©Craig S. Travis, Ph.D.

DDP184

DAILY DOSE OF POSITIVITY™

CHANGE STARTS WITH CHOICE

Changing your life for the better begins by choosing your attitude. How you see things in life greatly influences your success.

Your thoughts determine your actions.

Make the changes you want to by choosing to do so.
When you change your thoughts, you're likely to change your behavior.

And this changes everything.

Think differently and act differently and you bring about different results. Continue this growth and improvement of yourself and your success will follow.

Things will be different when you choose to make a difference.

©Craig S. Travis, Ph.D.

DDP185

DAILY DOSE OF POSITIVITY™

CONFIDENCE GOES A LONG WAY

Confidence stems in part from ability. It also develops out of successful experience. But what makes it blossom is your belief in yourself. The power in confidence is the belief that allows you to even try in the first place.

Believe in yourself and you know no bounds.

Your ability is limitless and what makes it grow is belief. Belief is what enables you to stop saying you can't and start seeing the possibilities. Without it you dare not try. Confidence is what allows you to push past your limits and drives your success.

Feed this belief and your confidence grows.

Self-reliance may breed success but know this: There is a difference between being sure of your self and being full of yourself. Confidence is endearing, cockiness abrasive.

Your confidence needs no bragging, let it speak for itself.

©Craig S. Travis, Ph.D.

DDP186

DAILY DOSE OF POSITIVITY™

WHERE THERE IS A WILL, THERE IS A WAY

There is no substitute for determination. It has been said that success is ten percent inspiration and ninety percent perspiration. When you have enough determination you can break through your barriers.

And hard work brings with it satisfaction.

When you put forth valiant effort, your satisfaction not only comes from the job being done but also from a job well-done.
The value you place on your accomplishments is proportional to the amount of effort needed to acquire them.

What you get is what you give.

In life, you get out of everything exactly what you put into it. Put forth half the effort and you receive half the reward. You may have wonderful dreams, but put forth no effort and they remain unreachable.

Inspiration may spark a fire but persistence makes it burn its brightest.

©Craig S. Travis, Ph.D.

DDP187

DAILY DOSE OF POSITIVITY™

GO AFTER YOUR DREAMS

Dare not dream and you lose your vision. Lose your vision and you lose your way. If you do not know where you are going how will you know when you get there?

So, make your goals clear.

Determine a path so that you may embark on your journey. You don't need a fancy strategy to pursue your dreams. You just need the will to start and persist. You can dream big and dream a lot but dreams without action will get you nowhere.

With clarity comes purpose.

Once your dreams are clear, establish specific attainable goals so that you can accurately measure your progress toward your dreams. Millions of people are sitting on a good idea; be one of the priceless ones that put ideas into action.

Meeting your dreams comes from acting on them not sitting on them.

©Craig S. Travis, Ph.D.

DDP188

DAILY DOSE OF POSITIVITY™

YOUR MIND CAN WORK AGAINST YOU, OR FOR YOU

Your mind has the capacity for both good and bad thinking. Healthy rational thinking and unhealthy irrational thinking, both forces inherent in who you are competing for power and influence. The beautiful thing about your attitude is that you have a conscious choice which one out duels the other.

Choose to use the power for good.

Both forces will continue to occur, but you can defeat the negative by putting forth effort to focus on the positive. What you choose is your choice.

You can choose your attitude.

This does not mean pretending that bad or unfortunate things do not happen; it is not denial of reality. It simply means you have control over how you choose to see your situation.

What do you want your mind to do?

©Craig S. Travis, Ph.D.

DDP189

DAILY DOSE OF POSITIVITY™

VALUES, NOT PLEASURE, BRING TRUE HAPPINESS

Be careful not to make pleasure the only focus in your life for pleasure based happiness does not last. Happiness based on pleasure and unattached to positive character is fragile and hollow.

The higher standard of value is what brings sincere happiness.

This does not mean don't do pleasurable things. Pleasurable activities do bring enjoyment and this is important in life. But understand that these alone will not make you happy.

Pleasure is finite, happiness transcending.

Confuse pleasure with happiness and you may end up miserable. Happiness is not the end product of your search for personal growth. It is the search itself. Happiness is abstract, a lofty state of mind. It is found in your attitude and reflected in values.

To be happy, you may have pleasure, but you'll need values.

©Craig S. Travis, Ph.D.

DDP190

DAILY DOSE OF POSITIVITY™

TAKE THE RISK TO TRY NEW THINGS

Every day can be an adventure when you allow yourself the joy of new experiences. There is a world of excitement when you delve into the unknown. This does not mean jump blindly.

It is wise to look before you leap.

Anything new involves risk for the new is uncertain. Have an idea of what you are getting into by knowing the risks that you need to overcome.

Stay focused and you will succeed.

Clarity comes from your goals. They provide the roadmap to the journey of your dreams. When you travel the road to your dreams, see the opportunity that is around every corner.

Dare not spread your wings and you will not learn to fly.

©Craig S. Travis, Ph.D.

DDP191

DAILY DOSE OF POSITIVITY™

YOU CHOOSE YOUR ATTITUDE

You are in control of your own mind. How you see things is controlled by your choice. See things as they are but also how they can be. Expand your horizon by thinking outside the box.

Don't let your mind limit yourself.

There are no limits unless you limit yourself. What may appear to be a problem at first may in fact be reframed upon further evaluation. One way to view it is that there are no problems, just solutions yet to be discovered.

From problem to solution, a change in attitude is a change in life.

Make your life what you want. Know that you determine your direction by the choices you make. Outside influences may shape you, but not as much as your attitude. No one controls this more than you.

Your attitude is in _your_ hands, don't drop it.

©Craig S. Travis, Ph.D.

DDP192

DAILY DOSE OF POSITIVITY™

POSITIVITY STARTS WITH YOU

What kind of world do you want yours to be, one that is negative, or positive? If Positivity is what you want, have you been living up to it? Your actions will be your legacy.

Set an example you can be proud to leave behind.

Positivity won't just happen. To make it happen you must practice what you preach. This is not easy for it takes strength and it takes courage.

Show you have the courage for Positivity.

©Craig S. Travis, Ph.D.

DDP193

DAILY DOSE OF POSITIVITY™

YOUR REPUTATION IS YOUR LEGACY

Others will judge your character by the actions and behaviors you have toward them. What do you want people to say about you? More importantly, what do people say about you when you are not there?

Your actions often speak louder than words.

What kind of difference will people say that you made? It is never to early or late to start thinking about your life and how you are living it. The life examined is the life worth living.

What impact do you want to make?

The mark you leave behind on the world depends highly on how you engage others. Your relationships are the seed of your success. Nurture these and watch them blossom. Treat others how they wish and your reputation will flourish.

What legacy shall you leave?

©Craig S. Travis, Ph.D.

DDP194

DAILY DOSE OF POSITIVITY™

PUT FORTH THE EFFORT

The quality of your life is directly proportional to your commitment to excellence. This is true regardless of the chosen endeavor. When you choose to do something, choose to do it well.

Commit yourself to your excellence.

Excellence does not mean perfection. Your perfection is unattainable, your excellence is not. While perfection leads to misery, excellence leads to mastery and success. Excellence is an indication of continued growth.

Let your effort lead you to excel.

Your ability to excel in your endeavors is governed by your effort. Striving to excel means putting forth a continued stream of effort to do your best in any given situation.

You will succeed because you excel.

©Craig S. Travis, Ph.D.

Craig S. Travis, Ph.D.

DDP195

DAILY DOSE OF POSITIVITY™

GROWTH IS RESPONDING INSTEAD OF REACTING

You may not always be able to control the circumstances that life presents to you. But, what you do determine is the impact they have on you. Your response to the surrounding world determines your success.

Your response is your choice.

You see, your life is governed by choices. Some are easy and some are hard; each brings with it its own consequence. You may not like from what you have to choose. However, you still get a choice in how you handle that, and that brings an essence of power.

In difficult times, your attitude is what pulls you through.

While you may not always be able to control what happens around you, you can still control yourself. Start with the choices you make. Choose to respond instead of react. Response suggests your power and control; reaction gives it to someone else.

Choose to respond and you keep your composure.

©Craig S. Travis, Ph.D.

DDP196

DAILY DOSE OF POSITIVITY™

SUCCESS IS MORE ATTITUDE THAN APTITUDE

There is more to success than being gifted. Talent will carry you only so far. Your success in life comes not from being dealt the right cards but from playing bad ones properly.

The world owes nothing to talent alone.

Endurance and perseverance is what allows you to successfully overcome life's setbacks. The right attitude enhances this effort. This bears the right fruit.

Plant the seeds for your success in the attitude you take.

What carries you past your ability and thus allows for success is the attitude you take in the effort you exert to achieve your dreams. Believe in yourself, develop the right attitude, put forth great effort and you will be rewarded greatly.

You see, ability determines what floor you get on, attitude how high your elevator will go.

©Craig S. Travis, Ph.D.

DDP197

DAILY DOSE OF POSITIVITY™

YOU NEVER KNOW WHAT YOU MIGHT ACCOMPLISH UNLESS YOU TRY

You can do anything that you want. The only thing that stops you is the limits you impose upon yourself. Any doubt in your own mind defeats your attempt.

What you think determines your accomplishment.

Successful accomplishment involves effort. Do not box yourself in simply because you think you can't for if you think you can't, then you will not try.

Never try and you'll never succeed.

There are two possibilities when you try: You may fail or you may succeed in your attempt. But if you do not try you are guaranteed not to succeed.

The only way you'll ever know success is when you try.

Engage success by attempting to be successful. If you do not take the risk to make the attempt, then success will surely elude you.

Your possibilities are endless when you try.

©Craig S. Travis, Ph.D.

DDP198

DAILY DOSE OF POSITIVITY™

FAILURE BRINGS WISDOM

Your fear of failure is often what prevents you from attempting something in the first place. Don't think about failure. Instead, think about the chances that you miss when you don't even try.

Stop trying now and you'll never know what the future could bring

It is not about how many times you get knocked down but how many times you get up. Your greatest glory is not in never falling, but in rising every time you do. If you never fell it stands to reason that you dared never to climb.

Don't be left with regret.

Regretting your mistakes means that you have not learned from them. Failure, in a curious way, is success for it brings with it wisdom. You see, failure provides the opportunity to begin again, more intelligently.

Failure or success? It's all in how you look at it.

©Craig S. Travis, Ph.D.

Craig S. Travis, Ph.D.

DDP199

DAILY DOSE OF POSITIVITY™

TAKING RISK MAKES YOU SUCCESSFUL

Continue to be afraid of risk and success will remain elusive. Challenge yourself to risk new endeavors everyday and you steadily move closer to your dreams. Build upon each accomplishment. These need not be monumental.

Small steps toward your goals still get you there.

Do not see the potential failure in risk. Instead see the chances you miss if you remain afraid to try. The greatest risk is the one not taken, for without risk you will not achieve your dreams. Yes, it is hard to fail, but it is worse never to have tried to succeed.

Only when you dare to fail greatly can you ever achieve greatly.

©Craig S. Travis, Ph.D.

DDP200

DAILY DOSE OF POSITIVITY™

BELIEVE IN YOURSELF, KNOW WHAT YOU WANT, AND MAKE IT HAPPEN

These are the key ingredients for you to live a successful, rewarding and fulfilled life. No matter what your goals are, success at anything starts with your belief in you.

Believe in yourself.

Have faith in your capabilities. Feed your confidence by building upon this belief. Stay grounded and centered in who you are and what you choose to do. This will propel you forward.

Know what you want.

Having a clear plan provides direction in your life. Without knowing what you want, you won't know how to get there. Create a vision in your mind and you will more likely pursue it.

Make it happen.

A well thought out plan is still only a plan unless acted upon. Thought without action will not bring accomplishment. Once you know what you want, actively seek it. The greater the effort the harder it is to give up. Put forth great effort and you will be rewarded as much.

Believe it, know it, do it.

©Craig S. Travis, Ph.D.

DDP201

DAILY DOSE OF POSITIVITY™

WHAT IS HEALTHY ISN'T ALWAYS WHAT IS EASY

Behavior often follows the laws of physics; you take the path of least resistance. It is human nature to choose what is familiar for familiarity eases the complexity in life. But, given the right circumstances, sometimes the healthy choice creates discomfort.

Making the right choices in life is often very difficult.

Standing up for what you believe in despite the reaction from others takes courage. Choosing the struggle because it is worth the fight although extremely challenging and sometimes lonely allows your character to outshine the circumstances.

Things that are worthwhile are worth the effort.

Healthy choices may not always be immediately popular but in the long run they are most beneficial. Do what is responsible and what you know to be right and the right people will respect and encourage you. There is no right way to do something obviously wrong.

The right path is often the most difficult to navigate.

©Craig S. Travis, Ph.D.

DDP202

DAILY DOSE OF POSITIVITY™

ATTITUDE IS EVERYTHING, EVERYTHING IS ATTITUDE

Everything in your life is reflected by your attitude. Your successes are largely a result of positive thinking and affirming beliefs in your self and your abilities.

Your attitude determines your direction.

It is also true that your attitude can bring about failure and defeat. Have no faith in yourself and you will not bring yourself to try.

You have a choice.

The great thing about attitude is that you get to choose which one you have: Positive or negative? There is no secret about it. It is that simple.

Have the right attitude and you will find success.

©Craig S. Travis, Ph.D.

REFERENCES: PART I

Amen, D. G. (1998). Change Your Brain, Change Your Life: The breakthrough program for Conquering Anxiety, Depression, Obsessiveness, Anger, and Impulsiveness. New York: TimesBooks.

Anchor, K. N., & Pautler, T. G. (1993). Theory and Practice of Medical Psychotherapy: Paradigm, Cases, and Office Practice Tools. Dubuque, IA:Kendall/Hunt

Annual Convention APA (2002), Daily Reports, PsychiatryMatters.MD.

Annual Data on Neutriceuticals. Nutrition Business Journal. 1997.

Annual Report Pfizer Pharmaceuticals (1998). www.pfizer.com/pfizerinc/investing//annual/1998/financials/review.html

Annual Report Lilly Pharmaceuticals (1998). www.lilly.com/financial/annual.html

Annual Report Smith-Kline Beecham (1998). www.sb.com/annualreport/opreview.html

APA Annual Convention (2002)

APA DSM-IV, 2000

Beck, A. T. (1967). Depression: Causes and treatment. Philadelphia: University of Pennsylvania Press.

Beck, A. T. (1985). Cognitive therapy. In H. I. Kaplan & B. J. Sadlock (Eds.), Comprehensive textbook of psychiatry (4th ed., pp. 1432-1438). Baltimore: Williams & Wilkins.

Beck J. S. (1995). Cognitive therapy: Basics and beyond. New York: The Gulford Press.

Bernard, M. E. (1995a). It's prime time for Rational Emotive Behavioral Therapy: Current theory and practice, research recommendations, and predictions. Journal of Rational-Emotive & Cognitive-Behavior Therapy, 13(1), 9-27.

Bernard, M. E. (1995b). Editor's note. Journal of Rational-Emotive & Cognitive-Behavior Therapy, 13 (2), 79-80.

Bond, F. W., & Dryden, W. (1996). Why two, central hypotheses appear untestable. Journal of Rational-Emotive & Cognitive-Behavior Therapy, 14(1), 29-40.

Borysenko, J. (1987). Minding the Body, Mending the Mind. Reading MA: Addison-Wesley Publishing Company,Inc.

Bradley, L. J. (1989). Counselor supervision: Principles, process, practice (2nd ed.). Muncie, IN: Accelerated Development Inc.

Butler & Beck (2000), cognitive therapy outcomes: A review of meta-analyses. Journal of Norwegian Psychological Association, 37.

Carter, R. (1998). Mapping the mind. Berkley: University of California Press.

Cheren, S. (Ed) (1989). Psychosomatic Medicine: Theory, Physiology, and Practice (vol. 1 & 2). Madison, CT: International Universities Press, Inc.

Chrousos GP, Gold, PW (1992). The concepts of stress and stress system disorders. Overview of physical and behavioral homeostasis. JAMA; 267(9):1244-52.

Corey, G. (1990). Theory and practice of group counseling (3rd ed.). Pacific Grove, CA: Brooks/Cole Publishing.

Cormier, L. S., & Hackney, H. (1987). The professional counselor: A process guide to helping. Englewood Cliffs, NJ: Prentice-Hall.

Corsini, R. J. (1995). Putting the "B" in RET: It had to be. Journal of Rational-Emotive & Cognitive-Behavior Therapy, 13(1), 5-7.

Czeh B, Michaelis T, Watanabe T, Frahm J, de Biurrun G, van Kampen M, Bartolomucci A, Fuchs E. (2001) Stress-induced changes in cerebral metabolites, hippocampal volume and cell proliferation are prevented by antidepressant treatment with tianeptine. PNAS vol 98(22) 12796-801.

Davison, G.C. (1995). Personal reflections on Albert Ellis and rational emotive behavior therapy. Journal of Rational-Emotive & Cognitive-Behavior Therapy, 13(2), 81-84.

DiGiuseppe, R. (1996). The nature of irrational and rational beliefs: Progress in rational emotive behavior theory. Journal of Rational-Emotive & Cognitive-Behavior Therapy, 14(1), 5-28.

Ellis, A. (1962) Reason and emotion in psychotherapy. New York: Lyle Stuart.

Ellis, A. (1973). Humanistic psychotherapy: The rational emotive approach. New York: Julian Press.

Ellis, A. (1979). Rational-emotive therapy. In R. J. Corsini (Ed.), Current psychotherapies (2nd ed.). Itasca, IL: F. E. Peacock.

Ellis, A., & Becker, I. (1982). A guide to personal happiness. North Hollywood, CA: Wilshire Book Co.

Ellis, A., & Harper, R. A. (1975). A new guide to rational living. Hollywood: Wilshire Book Co.

Ellis, A. (1994). Reason and emotion in psychotherapy: Revised and updated. New York: Carol Publishing Group.

Ellis, A. (1995). Changing Rational-emotive therapy (RET) to Rational emotive behavior therapy (REBT). Journal of Rational-Emotive & Cognitive-Behavior Therapy, 13(2), 85-89.

Ellis, A. (1996). Responses to criticisms of rational emotive behavior therapy (REBT) by Ray DiGiuseppe, Frank Bond, Windy Dryden, Steve Weinrach, and Richard Wessler. Journal of Rational-Emotive & Cognitive-Behavior Therapy, 14(2), 97-121.

Franks, C. (1995). RET, REBT and Albert Ellis. Journal of Rational-Emotive & Cognitive-Behavior Therapy, 13(2), 91-95.

Furmark, T., Tillfors, M., Marteinsdottir, I., Fischer, H., Pissiota, A., Bengt Långström, B., Fredrikson, M. (2002), Common Changes in Cerebral Blood Flow in Patients With Social Phobia Treated With Citalopram or Cognitive-Behavioral Therapy. Archives of General Psychiatry, 59, 425-433.

George, M. S., Ketter, T. A., & Post, R. M. (1993). SPECT and PET imaging in mood disorders. Journal of Clinical Psychiatry, 54 (suppl), 6-13.

George, M. S., Ketter, T. A., Parekh, P. I., Horwitz, B., Herscovitch, P., & Post, R. M. (1995). Brain Activity during transient sadness and happiness in healthy women. American Journal of Psychiatry, 152 (3), 341-351.

Goleman, D., & Gurin, J. (Eds.) (1993). Mind Body Medicine: How to use your mind for better health. New York: Consumer Reports Books

Gorman (1996-1997) Comorbid depression and anxiety spectrum disorders. Depress Anxiety, 4(4), 160-168.

Hall, N. (2001). Winning the stress challenge. Temple Terrace, FL: Institute for Health and Human Performance.

Heim, C, Newport, D. J., Heit, S., Graham, Y. P., Wilcox, M., Bonsall, R., Miller, A. H., Nemeroff, C. B., (2000). Pituitary-Adrenal and Autonomic Responses to Stress in Women After Sexual and Physical Abuse in Childhood, JAMA, 284 (5), 592-597.

Hirschfield, R. M. A., & Shea, M. T. (1985). Affective disorders: Psychosocial treatment—Cognitive behavioral therapy. In H. I. Kaplan & B. J. Sadlock (Eds.), Comprehensive textbook of psychiatry (4th ed., pp. 817-819). Baltimore: Williams & Wilkins.

Hothersall, D. (1990). History of Psychology (2nd ed.). New York: McGraw-Hill

Hudziak, J. (1999). Family Practice Residency Lecture on Brain Imaging
http://www.healthemotions.org/research/index.html
http://www.mhsource.com/expert/exp1100598h.html
http://www.news.wisc.edu/packages/emotion/
http://www.positivepsychology.org/institute2001shortsummaries.htm#JB3

Jarrett, R.B., Kraft, D., Doyle, J., Foster, B. M., Eaves, G. G., Silver, P. C. (2001), Recurrent Depression Using Cognitive Therapy With and Without a Continuation Phase, Archives of General Psychiatry, 58 no 4, 381-388.

Jarrett, R. B, Schaffer, M, McIntire, D, Witt-Browder, A, Kraft, D, Risser, R (1999) Treatment of Atypical Depression with Cognitive Therapy or Phenelzine, Archives of General Psychiatry, 56, 431-437.

Johnson, E.O., Kamilaris, T.C., Chrousos, G.P., & Gold, P.W. (1992). Mechanisms of stress: a dynamic overview of hormonal and behavioral homeostasis. Neurosci Biobehav Rev, 16(2): 115-30.

Kagan, J. (1984). The nature of the child. New York: Basic Books.

Kalin, N (2002) Fear: the emotion to save us or sink us, *The Magazine*, 36, PsychiatryMatters.MD

Kaplan, H. I., & Sadock, B. J. (Eds.) (1995) Comprehensive Textbook of Psychiatry (vol. 1) (6th ed.). Baltimore: Williams & Wilkins.

Lazarus, A. A. (1995). REBT: A sign of evolution or devolution? An historical perspective. Journal of Rational-Emotive & Cognitive-Behavior Therapy, 13(2), 97-100.

Ledoux, J. (1996). The Emotional brain: The mysterious underpinnings of emotional life. New York: Touchstone.

Leff, J., Vearnals, S., Wolff, G., Alexander, B., Chisholm, D., Everitt, B., Asen, E., Jones, E.,. Brewin, C. R., & Dayson, D. (2000). The London Depression Intervention Trial: Randomised controlled trial of antidepressants v. couple therapy in the treatment and maintenance of people with depression living with a partner: clinical outcome and costs
Br J Psychiatry 177: 95-100.

Leuchter, A. (2002) American Journal Of Psychiatry, 159, 122-129.

Lichtenberg, J. W., Johnson, D. D., & Arachtingi, M. (1992). Physical illness and subscription to Ellis's irrational beliefs. Journal of Counseling and Development, 71(2), 157-163.

Maier SF, Watkins LR. Cytokines for psychologists: implications of bidirectional immune-to-brain communication for understanding behavior, mood, and cognition (1998). Psychol Rev.;105:83-107.

Mayberg, H. (2002). Placebo, Antidepressant May Lift Depression Via Common Mechanism, NIH News Release.

Mayne, T. J. & Ramsey, J. (2001). The Structure of emotion: A nonlinear dynamic systems approach. In T. J. Mayne & G. A. Bonanno (Eds.), Emotion: Current issues and future directions (pp. 1-38). New York: Guilford Press.

Meichenbaum, D. (1977). *Cognitive-behavior modification: An integrative approach.* New York, NY: Plenum Press.

Meichenbaum, D. (1985). *Stress inoculation training.* New York, NY: Pergamon Press.

Messer, S. B., & Warren, S. (1990). Personality change and psychotherapy. In L. A. Pervin (Ed.), Handbook of personality: Theory and research (pp. 371-398). New York: Guilford Press.

Nesse, R.E. (1996). Feeling Hopeless and helpless: when anxiety symptoms coexist with depressive disorder. Postgrad Med., 100, 163-177

Nesse, R.M. (2000). Is depression an adaptation? Arch Gen Psychiatry, 57, 14-20.

Nesse, R.M., & Williams, G.C. (1994). Why we get sick. New York: New York Times Books.

NIH Backgrounder, (2002). Stress system malfunction could lead to serious, life threatening disease. www.nichd.nih.gov/new/releases.stress.cfm.

Osipow, S. H., Walsh, W. B., & Tosi, D. J. (1984). A survey of counseling methods. Chicago: The Dorsey Press.

Rachal Pugh C, Fleshner M, Watkins LR, Maier SF, Rudy JW. The immune system and memory consolidation: a role for the cytokine IL-1beta (2001). Neurosci Biobehav Rev.;25:29-41.

Rimm, D. C., & Masters, J. C. (1979). Behavior therapy: Techniques and empirical findings (2nd ed.). New York: Academic Press

Rosenhan, D. L., & Seligman, M. E. P. (1995). Abnormal psychology (3rd ed.). New York: W. W. Norton & Company.

Sapolsky, R. M. (1994) Why Zebras don't get Ulcers: An updated guide to stress, stress-related disease, and coping. New York: W. H. Freeman and Company.

Sapolsky, 2000; Newsweek

Sapolsky, 2001; PNAS, vol 98, no 22 (in a PDF file on work computer saved in DDP folder)

Sapolsky, 2001)

Sheehan, D., Dunbar, G.C., & Fuell, D.L. (1992). The Effect of paroxetine on anxiety and agitation associated with depression, Psychopharmacological Bulletin, 28, 139-143;;

Selye, H. (1956). The stress of life. New York: McGraw-Hill.

Silverglade, L. F., Tosi, D. J., Wise, P., & D'Costa, A. (1994). Irrational beliefs and emotionality in adolescents with and without bronchial asthma. Journal of General Psychology, 121, 199-207.

Smith, T. W., & Brehm S. S. (1981). Cognitive correlates of the Type A coronary-prone behavior pattern. Motivation and Emotion, 5(3), 215-223.

Sobel, D. S., & Ornstein, R. (1996). The Health Mind Healthy Body Handbook. New York: Patient Education Media, Inc.

Solomon (2001), The Noonday Demon: An Atlas of Depression, New York: Simon & Shuster

Stuart, M. R., & Lieberman, J. A. (1993). <u>The Fifteen Minute Hour: Applied psychotherapy for the primary care physician.</u> Wesport, CT: Praeger.

Sundberg, N. D., Taplin, J. R., & Tyler, L. E. (1983). <u>Introduction to clinical psychology: Perspectives, issues, and contributions to human service.</u> Englewoods, NJ: Prentice-Hall.

Thompson, C. L., & Rudolph, L. B. (1988). <u>Counseling children</u> (2nd ed.). Pacific Grove, CA: Brooks/Cole.

Tosi, D. J. (1980). Conceptual innovations in cognitive experiential therapy (RSDI-H). Paper presented at the Third Annual Conference on Rational Emotive Therapy, New York.

Tosi, D. J., Leclair, S. W., Peters, H. J., 7 Murphy, M. A. (1987). <u>Theories and applications of counseling: Systems and techniques of counseling and psychotherapy.</u> Springfield, IL: Charles C. Thomas.

Tosi, D. J., & Murphy, M. A. (1994). Cognitive hypnotherapy in psychosomatic illness: A cognitive experiential perspective. <u>Journal of Cognitive Psychotherapy: An International Quarterly, 8</u>(4), 313-329.

Tosi, D. J., Rudy, D. R., Lewis, J., & Murphy, M. A. (1992). The psychobiological effects of cognitive experiential therapy, hypnosis, cognitive restructuring, and attention placebo control in the treatment of essential hypertension. <u>Psychotherapy, 29</u>(2), 274-284.

Wedding, D. (1995). <u>Behavior and Medicine</u> (2nd ed). St. Louis: Mosby

Weeks, G. R., & Treat, S. (1992). <u>Couples in treatment: Techniques and approaches for effective practice.</u> New York: Brunner/Mazel.

Weiner, H. (1989). The dynamics of the organism: Implications of recent biological thought for psychosomatic theory and research. <u>Psychosomatic Medicine, 51,</u> 608-663.

Wessler, R. L. (1996). Idiosyncratic definitions and unsupported hypothesis: Rational emotive behavior therapy as a pseudoscience. <u>Journal of Rational-Emotive & Cognitive-Behavior Therapy, 14</u>(1), 41-61.

Wittchen, H-U., Lieb, R., Wunderlich, U., & Schuster, P. (1999). Comorbidity in primary care: presentation and consequences. Journal of Clinical Psychiatry, 60, (suppl 7), 29-36.

Woods, P. J. (1996). A note on the "B" in REBT. <u>Journal of Rational-Emotive & Cognitive-Behavior Therapy, 14</u>(2), 91-95.

REFERENCES: PART II

Afflect, G., & Tennen, H. (1996). Construing benefits from adversity: Adaptional significance and dispositional underpinnings. Journal of Personality, 64, 899-922.

Allen, J. (1987). As a man thinketh. Harrington Park, NJ: Robert H. Somner Publishers.

Arnold, M. (2001). Preface. In T. J. Mayne & G. A. Bonanno (Eds.), Emotions: Current issues and future directions. New York: The Guilford Press.

Ashby, F. G., Isen, A. M., & Turken, A. U. (in press). A neuropsychological theory of positive affect and its influence on cognition. Psychological Review.

Aspinwall, L. G. & Fredrickson, B. L. Positive Subjective Experience. Appendix, http://www.psych.upenn.edu/seligman/ppappend.htm.

Beck, A. T. & Rush, A J. (1995). Cognitive therapy. In H. I. Kaplan & B. J. Sadock, (Eds.), Comprehensive textbook of psychiatry (6th ed.) (pp. 1847-1857). Baltimore, MD: Williams & Wilkins.

Buss, D. M. (2000). The evolution of happiness. American Psychologist, 55(1), 15-23.

Page: 366

Carter, R. (1998) Mapping the mind. Berkley: University of California Press

Casacalenda, N., Perry, J. C., & Looper, K. (2002). Remission in Major Depressive Disorder: A Comparison of Pharmacotherapy, Psychotherapy, and Control Conditions. Am J Psychiatry 159: 1354-1360.

Davis, C. G., Nolen-Hoeksema, S., & Larson, J. (1998). Making sense of loss and benefiting from experience: Two construals of meaning. Journal of Personality and Social Psychology, 75, 561-574.

Diener, E. (2000). Subjective well-being: The science of happiness and a proposal for a national index. American Psychologist, 55(1), 34-43.

Diener, E., Horowitz, J., & Emmons, R. A. (1985). Happiness of the very wealthy. Social Indicators,16, 263-274.

Estrada, C. A., Isen, A. M., & Young, M. J. (1997). Positive affect facilitates integration of information and decreases anchoring in reasoning among physicians. Organizational Behavior and Human decision Processes, 72, 117-135.

Folkman, S. (1997). Positive psychological states and coping with severe stress. Social Science Medicine, 45, 1207-1221.

Folkman, S., Chesney, M. A., Collette, L., Boccellari, A., & Cooke, M. (1996). Post bereavement depressive mood and its pre-bereavement predictors in

HIV+ and HIV-gay men. Journal of Personality and Social Psychology, 70, 336-348.

Folkman, S., Moskowitz, J.T., Ozer, E. M., & Park, C. L. (1997). Positive meaningful events and coping in the context of HIV/AIDS. In B. H. Gottlieb (Ed.) Coping with chronic stress (pp. 293-314). New York: Plenum.

Frankl V. (1963). Man's search for meaning. New York: Washington Square Press.

Frederickson, B. L. (1998). What good are positive emotions? Review of General Psychology, 2(3), 300-319.

Fredrickson, B. L. (2000). Cultivating positive emotions to optimize health and well-being. Prevention and Treatment, 3, Article 1. Washington: American Psychological Association.

Friedman, R. A. (2002). Like Drugs talk therapy can change brain chemistry. New York Times.

Frijda, N. H. (1986). The Emotions. Cambridge, England: Cambridge University Press.

Frijda, N. H., Kuipers, P., & Schure, E. (1989). Relations among emotion, appraisal, and emotional action readiness. Journal of Personality and Social Psychology, 57, 212-228.

Gillham, J., Reivech, K., Jaycox, L., & Seligman, M. E. P. (1995). Prevention of depressive symptoms in school children: Two year follow up. Psychological Science, 6, 343-351.

Inglehart, R. (1990). Culture shift in advanced industrial society. Princeton, NJ: Princeton University Press.

Isen, A. M. (1987). Positive affect, cognitive processes, and social behavior. Advances in Experimental Social Psychology, 20, 203-253.

Isen, A. M., & Daubmen, K. A. (1984). The influence of affect on categorization. Journal of Personality and Social Psychology, 47, 1206-1217.

Isen, A. M., Daubmen, K. A., & Nowicki, G. P. (1987). Positive affect facilitates creative problem solving. Journal of Personality and Social Psychology, 52, 1122-1131.

Isen, A. M., Johnson, M. M. S., Mertz, E., & Robinson, G. F. (1985). The influence of positive affect on the unusualness of word associations. Journal of Personality and Social Psychology, 48, 1413-1426.

Jaycox, L., Reivich, K., Gillham, J., & Seligman, M. E. P. (1994). Prevention of depressive symptoms in school children. Behaviour Research and Therapy, 32, 801–816.

Kaplan, H. I. & Sadock, B. J. (1998). Synopsis of psychiatry: Behavioral sciences/clinical psychiatry. Philadelphia: Lippincott Williams & Wilkins.

Larsen, R. J. (2000a). Toward a science of mood regulation. <u>Psychological Inquiry, 11,</u> (3), 129-141.

Larsen, R. J. (2000b). Maintaining hedonic balance: Reply to commentaries. <u>Psychological Inquiry, 11,</u> (3), 218-225.

Lazarus, R. S. (1991). <u>Emotion and adaptation.</u> New York: Oxford Universtiy Press.

Levenson, R. W. (1994). Human emotions: A functional view. In P. Ekman & R. Davidson, (Eds.), <u>The nature of emotion: Fundamental questions</u> (pp. 123-126). New York: Oxford University Press.

Lewinsohn, P. M., & Gotlib, I. H. (1995). Behavior theory and treatment of depression. In E. E. Beckman & W. R. Leber (Eds.), <u>Handbook of depression</u> (2nd ed., pp. 352-375). New York: Guilford.

Lykken, D. & Tellegan, A. (1996). Happiness is a stochastic phenomenon. <u>Psychological Science, 7,</u> 186-189.

Moon, M. A. (2000). Positive psychology halved depression in kids. <u>Clinical Psychiatry News, 28</u> (5), 29.

Myers, D. G. (1993) <u>The Pursuit of happiness: Who is happy and why</u>. New York: Avon.

Myers, D.G. (2000). The funds, friends, and faith of happy people. <u>American Psychologist, 55</u>(1), 56-67.

Myers, D. G. (2001). <u>Psychology</u> (6th ed.). New York: Worth Publishers.

Oatley, K., & Jenkins, J.M. (1996). <u>Understanding emotion</u>. Cambridge, MA: Blackwell.

Pert, C. B. (1997). <u>Molecules of emotion: Why you feel the way you feel</u>. New York: Simon & Schuster.

Pinker, S. (1997). How the mind works. New York: Norton.

RAND Partners in Care http://www.rand.org/pubs/monograph_reports/MR1198/MR1198.8.pdf

Reiss, S. (2001). Secrets of Happiness. <u>Psychology Today</u>.

Reiss, S. (2000). <u>Who am I: The 16 basic desires that motivate our happiness and define our personalities.</u> New York: Tarcher/Putnam

Schopenhauer, A. (1969). <u>The world as will and representation,</u> (3rd ed.). New York: Dover.

Seligman, M. E. P. (1990). <u>Learned optimism: How to change your mind and your life.</u> New York: Knopf.

Seligman, M. E. P., Schulman, B. S., DeRubeis, R. J., & Hollon, S. D. (1999). The Prevention of depression and anxiety. <u>Prevention and Treatment, 2,</u> Article 8. Washington: American Psychological Association.

Seligman, M. E. P., & Csikszentmihalyi, M. (2000). Positive psychology: An introduction, <u>American Psychologist: Special Issue on Happiness, Excellence, and Optimal Human Functioning, 55</u>(1), 5-14.

Seligman, M.E.P., & Peterson, C. (in press). Positive clinical psychology. In L. G. Aspinwall & U. M. Staudinger (Eds.) <u>A psychology of human strengths: Perspectives on the emerging field</u>. Washington, DC: American Psychological Association.

Simon, C.C. (2002). A change of mind. <u>The Washington Post.</u>

Thase M. E. & Wright, J. H. (1997). Cognitive and behavioral therapies. In A. Tasman, J. Kay & J. A. Lieberman (Eds.), <u>Psychiatry</u> (pp. 1418-1438). Philadelphia: W. B. Saunders Company.

Tooby, J., & Cosmides, L. (1990). The past explains the present: Emotional adaptations and the structure of ancestral environments. <u>Ethology and Sociobiology, 11</u>, 375-424.

The Vancouver Sun (Canada), 2 June 2001

Volz, J. (2000). In search of the good life: Psychologists outline a plan for promoting human strengths through a positive approach. <u>Monitor on Psychology, 31</u>(2), 68-69.

World Health Report 2001

978-0-595-39987-1
0-595-39987-8

Printed in the United States
60876LVS00005B/9